T0186271

Manufacturing Databases and Computer Integrated Systems

Manufacturing Databases and Computer Integrated Systems

Dimitris N. Chorafas

CRC Press

Boca Raton   Ann Arbor   London   Tokyo

Library of Congress Cataloging-in-Publication Data

Chorafas, Dimitris N.
  Manufacturing databases and computer integrated systems / Dimitris N. Chorafas
    p.   cm.
  Includes bibliographical references and index.
  ISBN 0-8493-8689-6
  1. Computer integrated manufacturing systems.   2. Data base management.   I. Title
TS155.6.C496 1993
670'.0285—dc2   93-18348
                                                                                 CIP

This book represents information obtained from authentic and highly regarded sources. Re-printed material is quoted with permission, and sources are indicated. A wide variety of references are listed. Every reasonable effort has been made to give reliable data and information, but the author and the publisher cannot assume responsibility for the validity of all materials or for the consequences of their use.

Neither this book nor any part may be reproduced or transmitted in any form or by any means, electronic or mechanical, including photocopying, microfilming, and recording, or by any information storage and retrieval system, without permission in writing from the publisher.

CRC Press, Inc.'s consent does not extend to copying for general distribution, for promotion, for creating new works, or for resale. Specific permission must be obtained in writing from CRC Press for such copying.

Direct all inquiries to CRC Press, Inc., 2000 Corporate Blvd., N.W., Boca Raton, Florida 33431.

© 1993 by CRC Press, Inc.

No claim to original U.S. Government works
International Standard Book Number 0-8493-8689-6
Library of Congress Card Number 93-18348
Printed in the United States of America   2 3 4 5 6 7 8 9 0
Printed on acid-free paper

Contents

Preface

Many of my colleagues who reviewed this book when still in manuscript form were of the opinion that it reflects a field of knowledge that, in the course of the last few years, has developed from empiricism to science. While this may be a far-reaching statement, it is true that a great deal has changed in the way we view computer integrated manufacturing (CIM).

We have come to appreciate that, more than anything else, the able implementation of CIM requires seamless access to heterogeneous manufacturing databases. This book explains why, and through numerous examples, what has to be done:

- Resources should be capable of integration no matter where they reside.
- The architecture should not have to change when additional resources are taken on.
- Existing information elements should not have to permanently migrate or be filtered or modified in order to achieve integration.
- Existing applications should not have to be altered for CIM, unless they are needed to access new database resources.
- Users should not have to adopt strange languages for communicating with the computer integrated manufacturing system.

The typical reader of this book, and the one who stands to benefit the most, is the practical person who must solve problems connected to CIM and the integration of heterogeneous databases — from computer aided design and robotics to inventory management and merchandizing requirements.

In accordance with the principles stated in the list above, the book is divided into three parts. Each addresses a specific field of knowledge in manufacturing technology.

Part I focuses on strategic directions in the manufacturing industry. Starting with the fundamentals, Chapter 1 focuses on what makes the market tick, specifically, which product policies best fit the competitive nature of manufacturing in this modern age.

Chapter 2 explains what it takes to bring high technology into manufacturing, all the way to introducing fuzzy controls for plant operations. Chapter 3 gives the advantages to be derived from concurrent engineering, and Chapter 4 shows the practical applications of expert systems.

Chapter 5 concludes Part I by addressing a subject often left aside, in spite of being most fundamental. It concerns the organizational prerequisites that, if not answered in an able manner, tend to create major handicaps. No amount of money thrown at computers will provide an integrated manufacturing landscape without the proper organization.

Part I is oriented towards management issues, which should dominate any systems study in the manufacturing industry. Without a strategic orientation, the money a company invests in technology is essentially thrown down the drain. Therefore, Part I is most important both to senior managers and to information systems specialists.

Part II defines the nature of the multidatabase challenges and outlines the best possible solutions. This discussion starts with the issue of what can be done with heterogeneous database environments, treated in Chapter 6.

Having set the multidatabase perspective, Chapter 7 explains why object-oriented databases are a good bet in manufacturing. This theme is carried further in Chapter 8, which discusses integration and interoperability within a distributed operations perspective.

Chapter 9 explains how to answer the need for real or virtual homogeneity in database functions. The requirements for virtual database integration are further explained in Chapter 10, along with a good deal of practical examples.

Part II is more technical than Part I. Here the argument is that managers should understand and appreciate what can be achieved through technology. Short of this, the so-called computer/management gap will never be closed.

Part III is dedicated to case studies, that is, representative projects that permit the reader to gain insight and foresight by seeing what other companies have done as well as the results they got. Chapter 11 treats the TRW solution applied to Operation Desert Storm; it also covers project CRONUS by BBN.

The subject of Chapter 12 is two cross-database applications designed and managed by Hughes Aircraft. Also two integrative financial systems solutions elaborated in Japan. These projects satisfied the basic principles of database integration in different ways:

- The Japanese based their approach on schema heterogeneity.
- The Hughes projects crafted a new schema for each collection of information resources to be integrated.

Chapter 13 presents, in a fairly detailed manner, the Intelligent Database Assistant (IDA) by GTE. Chapter 14 examines the DATAPLEX solution by General Motors, and compares the background concepts and results of DATAPLEX and IDA.

Chapter 15 is dedicated to Project Carnot by the Microelectronics and Computer Development Corporation (MCC). It presents the Carnot concepts of physical and logical connectivity, places emphasis on a framework approach for developing cross-database applications, and evaluates alternatives to schema integration.

To a very large measure, the references given in this book are solid; they make both technical and business sense. A number of practical examples demonstrate that the foremost companies today:

- Use high technology, not brute force to integrate their databases
- Break down the wall of database incompatibility through object orientation and knowledge engineering.
- Try to increase the quality and value of CIM solutions, using high technology to lower the costs.

Companies that behave in this way do not have to be afraid of competition; they are leaving other companies in the dust.

Let me close by expressing my thanks to everyone who contributed to making this text successful: my colleagues for their advice; the organizations visited for communicating selected parts of their work; and Eva-Maria Binder for the artwork, typing of the manuscript, and the index.

Dr. Dimitris N. Chorafas
Valmer and Vitznau

I

Strategic Directions in Manufacturing

1

Markets, Products, and the Manufacturing Industry

Introduction

The U.S., Western Europe, and Japan are going through a profound economic shift, prompted in great part by the *globalization* of manufacturing. This global perspective and the change in markets which follows is rendering some basic industries obsolete — and the same is true of time-honored industrial practices.

As global competition intensifies and the artificial barriers that were protecting certain markets (as well as a number of industries) crumble, it becomes increasingly apparent that companies must have certain characteristics to survive:

- · Rapid time-to-market requirements
- · Low cost producers and distributors
- · High quality products and services

Technology can be instrumental in achieving such goals provided the tools it makes available are used with imagination. This is not always the case; proactive management policies do not come as a matter of course.

Factory automation, decision support systems, scheduling and optimization algorithms, computer aided design (CAD), robotics, and computer integrated manufacturing have been efforts in harnessing technology to make its fruits available for competitive reasons. But not all projects and companies were able to collect the promised fruits.

Advanced projects often come and go. One of the latest is aimed at providing a quantum leap and is known as the Intelligent Manufacturing System.[1] In 1992 manufacturing representatives from the U.S., Canada, Australia, Western Europe,

---

1 Use of the IMS abbreviation is unfortunate because it gets confused with the IBM Information Management System (IMS), a hierarchical DBMS that is 25 years old and obsolete.

and Japan met in Switzerland to draw up guidelines for a 2-year study which, by all likelihood, is going to cost over $1 billion.

This Intelligent Manufacturing System initiative has provoked thoughtful responses such as a new study from Lehigh University that practically states:

· The challenges in the next century are too big for any one country to undertake alone.
· Cross-border intelligent manufacturing projects need a clear commitment.

The commitment is to a spirit of global cooperation able to deliver tomorrow's technology to the factory floor, enterprise nerve centers, and the market place.

Setting Priorities in the Practice of Manufacturing Management

The manufacturing industry of the First World[2] is in transition, and transitions come with costs. But what are the choices? Failure to undertake the needed transition ends in much higher costs, as well as lost competitiveness.

A manufacturing enterprise can go out of business if it does not renew itself by steadily revamping and updating its products, processes, and markets — also, if not primarily, by renewing its human capital, its culture, its structure, and its organization.

Therefore, the management of change should be the number one goal of industrial strategy. A company's strategy is the master plan against its corporate opponents. As shown in Figure 1, it integrates other strategies focused by subject area:

· Human capital strategy
· Product strategy
· Market strategy
· Financial strategy
· Technology strategy

Human resources is written first because of all the assets a company has the two most important are *people* and *people*. People are the shareholders, managers, professionals and other employees, and people are the clients.

When human resources get obsolete, the strength of a manufacturing company declines. In this age of globalized competition, human resources get obsolete very fast. How can top management keep human resources on the move?

"The human donkey will not move," Winston Churchill is rumored to have said at the end of World War II, "unless it sees a carrot in the front and feels a stick

---

2   America, Western Europe, and Japan.

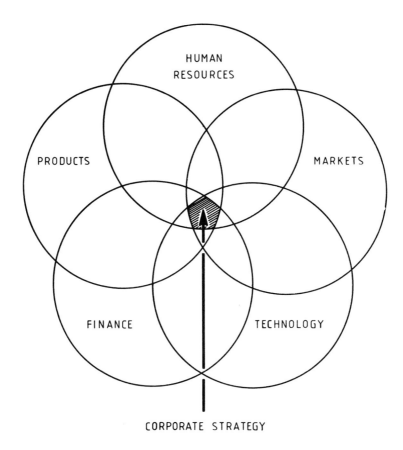

HUMAN
RESOURCES

PRODUCTS

MARKETS

FINANCE

TECHNOLOGY

CORPORATE STRATEGY

**Figure 1   Strategy is a master plan that integrates other strategies focused by area
of endeavor.**

in the back." The carrot in the front is the *incentives,* the stick in the back, the
demerits and penalties: no promotion, no pay raise, stagnant career.

The best incentives can be of two types. One is company-sponsored *lifelong
learning,* which only leading edge organizations are wise enough to practice. The
other is setting *priorities* as well as *quotas* and attaching *bonuses* to them. This is
by far the wider practiced carrot.

But priorities can get out of focus and bonuses may at times be paid in a
counterproductive manner:

·   Quite often companies are missing their market goals as well as their
     internal profit targets for years running.
·   Yet most managers are still collecting bonuses of 20, 30, or 40% of yearly
     pay.

It is easy to say that this practice should stop. However, once a bureaucratic mechanism sets in, it is not that simple to dethrone. Such a statement is even more true when the board and the top management are complacent.

Targets are often set in a way which is more or less counterproductive — or was good in the past but no longer responds to new requirements. For instance, bonuses may be tied to sales growth without regard to profitability, or they may be associated to tiny profit improvements that do not warrant a bonus.

Properly targeted bonuses should reflect priorities, which must never be the same from year to year. It is most important to keep the incentive-based compensation for managers and professionals dynamic, conditioned not by old concepts but by the DO list.

While goals should assure continuity, each year also has its own targets, for instance, slashing spending, shrinking overhead, significantly improving products and service quality, speeding up inventory turnover, and swamping inventories through just-in-time (JIT) deliveries. The common ground of these references is *cutting down* in excesses of people as well as assets. It is a culture focusing on *results* rather than complacency about faraway potential.

The furtherout fields are always greener and the risk of pouring billions down the drain never ceases. Yet, it is often misperceived or even not perceived at all by management.

When KKR bought RJR Nabisco through a leveraged buyout, it unearthed and stopped the "Premier" project sponsored by the previous management. This grandiose project represented an ill-fated $1 billion attempt to develop a smokeless cigarette nobody seems to have wanted.

In his book *Merchants of Debt*[3] George Anders wrote that the "Next to go was Cookeville, an ambitious $2 billion plan to build two high tech bakeries using robots and optical sensors, instead of human beings, in making cookies." It was ludicrous: "In one instance, Cookeville planners wanted to install $10 million of robotics to eliminate three jobs held by forklift operators."

It is unimaginable what bureaucrats and planners will do when left to run wild. Living in an ivory tower and detached from the salt of the earth, they have trouble finding their footing as the market environment paces ahead. Priorities should therefore be targeted to bring everybody down to earth — or move him or her out of the system.

Product Leadership and Market Leadership

There is an academic argument recurring every few years about what comes first, market or product leadership? Each strategy has its proponents and opponents. Both miss the fact that the two integrate. They cannot be separated from one another in any meaningful sense.

Figure 2 presses this point. Markets create the demand for products, and products exploit the potential of markets. Even better, appealing products open up

---

3 Basic Books, New York, 1992.

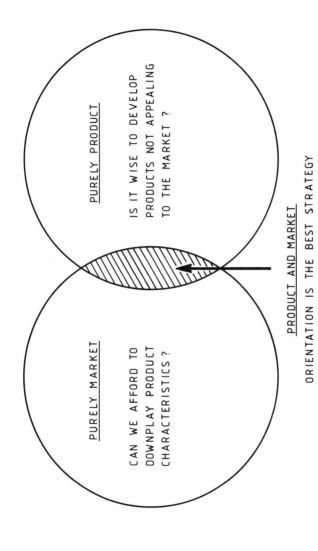

Figure 2   Is there really a choice between product and market orientation?

new business opportunities. The sense of market leadership and product innovation lies in this short sentence.

We do not innovate if there is no benefit to be derived from the change. Therefore, we must first look at the benefit part of the equation by taking a long hard look at

- Markets and their evolution
- Changing pattern of client requirements
- New possibilities for major improvements through technology
- What the competition has in store

Being proactive, and not reactive, we should look at the markets first — as well as at our clients' needs. Though the plans and acts of our competitors have to be part of the picture, we can never adopt a "me too" attitude.

- The term "competitor" which appears so often in our vocabulary has to be replaced by "market."
- Who are the beneficiaries of *our* plans and acts? Of our services and our products?

Research and development is not done to satisfy the ego of technology freaks. Therefore, top management has to be very careful in defining what a project *is* and should *do,* as well as defining the timeframe within which there should be a market launch, that is, the time to market,

- This can never be really achieved without consulting the user — hence the wisdom of market research.
- Yet many companies engage in grandiose projects, and *after* the product is nearly ready, three years or more down the road, they try to find a market for it.

"This company deteriorated faster than the economy," said a securities analyst of a certain manufacturing firm during a Wall Street meeting. "After having lost $3 billion over the years, it floated largely by selling assets. Now it reached the end of the line. There are no more valuable assets to sell."

This case is not a rare exception. It happens practically every day, particularly when top management forgets that the manufacturing industry can survive only if it shifts from being labor intensive to knowledge intensive. For many years we said:

- Operators at the factory floor getting high wages for doing unskilled, repetitive work must be replaced by robots.

Provided the replacement is cost-effective, that statement is old hat as a principle and nobody would really argue with it. But the underlying message is often forgotten:

· We should pay people for using their brains, not their hands and feet.
· Knowledge workers should be rewarded with premiums for designing, controlling, and servicing process and products through the able management of information.

Why do we fail to make this happen? A major reason is inertia, and inertia is propelled by bureaucracy and the aversion to any change. Another reason is lack of imagination. We simply don't put our heart and mind into new departures.

Inertia is damaging. A spirit of innovation and new departures are necessary to serve both markets and products. Top management tends to forget that a policy of managing changes responds to practically every interest, because it fits well with demographics.

In every First World country more and more young people, and especially young males, stay in school beyond the secondary level and are no longer available for blue collar jobs, even well paying ones. To make capital work well, business needs an educated, skilled work force that cares about what it is producing. This becomes clearer as new manufacturing technologies are introduced.

Getting the kind of labor force necessary to make flexible automation work requires management and unions that abandon the old adversarial attitudes and strive for cooperation:

· When unions resist change, they guarantee a continuing loss of production, and therefore of jobs, to foreign competitors.
· Manufacturers can flee a given country, but they can also make their domestic operations pay better by investing more in training and encouraging white and blue collar worker participation.

There is no better example to prove this statement than the near miracle Japanese manufacturing companies have done in less than 20 years — from the early 1960s to the late 1970s. Since then, many Japanese manufacturers found themselves at the top of global competition, and stayed there.

Product leadership and market leadership come together or not at all. There is no way of gaining an edge through half measures. Essentially, there are two reasons why companies, even small ones, wield clout:

1. In terms of human capital, they capitalize on quality not numbers.
2. In business practice, they use knowledge not rudeness and brute force to gain power.

Companies at the pinnacle of industry don't need to show their power. The fact that they have resources is widely known. But they have to be careful to preserve and grow the resources they possess. Otherwise, they will go into decline and their time will pass.

What's the Sense of a Dynamic Organization?

It is the nature of some people that they flower in emergencies and fail in normal times. This is true in politics and is also the case in business; it is valid for organizations as well, since companies are made up of people.

The stumbling blocks to good business sense are often invisible. They can be detected by studying company decline over a long time period, not by examining snapshots. The reason is that the challenger is

· Conceptual
· Cultural

rather than only technical in its nature. There is plenty of evidence that people and companies stumble backwards into the future because of laziness, inertia, fear of the unknown, and love of the status quo.

Every time I talk to members of the Board and other senior executives and I see some of them admiring their grades and their perks, I know that their company is in trouble. They care more about what happened in the past, and the wave which brought them to their current level of incompetence, than what is going to happen to themselves and their company in the future.

The "love your grade" rotten spirit is being fed largely by the hierarchical structure of an organization, as well as the survival and perpetuation of obsolete policies and inadequate procedures. Often the factors in reference are so ingrained that they become second nature. Yet,

· Traditional hierarchical attitudes and habits are incompatible with the requirements and capabilities of an advanced society.
· Piecemeal changes vastly underutilize the potential of new manufacturing investments.
· Some managers are slow in appreciating the essence of new technologies, because they are fearful of their position.

All this is alien to a dynamic organization, but in business and industry it is often the practice — a practice that costs dearly for those foolish enough to espouse it. Restructuring and renovation is widely feared in many companies, because bureaucrats know that reform means nothing short of a new manufacturing culture. Reform requires structures able to accommodate interactive, cooperative relationships that separate the loafers from the doers.

Moribund manufacturing companies remain hierarchical and monolithic. Dynamic organization restructure themselves into *independent business units,* a federation of smaller enterprises where one impacts on the other through leadership and knowhow not flat orders. Reform also means

· Changes in procedures all the way from production planning and inventory management to performance measurement and capital budgeting.
· New technology strategies that reflect long-term thinking but short-term delivery of concrete results.

This of course calls for a change in culture. "Sunshine is the best disinfectant," Judge Louis Brandeis once suggested. That's why the obsolete EDPers[4] are so afraid of bringing to light their projects on which millions are being spent. They are scared of the void they themselves have created and of the rotten software that they hide.

The successful use of technology requires people who can work with machines and with each other. As we begin to implement new methods, we have to guard against too much automation and too little training. We need to keep redesigning some of our processes, and we always have to broaden our training efforts.

Maybe we all know these truths, but so far only the Japanese companies created, in significant numbers, manufacturing infrastructures that can quickly respond to market demands and changing opportunities. Through flexible automation products are practically designed from scratch:

· Made with high quality
· Planned for ease of assembly
· Emphasize simplicity
· Use the fewest parts possible
· Have a concept that is modular for easy modification

Unlike many American and European manufacturing operations, Japanese operations have practically no work-in-process waiting for a drilling machine, then moving onto another queue, then processing on a grinding machine. The whole production is orchestrated with such precision that it runs with virtually no inventories of purchased parts and materials or partly finished products. All of these intermediate stocks tie up money.

The Japanese also put the craft back in manufacturing by making quality the responsibility of each worker, not of the after-the-fact inspectors. Jobs that basically need only hands are delegated to robots, yielding products that have both higher quality and less cost. As suggested in an earlier paragraph, the people who are paid to work are paid for their brains, not for their hands.

Mathematics make a major contribution to good management. Many people think of statistical quality control only in terms of outgoing product quality. This

---

4 In the 1950s EDP stood for Electronic Data Processing. Today it is synonymous to Emotionally Disturbed People. See also IBM's decline.

is a small part of what statistical probability theory can help achieve. The same principles can be applied just as well to other areas of management:

- · Cost Control
- · Cash flow evaluation
- · Risk management
- · Return on investment
- · Profitability analyses
- · Productivity
- · Production rates

A dynamic organization appreciates that there are unique opportunities in engineering and finance to be gained through experimentation. Therefore, it plans, designs, executes, and analyzes experiments that can lead to dramatic improvements in performance at minimal costs. This is the essense of competitiveness.

Competitive Results and Cultural Change

Dynamic organizations are created by people, not by circumstances, just as neither structural nor technological changes happen by themselves. Major changes are made by people and sometimes such changes take a long time to mature.

If economic and industrial life teaches us one lesson, it is that with inaction the gap is widening. Let's first bring the national economy into perspective. Today, as percent of gross national product (GNP), *high technology* manufacturing represents:

- · 10% of GNP in Japan
- · 5% of GNP in the U.S. and England
- · 4% of GNP in Germany

In other First World countries it is less than 3%. These are the countries whose economies are shrinking with a corresponding loss of competitiveness, but their governments, industrialists, and business leaders fail to understand the underlying ills.

Governments that do not know how to sort out their priorities for economic growth are in trouble. The same is true of companies as well as individuals. Keeping the perspective of the next 10 years as a yardstick for survival, Japanese emphasis is placed on three sectors:

- · High technology manufacturing
- · Banking, finance, and insurance
- · Personal and social services

Table 1   Production and consumption of microelectronics and semiconductors

	1990		2000 (est.)	
	Production	Consumption	Production	Consumption
Japan	100[a]	80	425	290
U.S.	72	60	240	240
Europe	20	40	80	130
Rest of World	8	20	55	140
	200	200	800	800

[a]   The 1990 production data in Japan are taken as a point of reference.

The shrinking industrial sectors are low technology manufacturing, construction, and agriculture. The booming sectors are microelectronics, semiconductors, and the machinery made out of them.

Table 1 tells the quantitative part of the story, taking the 1990 level of microelectronics and semiconductors in Japan as the 100% level of reference. Japanese production and consumption in these high tech industries is today the largest in the world. It will be even more so in the future, but look more closely into the numbers.

If America is today an exporter of microelectronics, it will cease being so by year 2000, barely covering its needs through its own production. The deficit Europe has today in high technology will widen, with Japan taking that share of the market.

No wonder the Japanese are already planning and tooling for year 2000. The chief executive officer of Fujitsu is said to have in his office a chart like the one in Figure 3. It points to overtaking IBM in total sales at time "X". This is not an unlikely feat:

·   Fujitsu is strong not only in computers but in communications, where IBM is weak.
·   By the end of this century the communications market will far exceed the computer market as networks will link companies to their customers and suppliers.

Another interesting case study of manufacturing policy, is that of Komatsu vs. Caterpillar. Komatsu makes construction machines: excavators, bulldozers, dump trucks, wheel loaders. It also makes industrial machines and robots, and is today a world leader.

In the 1960s, when Komatsu was still a small company, its management developed the strategy "Encircle Caterpillar". This is based on six pillars:

·   Quality first

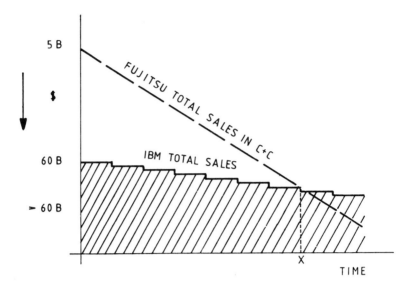

Figure 3 **Corporate strategy by Fujitsu: "surpass IBM at time X"; rationale for inverse money scale: "it is easier to understand, and therefore to achieve."**

- · Product range
- · Value differentiation
- · Dealer network
- · Cost swamping
- · Competitive pricing at 130 ¥/$

When this decision was reached, the yen to dollar exchange rate was 180, giving Komatsu a huge price advantage. But Komatsu management planned for the competitiveness of its products with an exchange rate of 130¥ to the dollar and kept way ahead of price fluctuations.

Nations, companies, and persons that wish to survive the changing fortunes of the market place look to the future — not to the past. But they use what has happened in the past as part of their wider background, to learn a lesson and avoid repeating the same mistakes.

It is said that the master plans for industrial strategy that the Japanese Ministry for International Trade and Industry (MITI) has set up, derive their emphasis from a thorough analysis of the Japanese failure in World War II. A thorough study done to that effect identified the top reasons:

1. Lack of leadership in the high technology of the time
2. Lack of mass production capability

Both have become the goals of today. What many people fail to see is that these two factors work in synergy. Also, the policy they need is based on experience, guts, sensitivity to environmental factors, and wisdom.

At the bottom line, the wisdom emphasizes the role of the individual. The German general Clausewitz[5] categorized the various types of strategies in a logically structured manner. But the Musashi techniques are inner-directed, speaking to the soul of a person. This is how the Japanese samurai thinks.

Study, meditation, and mental preparation is the Musashi approach. "My way of strategy is the sure method to win when fighting for your life," Musashi writes in *A Book of Five Rings*.[6] That's how the high-grade professional works. It is a matter of *culture*, not just logical behavior.

The Question Mark Hanging over Car Makers

Industries can be broken into high, medium, and low technology. Car manufacturing is in the well-established, medium-technology class with few surprises over the years; it is sensitive to low cost production and distribution policies most companies are ill prepared to support.

No matter how one looks at it, there is no getting around the fact that many auto companies, even whole nations, produce too expensively. Most car manufacturers in America and in Europe have been slow to respond to new Japanese competition:

· From the comfortable compact auto to the luxury end of the car market

Because of globalization, there is increasingly fierce competition from all sides. Old, established companies in the auto industry are now scrambling to learn many of the new manufacturing techniques pioneered by Japanese rivals, which have already swept through the international car industry over the past few years.

Take the French Renault as a case study. Experts think that, to survive, it needs to resolve two essential problems at the same time and do so rapidly:

· Increase its producivity at the order of 8 to 10% per year from today to the end of this century
· Put in place the needed preconditions for thorough structuring and cultural transformation.[7]

Without these two turnarounds Renault will remain uncompetitive and therefore unable to position itself against the onslaught of Japanese competition which, according to standing agreements, will have a free hand in Europe by the end of this decade.

If the reader thinks that this is the case because Renault is nationalized, they would be wrong. General Motors is not really in better competitive shape, as it also suffers from a huge immovable bureaucracy. "I could never understand," said

---

5 Father of the modern military strategy.
6 The Overlook Press, New York, 1974.
7 Which, in the case of Renault, includes its privatization.

Ross Perot, a former GM executive, "why it takes 5 years to bring a new car to the market, when it took us 4 years to win World War II.""

As 1991 came to a close, the verdict of the board of directors fell on the mismanagement of GM. The Board had long advised change but Chairman Robert C. Stempler and his top lieutenants resisted. They too had a plan, but their plan did not address the real problem affecting the company:

> The big gap in the amount of man-hours that GM needs to make a car compared to the time needed by its competitors

According to an internal report done by the Chevrolet-Pontiac-GM of Canada Group, GM's most efficient plant requires 30 man-hours per vehicle, compared to 18 man-hours per vehicle at Ford's most efficient plant.[8]

Until a manufacturing company does something to eliminate those differences, it hasn't addressed its basic problems. This can be seen by the fact that GM has been losing about 5% of its market share every 7 years, as well as suffering from runaway costs.

According to Wall Street analysts, the cost of medical expenditures for personnel at GM exceeds the cost of steel that goes into a car in terms of sharing the dollar input. Something similar in terms of lopsided cost allocation happens in the auto industries of England, Italy, France, and Germany. This is no way to run a manufacturing firm.

The huge differences between the way Japanese and Western manufacturing companies make cars are vividly illustrated in "The Machine That Changed the World", a 5-year study of the international car industry by researchers at the Massachusetts Institute of Technology. This document should become the bible of key manufacturing personnel.

MIT has found that a German luxury car plant required up to *four times* as many man-hours as a Japanese factory to build a similar car. After this finding, the researchers coined the term "lean manufacturing" to describe how the Japanese

·   Use flexible teams of workers
·   Steadily eliminate waste and improve quality

Instead of stopping the production line to deal with defects when they occur, as the Japanese do, western factories use large repair areas at the end of the production line. At one German plant, the MIT team said, armies of technicians in white laboratory jackets labored to bring the finished vehicles up to company quality standards.

---

8   International Herald Tribune, January 7, 1992.

In America, car companies wounded by the Japanese have already begun to cut costs sharply and to introduce their competitors' methods of production. But until recently, emulating the Japanese was something unthinkable to the Germans — who finally got rightly worried.

E. Reuter, chief executive officer of Daimler Benz, reckons that Mercedes-Benz, his company's car-making subsidiary, needs to shed 20,000 out of 237,000 jobs over the next 3 or 4 years. At the same time:

- Mercedes began small-scale assembly of cars in Mexico.
- BMW is considering opening an American plant.
- Audi has been actively seaching for lower-cost assembly in Mexico and America.

The globalization of manufacturing has practically no bounds and can hit markets, products, companies, labor unions, and jobs just as fiercely. Many people have yet to wake up to these facts, but they should. If they sleep too long, when they finally try to do something it is going to be too late.

Betting on a Rapid Innovation Cycle

Banking and manufacturing have this in common: the old *innovation cycle* of 10, 20, and 30 years has been replaced by 3 to 5 years — and for some products less than that. A recent American study found that, in order to survive, a high technology company must

- *Reinvent* itself every 2 1/2 years

Another study done in Europe by a leading manufacturer established that it is not the stocked-up products that create market demand:

- *Demand* is created by changing circumstances in terms of market drives and desires.

The more the market drives change, the more business tends to expand, but the amount of necessary innovation to remain competitive and survive becomes greater.

All leading-edge manufacturing companies today espouse the principle that commitment to product and market leadership is a necessary ingredient of a success. This is true at all levels: personal, corporate, and national. The spirit of innovation is no magic that will make problems disappear. It is a state of mind, and the results we obtain are proportional to

- The commitments we make
- The imagination we use in doing our business

Japanese companies achieve an enormous advantage in innovation through a process of incremental, steady improvements that keep them ahead of their competitors. In part this provides market leadership, it also enables companies to surprise their adversaries through novel and (for them) deceptive situations — deceptive because these companies move at a tempo not easy to match.

Any novel product/market situation presents numerous potential interactions made out of a large number of variables. These tasks are well-suited for strategic moves that keep *our* company ahead of its corporate opponents.

Sophisticated information technology comes into play as the interpretation of operating conditions requires the analysis of large volumes of apparently incoherent and incomplete signals, aimed at detecting a small number of highly significant features. Knowledge-based solutions assist management strategy because the artifacts they use, such as fuzzy engineering models, feature

- Inexact reasoning
- Inductive and deductive approaches
- Constraint-directed evaluation
- Semantic-based response to queries
- Natural language capabilities

The rapid flow of technology, the improving means of production around the globe, and the clear trend for many companies to gear their strategies and management attitudes to the global market all point to the wisdom of paying attention to the ways and means high technology provides to help improve *our* competitiveness.

The statement made in the preceding paragraph is not only true of the emerging new, global enterprises but also of smaller firms that must move even faster than their big-size competitiors to survive. Stagnation results from a lack of policies with innovation at the core.

However, let's be careful with the interpretation. It is not just product innovation we are talking about, but the four strategic "Cs":

1. *Clients* — We must offer our products and services to the client base in the most cost-effective manner, but with a significant innovation content to distinguish them from the products of the competition.
2. *Communications* — Sophisticated clients depend on a growing range of communications, and so does our company. Interactivity with business partners is one of the most efficient handholding forms.
3. *Computers* — Implementation must move well beyond data processing into environments enriched with expert systems able to produce individualized services.
4. *Costs* — Technology should be used to cut costs to the bone, weeding out paper and manual labor while at the same time improving quality and the dependability of products.

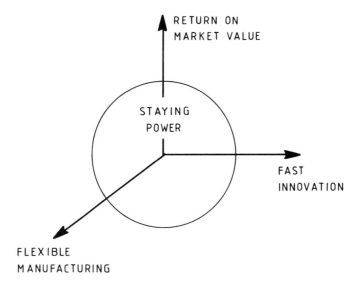

Figure 4   Three top metrics for judging the performance of a manufacturing enterprise — staying power is a function of human capital, product market, finance, and technology.

Few companies have the image of the four strategic "Cs", and not all management teams know, or even care, to differentiate between the sectors where technology is applied for innovation purposes, improving quality, and swamping costs. There is plenty of evidence that the indiscriminate use of investments is far from producing desired results.

A careful study of industrial history during the last 20 years demonstrates that the most successful output is obtained by companies and professionals using a fast cycle, time-based competitive strategy. This is the strategy that supports and promotes

- · Positive market response
- · Rapid product innovation
- · Flexible manufacturing operations
- · Financial staying power

Figure 4 shows the axes of reference around which management decisions must revolve. Staying power is a function of products, markets, human capital, finance, and technology — the five strategies integrating into the master plan of which we spoke in Figure 1.

Flexible manufacturing is the alter ego of the accelerating pace of innovation, and as such, contrasts with the cumbersome mass production techniques. Many people tend to forget that

- · Mass production originated at the beginning of this century.
- · Today it is outmoded but still dominates industrial thinking in the West.

The practice of flexible manufacturing helps explain why some companies can respond much more rapidly to changes in consumer tastes than others. They are able to generate a variety of novel products to overwhelm their competitors.

Fast product innovation and flexible manufacturing have to be balanced against *return on market value*. The algorithm can be simple, but contrary to return on investment (ROI) it has to be personalized, company by company, considering its client base, products, sales structure, and market moves.[9]

An analogy from the military can help explain this concept. General Guenther von Blumentritt, of World War II, described the German blitzkrieg in this way: "The entire operational and tactical leadership method hinged upon ... rapid, concise assessment of situations ... quick decisions and quick execution, on the principle that each minute ahead of the enemy is an advantage."[10] That is what global business is all about today.

The key to winning is to operate at a faster tempo than the adversary — to beat him in the time cycle loop. This is the whole sense of

- · Flexible manufacturing
- · Time to Market

Without the synergy of both concepts product innovation never reaches the market to beat the competitors. Yet, to make it into the 21st century a manufacturing company needs to create revenues from entirely new products. People and companies who live on past laurels are those who are already logically dead.

---

9 See also D. N. Chorafas, *Measuring Return on Technology Investments,* Lafferty Publications, London and Dublin, 1993.

10 *Forbes,* December 9, 1991.

2

Bringing High Technology into Manufacturing

Introduction

Technology is always opposed to the mythology that many people in business and industry, unfortunately for them, espouse. The products of industry are not susceptible to becoming monuments around which myths are built, because historical monuments have to have some sort of supranatural qualities and should not change over time.

By contrast, change is the keyword of science and industry, though in many quarters there is widespread resistance to change and renovation. Experiences teach that resistance to change mainly comes from those who

· Stand to lose significant advantages they have today
· Have advantages built around the many inefficiencies of the current system

Only the leaders of industry understand and appreciate that, in an economy accustomed to shopping for value, failure to change condemns a company to *decay.*

As we saw in Chapter 1, a recent American study has shown that, to survive, a technology company must reinvent itself every 2 1/2 years. This 2 1/2-year reinvention cycle characterizes not only computer and communication firms but other industrial sectors, including financial institutions whose survival rests on the able use of high technology:

· The merging of product development with advanced computers and communications in order to be, not only an innovator, but a low cost producer and distributor of products and services.

Astute management can appreciate that a great deal of change has come and continues to come through channels, such as networked workstations that make

21

multimedia communications feasible, large distributed databases that act as information repositories, intelligent broadband networks that interconnect cooperating units in realtime, as well as a widening amount of implemented simulators and expert systems.

To exploit the available facilities in an able manner, we must lay down a corporate architecture that assures that, within our organization, everybody's new automation project will work with everybody else's. This underlines the need to approach integration as a basic design characteristic rather than a series of random fires.

There are many things a company can do to stay competitive, and some are more important than others. A wise solution starts with a forward-looking top management initiative, as we will see in the next section. The implementation of high technology is an indispensable part of a rigorous solution, but a new management culture is the best way to start.

Databases and the Strategic Vision of Manufacturing

In the summer of 1990, 15 executives from leading U.S. companies spent 2 days a week doing what they believe must be done by American industry as a whole. They cooperated on a strategic vision for manufacturing in the 21st century.

These meetings laid out a blueprint for industry to reinvent basic manufacturing concepts. The plan envisions automakers taking orders online, then using expert systems to build and deliver custom-made, defect-free cars in only 3 days.

Assembled from modular components, car manufacturing would benefit from a large base of diversified suppliers linked to a computer network. Internetworking will foster collaboration on *virtual ventures* created for one project, then the ventures will be disbanded:

- The intelligent network will facilitate concurrent engineering, developing a product as a collaboration of the design, production, marketing, purchasing, and service departments of different companies as well as among corporate partners.
- The factories can be quickly reconfigured along flexible manufacturing lines to exploit unanticipated opportunities, using software to command processes that could be easily changed within the manufacturing system.

There is no doubt in my mind that the organizational solutions we adopt should support this concept. As an example, Figure 1 outlines a structure that integrates but also distinguishes between two objectives: the assurance of long term survival and the guarantee of financial staying power for the manufacturing enterprise.

As far as long term survival is concerned, the approach is no different than that adopted by the Intelligent Manufacturing System of which we spoke in Chapter 1.

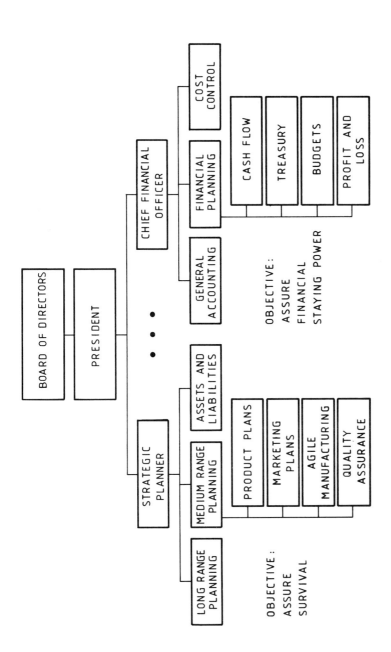

Figure 1   Strategy and structure must be tuned to corporate goals in order to assure survival.

Blending organization and technology, the scenario should envision using the network to form instant online partnerships to go after fast-moving markets.

In terms of business policy, virtual ventures thrive on instant response. Companies still wedded to mass production will lose out to competitors who use reconfigurable factories and computer integrated systems to produce customized products in a growing range of choices.

Many manufacturing executives in America today seem interested in the benefits such strategic plans can provide. But few realize that agile manufacturing cannot be done without *rich databases* interactively accessible online.

1. A database is an organized collection of *information elements* (IE) that serves as an infrastructure to transaction processing and is accessed by endusers through a query language.
2. The database is a corporate resource whose able exploitation can provide a roadmap to the company's activities, from design to marketing action.
3. As a repository of information elements, the database is structured according to a model into which is mapped the business cycle of the company.
4. Information elements stored in the database can be multimedia (text, data, graphics, image, and voice) as well as programming modules and commands.

In an environment of major technological change, databases are a foundation technology. It is through *database mining* that organizations seize the opportunities offered to them by technology and the market place.

Online exploitation of databases is connected to advances in computer processing. They range from realtime transactional applications to export systems for trading operations, decision support, and experimentation on market conditions.

Successful organizations have always capitalized on data resource management, and they have done so in the context of migrating from classical data processing to more sophisticated application domains. Examples from the manufacturing industry include

·   Computer aided design (CAD)[1]
·   Computer integrated manufacturing (CIM)[2]
·   The able use of expert systems[3]
·   Just-in-time (JIT) inventory
·   The exploitation of marketing databases
·   Computer assisted software engineering (CASE)

---

1   See Chapter 3.
2   See Chapter 4.
3   Examples provided in Chapter 5.

But while it is rewarding to think of Intelligent Manufacturing Systems as the way of the future, there are prerequisites to their implementation. These prerequisites have to do with the able design, integration and mining design, and manufacturing and marketing databases.

Choosing an Interactive Database Strategy

Manufacturing databases are a pivot point in the road toward Intelligent Manufacturing Systems. But their deployment and use should follow the corporate strategy laid out for growth and survival. As we saw in the previous section the strategic vision has precedence.

Only top management can establish the strategic vision of the firm. Once this is done, the manufacturing database should be tuned to support that vision in an agile, flexible manner — adaptable to the changing market conditions as well as the evolving product line(s) of the firm.

One of the best examples on what it takes to work out a valid strategy is offered by Cypress Semiconductors of Silicon Valley. Cypress is a niche player, specializing in a fast memory chip known as the static random access memory (SRAM).

"Mediocre management is the cause of most chip industry problems, not unfair competition from Japan," says T. J. Rodgers, the founder of this fiercely competitive chip company.[4] Run with bowstring tightness, Cypress has combined technical brilliance with business acumen to become an innovative firm.

Organized along the principle of smaller, independent business units, Cypress has positioned itself into new growth markets such as high-speed microprocessors and memory chips capable of powering supercomputers. The founder himself, not the underlings through delegation, has designed software programs to help manage everything:

· Sniffing out production problems
· Keeping plans and people within deadlines
· Noting the names of managers whose goals are overdue

Databases are steadily exploited for *plan/actual* comparisons. *Accountability* is constantly evaluated and upheld, with offending managers likely to get a handwritten memo from a pad inscribed "From the Desk of God" — after database mining exposed the discrepencies.

T. J. Rodgers and his small company compete with Japanese giants by using a flexible manufacturing process that can make hundreds of specialized types of chips. The secret is to

---

4 *Business Week,* December 9, 1991.

· Move fast from design to production
· Make small amounts of the types customers want
· Change quickly from one product to another

Online databases steadily enriched with concurrent engineering work and updated manufacturing schedules are instrumental in this process. But underpinning all this is the Cypress basic theory of management.

American companies, Rodgers suggests, should not build huge plants in an effort to go head-to-head with the Japanese, who have cheap capital and government support. Rather, American companies should stay small, exploiting their unique design technology and perpetual entrepreneurship through independent business units.

It takes either many layers of supervisory management or interactive exploitation of networked databases to hold these independent business units together. In terms of costs and effectiveness, the interactive database solution is by far the better alternative.

The able exploitation of databases can also be instrumental in setting up every independent business unit, and virtually every one of its functions, as *profit-and-loss* center. "Free money is one of the biggest problems of a large company," Rodgers suggests. "We have gotten rid of socialism in the organization."

An independent business unit that uses its own money has to be extremely careful on how it spends it. Developed for a leading manufacturing firm, Figures 2 and 3 give an idea of interactive reports that closely follow the strengths and weaknesses according to the profit center.

Within the implementation environment from which these two figures have been derived, all plan/actual results, as well as other crucial information, were databased in an interactive corporate memory facility. Knowledge engineering-enriched decision support systems steadily exploited incoming information:

· They made efficiency comparisons within the enterprise.
· They evaluated internal data against the best external results

Such just-in-time interactivity keeps management on its toes. But this policy is applicable only with dynamic enterprises driven in a "DO IT OR DIE" manner, not when bureaucracy has the upper hand.

Even if evaluated at the public company level, government-sponsored efforts are never characterized by such accountability. It therefore comes as no surprise that, to Rodgers, Sematech[5] is the great American cop-out. He believes improved U.S. quality from the best companies, not government handouts, has virtually stopped any real erosion in the last few years, and he cites his experience in this respect.

---

5 The U.S. Government sponsored this cooperative effort for microchip technology.

Criteria / Main Line	3 Years Hence					Our Position				
	Total Market		Our Share			Strength Neutral Weakness	Major Competitor	Corrective Action Short-term	Corrective Action Medium-term	
	Value	Pieces	Value	Pieces						

Figure 2 This chart obliges a unit chief executive to think ahead in qualitive and quantitative terms regarding the position he is choosing.

Criteria	Last Year				Next Year			
	Total Market		Our Share		Sales	Total Market		Our Share	
Main Line	Value	Pieces	Value	Pieces	Margin	Value	Pieces	Value	Pieces

Strengths and Weaknesses Report / "X" Market

Figure 3   This chart focuses on strengths and weaknesses of the market to which the independent business unit appeals, combining year-to-date statistics with short-term forecasts.

In 1990, Cypress offered to let Toshiba make its own version of a chip it now buys from Cypress. After evaluating the part, Toshiba said it could make the chip only by

·   Building it 30% larger
·   Having a higher defect rate

Cypress suggests that when its people called Toshiba's bluff, they found out that company did not have the technology. That is the strategy American manufacturing companies need: bright, iconoclastic, able to shake things up, and ready to bring the real problems to the debate.

Are We Ready to Face the Competition?

The case of Cypress Semiconductors is a refreshing example in a manufacturing industry often paralyzed by complacency, even within sectors that should know better than to sleep on laurels. T. J. Rodgers correctly criticizes companies like the Detroit dynosaurs which are trying to become more efficient by having a centralized fin design department.

But restructuring into independent business units, each responsible for its own profit and loss (P+L) supposes important organizational prerequisites. Happily for the companies that want to move ahead, the solutions necessary to meet these challenges fit hand-in-glove with the more sophisticated client demands. There is much to be learned from client needs:

·   Seamless access to heterogeneous databases
·   Object-oriented solutions
·   The use of knowledge engineering

These are three component parts of a successful strategy and can be applied all over the manufacturing enterprise. An example of a most fruitful area for their implementation is shown in Figure 4 — the large domain of factory scheduling and production control, all the way to quality management.

Evaluating our company's potential for change brings existing bottlenecks and inefficiencies into perspective, but it also presents opportunities through the effective use of technology. Much of this information can be found through an ingenious exploitation of databases.

If the examples on Cypress Semiconductors focus on a relatively small company, big firms are by no means hopeless situations, provided they are really determined to survive. From 1988 to 1992, in nearly 4 years as chairman and CEO of AT&T, Robert E. Allen

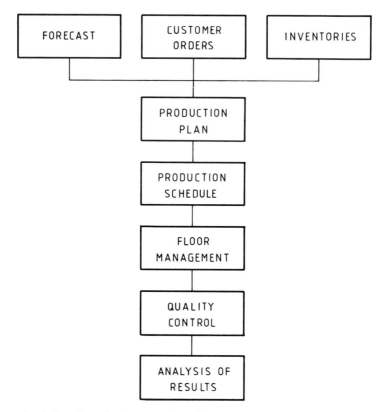

Figure 4   A flowchart for factory scheduling and production control.

·   Decentralized management
·   Fended off competitors in long-distance traffic
·   Slashed costs and increased profits

Unit by unit, the company is improving. Now Allen wants to create global computer networks as easy to use, as efficient, and as accessible as the phone network itself. Databases would be at the pivot point.

Able solutions demand a great amount of system integration, and here again the database reference is most important. Working along this line of reasoning, Japan's NTT (whose activities roughly correspond to those of AT&T) developed the Multivendor Integration Architecture (MIA).

As we will see in Chapter 6, the concept of MIA is simple. It aims at providing a software reference level that permits a multivendor procurement policy through compliance to a software standard established by MIA itself. The work started in 1988 and the detailed specifications were published in February 1991 in partnership with IBM, DEC, Hitachi, Fujitsu, and NEC.

Since the conceptual phase of the MIA project, the partners realized that flexibility is very important, and this requires changes in the way individual systems are designed and built. This is true all the way from macroengineering to the development of portable programming products that can work different machines due to the common software standard.

From Cypress to AT&T and NTT, clear-eyed management realizes that databases and sophisticated computer programs can be dramatic productivity-enhancing tools. This reference is particularly valid for knowledge engineering applications, e.g.,

· Expert systems for purchase orders to forecast delivery dates that most likely will not be met
· Expert systems for quality records that fail to meet specifications or drift toward that status.

Different strategems can be used in this connection. Cypress Semiconductors, for example, capitalizes on vital software support in two ways: by turning it *on* and by turning it *off*.

The idea was born in the late 1980s, when managers found 500-day-old parts languishing in inventory. The company started tracking parts and their usage electronically, creating a software routine that would shut down the inventory system if parts sat more than 200 days. Then management gradually speeded up the timing, until the limit reached just 10 days.

A finance department version works in reverse, automatically restoring credit to customers put on the credit risk list if their status is not reviewed within a pre-established period of time. Another one of the company's premier artifacts is designed to give employees more autonomy. Called the *goal system*, it is a project tracking proposition that helps people organize their work and lets top management monitor the output of some 11,000 employees. The idea is to

· Let each person set their own goals and deadlines
· Intervene only when goals are not being met

T. J. Rodgers designed this system himself over the years from a chalkboard to its current form. It operates on a network of computers and databases.

On each line of a spreadsheet, employees list all their current tasks or goals along with codes that identify the date a project was started, the original due date, and a revised due date if it slips behind schedule. Updated lists are loaded into the database and sent up the ranks to managers and vice presidents.

The CEO himself has interactive access on databased information, such as the status of projects and the names of managers whose subordinates have a high number of delinquent goals.

- With interactivity as the supporting infrastructure, the Cypress record for ontime shipments to customers rose from 65 to 90%.
- Managers say the goal system improves morale, since people are informed in time and always get credit for what they have done.

This is, in a nutshell, the spirit companies need to meet and beat competition. It is counterproductive to work uninformed, and it serves nothing to hide the facts. The result of hiding is that the situation deteriorates and then gets out of control.

Building on the Knowledge of What Technology Can Offer

The more knowledgeable we are when we make a choice, the more responsible the choice is going to be. Yet, when nearly 40 years ago computers came into manufacturing,[6] they were mainly used for data processing purposes, not for knowledge acquisition.

During the 1950s and much of the 1960s, even for scientific purposes, computer applications were made offline, in a batch mode. Interactive computer aided design (CAD) only started in the 1970s. It is not yet 20 years old.

By now there is enough evidence to document that the new implementation domains, which provided the best return on investment (ROI) with computers and communications are knowledge intense. Not only have our concepts of what a computer is and how it should be used changed, but we can capitalize on technological leaps.

During the last 18 years, computers have developed in speed and power by a ratio of at least 10,000 while costs have shrunk. But few manufacturing companies are really capitalizing on this tremendous evolution:

- In 1975, the IBM 370/145 reached the benchmark million instructions per second (MIPS), which subsequently became a standard of computer speed.
- In 1989, the Thinking Machines Connection Machine-2 had a peak power of 10,000 MIPS at roughly the same cost as the 1 MIPS — $3.5 million.
- In 1992, Mas-Par had a smallest configuration of 1000 nodes that delivered 2600 MIPS power at a cost of $125,000 — an 80:1 greater cost to benefit ratio than a mainframe.

This is not the last that we hear from unparalleled effectiveness in technology. Even greater enhancements are coming during the next 4 years. But how many companies today are using CM-2 or Mas-Par?

---

6 The first installation for commercial (nonmilitary, nonacademic) purposes was a Univac machine at General Electric in the early 1950s.

The challenge is not only to make low cost computer power available, but also to put it to proper use without loss of time, deriving benefits due to its existence. Short of productive results, which bristle with imagination, more MIPS will not mean power but "meaningless indication of processing speed".

The purposeful and profitable use of greater computer power at a steadily shrinking cost is becoming increasingly important in a number of tasks that underpin manufacturing. From computer aided design to robotics, man-made systems have largely supplanted human beings in the aiming and direction of factory operations.

· Man-made systems have been making considerable strides in the processing of huge amounts of industrial information.
· It is true that more large scale computers have been built in any recent 2-year period than in all the history of mankind up to that time.

Therefore, it is to be expected that in the 1990s computers will become an even more important factor in the manufacturing landscape. Enriched with artificial intelligence, they will be taking over much of the information processing activity currently handled by human beings and eventually revolutionize the role workers play in the First World.

However, as the management of the foremost manufacturing companies knows by experience, we benefit from technology only when we have clear policies regarding the usage of our productive resources:

· Clear planning and control goals, as well as well thought out policies, should be established.
· Overall objectives should take precedence over the more limited objectives the firm is following.
· Forecasting models must be used to pretell oncoming marketing and production requirements to shrink the time to market.

Human and materials availability should be assured to substantiate the planning premises. A range of tools should be available to assist and enhance the human intellect, from planning to production and sales.

The use of expert systems in production planning and scheduling is an example of state-of-the-art in manufacturing. It has helped the move toward flexible automation and the integration of resources.

The efforts spent on bringing CIM to the factory floor is to a large extent, motivated by the overall thrust to increase the speed of bringing new products to the market. Therefore, it is not surprising that one of the links in CIM is a sophisticated plant floor schedule concerned with meeting customer demand by responding quickly to changes on the floor:

· We plan and give a forecast and a set of orders.
· The plan has to be fine tuned through scheduling.
· Quality needs to be steadily followed and controlled.
· Analytical models should help in evaluating the results.

The change toward wider implementation of knowledge engineering is not incidental, and it did not happen by chance. To a very large extent it has been motivated by competitiveness — due to the fact that old tools and classical programming efforts have been dulled by years of poor usage with substandard results.

Capitalizing on new technology and algorithmic and heuristic solutions should assist manufacturing management in meeting cost control and factory planning crtiteria, helping to determine how to produce on schedule by using available production resources:

· A given quantity of specified quality

The optimization of production plans requires interactive evaluation. Once the experimentation and optimization is done through computer based models, networks must transmit the production plans online for immediate execution purposes, and an expert system should control plan/actual results.

As the fourth section in this chapter already outlined, for agile manufacturing reasons it is always advantageous if people and programs for ordering, producing, and selling are interconnected online in real time. This is true within the manufacturing company as well as between the company and its business partners (clients, suppliers) who both affect and are affected by *our* production plans.

Automated Manufacturing and Robotics

The evolution in technology has made significant contributions to the increasing automation of production lines. This not only involved process control devices, numerically controlled machine tools, and eventually robots, but also communications equipment, computers, and databases.

After gaining experience in marketing numerical control systems for machine tools, as well as precision mechanics, many tool companies advanced into the field of industrial robots. However, by and large the major breakthroughs came from newcomers.

· Industrial robots were introduced into the manufacturing environment around 1965. Since then, they are growing in numbers and sophistication with successive improvements in productivity, quality and cost.

There are many types of robots in the manufacturing industry today. Among the earliest are Cartesian robots, horizontal multiarticulated robots (floor-mounted and desktop), and pneumatically actuated robots.

By the mid1980s robots that met precision assembly applications were introduced. Variations of high-speed, high-precision, horizontal, multiarticulated robots were constructed with the building block method.

Modern robots go well beyond digital servo-control to feature sensory control with image processing as well as high-level robot languages. They are designed for mechanical and electrical manufacturing, for precision assembly (e.g., semiconductor devices), and for inspection.

With electronic components becoming denser and smaller, human inspection for high reliability becomes more difficult. It also requires increased inspection time, higher skills, and bigger cost. But high-sensitivity sensors, very fast memories, first class image processors, and powerful heuristics permit an extended application area of robot vision. The following are the overriding criteria:

- Process speed
- Resolution
- Image measuring algorithms
- Affinity to robot controller
- Physical compactness
- High reliability
- Cost-effectiveness

Modern designs enable robot eyes to see precisely what a robot arm is doing right down to its fingertips. By contrast, with more conventional robots, precision is limited by the separation of the robot eye, usually a camera, from the robot arms, which means that each had to be highly accurate.

- Each had to define where it was and where this position was in relation to the other.
- But cameras and lenses have optical distortions with a resulting decrease in accuracy.

This difficulty was compounded if the eyes had difficulty in communicating with the robot brain. Modern solutions see to it that the vision system and the computer are integrated.

In a similar manner robot eyes and robot arms are well coordinated. In one implementation, for example, the eyes glance repeatedly at where the robot arm is moving every 20 thousandths of a second.

Advanced systems use a direct feedback of information from the camera to the vision identification and location mechanism, as well as the robot tracking

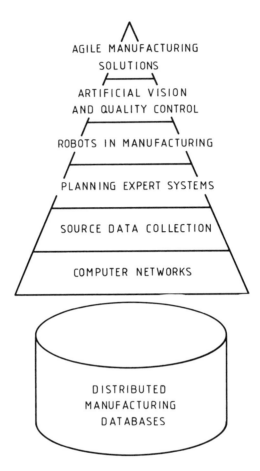

Figure 5   A layered design for integrative solutions in manufacturing.

system. This compensates for errors in the equipment or possible distortion problems.

Leading-edge organizations look toward layered design in robot implementation both macroscopic and at the microscopic level. Figure 5 presents an example of the former reference with a seven layer structure starting with distributed databases and ending with agile manufacturing solutions.

A microlevel layered structure has been adopted with ALLEN, a robot designed by the MIT Artificial Intelligence Laboratory to roll around exploring its environment. Each layer both uses and constraints the capabilities of those beneath it. The rolling robot has a collision avoidance layer which overrides any instructions from the exploring lower layers when an obstacle threatens. It then goes quiet again, when ALLEN is safely out of a collision danger.

Alertness is one advantage of this layered design. Another is speed. Each functional layer is relatively simple, requiring little computation, and implemented by interfacing to its upper and lower neighbors in the hierarchy. Such design is also robust. If a failure happens at a higher layer, or the sensors on which it depends, the layers beneath it are unaffected and can keep on operating.

Systems for Fuzzy Plant Operations

Plant operations support requires decision systems. Major contributions are done today by fuzzy control of processes, image understanding, planning and control of motion, as well as scheduling routines. Increasingly, there is a need for parallel information processing and fuzzy computer usage.

The main goal of a project undertaken by LIFE[7] is to determine the best method of applying fuzzy engineering theory in an operating support environment. The basic aim has been to provide machine intelligence to assist human plant operators.

This research effort also aimed at the development of an event description system, capable of representing the knowledge of a designer as one type of intelligent support. A third goal was to evaluate fuzzy engineering approaches vs. deterministic control methods.

The LIFE researchers looked for a solution capable of understanding events in a plant and evaluating measures that may be needed in dealing with such events through the utilization of specific knowledge of the type held by specialists in the field. They centered on investigating qualitative models and the associated theory for knowledge representation, including

- Investigation of a qualitative model description for a factory and a suitable model building method
- Examination of the use of case-based theory in the formulation of a qualitative model
- Experimentation on a system capable of generating suitable descriptions of events and actions in response to events

The decision was made to focus on diagnostics as one of the most important elements of plant operating support. Therefore, a survey was conducted of conventional diagnostic technologies to choose relevant topics of investigation.

The LIFE study showed that conventional diagnostic approaches embrace a number of factors that do not always work in synergy. Principal among them are

- Investigation and improvement of materials through tests and inspections

---

7 Laboratory for International Fuzzy Engineering, Yokohama, Japan.

- Monitoring observations using dynamic mathematical models and probabilistic schemes
- Reliability improvements based on measurements and algorithms
- Approaches for finding the cause of accidents by employing a fault tree
- Diagnostics using expert system support, mainly through shallow knowledge

While these approaches, each on its own merits, has made contributions, the systems analysts also found that intelligent information processing capable of understanding events can significantly improve upon current performance. Yet, they are not used as widely as one might expect.

The LIFE study documented that in most industrial accidents being surveyed, indications of a forthcoming event were present.

- If at that early warning signal a specialist module with knowledge concerning the plant processes and equipment had been present, the ensuing accident could have been prevented.
- Even accidents that were unforeseeable at the design stage could be described and understood, hence predicted, given a deep enough knowledge of the plant itself.

The project LIFE focused on utilizing a qualitative model for the representation of specialized knowledge. Input/output capabilities and necessary functions were investigated. Emphasis was placed on developing a system that checks early indicators of manufacturing process information against case-based reasoning and uses a qualitative model to represent specialized knowledge.

The predictive control system rested on fuzzy dynamic processing. It was evaluated on its mapping and control performance, leading to the development of algorithms and heuristics derived from time series and analytical statistical methods.

- Design heuristics were developed for prediction control based on fuzzy dynamic modeling.
- A fuzzy state estimation method was elaborated and then combined with a fuzzy model predictive control.

This system was tested by applying it to control problems regarding ill-structured processes such as fermentation and environmental control.

To develop artifacts through analogical reasoning, theoretical research was undertaken on modeling and control heuristics. Application studies were also carried out to evaluate interim results using reallife process data, e.g., input/output data collected from running processes.

·   One case involved a distillation process another, a rotary-kiln sewage sludge incineration.

The first of these processes was chosen as a complex chemical example. The second, as an environmental ill-structured problem. In both cases basic control problems have been considered on which to apply fuzzy theory. Subsequently, the fuzzy control system was compared to usual modeling algorithms in order to evaluate advantages of the proposed method. Special attention was given to multimodel control capabilities based on possibility theory.

The result of the LIFE research has been a model capable of controlling performances, particularly within the high-purity distillation processes. As with other domains of implementation, fuzzy engineering presented significant advantages over deterministic control methods.

3

Advantages from Concurrent Engineering

Introduction

Computer aided design changed several times in terms of concept and facilities since it was introduced into practical use in the 1970s. It started as drafting, graduated into designing, and today its prime importance is that of helping engineering professionals to communicate, learn, work, and create as a team.[1]

To properly manage CAD projects we don't just look at one of these component functions; just like when we design a new product we don't only focus on one of its parts. It is the totality of the effort that counts. Everything contributes to the results.

A concurrent engineering design charter requires a breadth of authority that many companies loathe according to their designers. Many firms ask: "How can we become a premier design company?" They are looking for a formula, and there is none because every company is different. But there is a common denominator, and that is the commitment at a senior management level that concurrent engineering is a priority for the corporation.

Designing through concurrent engineering has prerequisites and the engineering database is one of them. Typically it contains multimedia: text, data, graphics, images from which new graphics will be done, and bills of material regarding

· The products in design and their component parts
· The processes on which these products will be manufactured

Not all companies are sharp in bringing their efforts together to excel in concurrent engineering work. Many relegate their responsibilities to other

---

1 See also D. N. Chorafas, *Engineering Productivity Through CAD/CAM,* and *The Engineering Database* (with Steve Legg), Butterworths, London, 1989 and 1988.

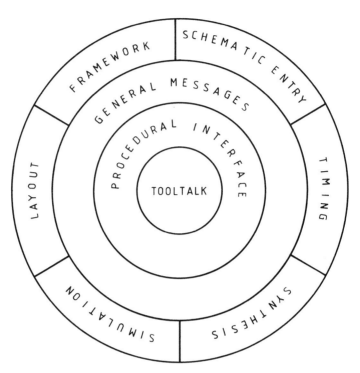

Figure 1   Cross-probing between CAD tools at the pilot project by Sun Microsystems.

organizations or initiatives like the CAD Framework Initiative 1.0 (CFI 1.0). In this delegation or relegation process, they are discovering that a preliminary set of standards cannot go toward solving real world integration problems in a meaningful sense.

This does not mean that the CAD Framework Initiative is worthless. It is the spirit of letting somebody else do the needed job that is criticized in this reference. The list of CAD vendors working on Framework Initiative 1.0 is the "Who's Who" in CAD: Hewlett-Packard, Sun Microsystems, IBM, and Siemens-Nixdorf. But it will be foolish to expect results by delegation.

Hewlett-Packard is working with the design representation (DR) specification to transfer connectivity data. Sun collaborates with five other vendors to test the interpool communications (ITC) specification, which will allow interative cross-probing of logic and timing data. Figure 1 presents in a nutshell the work being done.

IBM also addresses the ITC specs but is focusing on the transfer of design/ management data among frameworks. Siemens-Nixdorf looks at the integration of CFI standards into the European Jessi framework. But nobody seems to care about the most important issue of them all: the integration of engineering databases.

Investing in Advanced CAD Technology

A major impetus for manufacturing companies to invest in CAD is to increase their competitiveness in the global market place. The Japanese are known for investing time, effort, and money to design the product right the first time. By exploring

· CAD tools
· Engineering databases

they are significantly decreasing design time, costly re-engineering changes, useless tooling, obsolete inventories, and manufacturing process mismatches.

As the Introduction brought into perspective, today we look further than CAD into *concurrent engineering*, linking far away laboratories and design centers into one virtual space.

· Concurrent engineering permits the "co-location" of development teams. The aim is to assure that different labs and different specialists work on a specific project *as if* they were in a single site.

"There is a 10% cost penalty of having two separate, disconnected sites," suggests a cognizant engineering executive. "We carry many more people than we need." Other engineering executives think that penalty might be closer to 20%.

Interactive engineering solutions are part and parcel of a strategy of applying disciplined approaches to basic manufacturing chores. Such approaches start with experimental design and follow up with quality optimization, cost reduction, interactive bills of materials, and just-in-time inventory management.

This policy pays dividends. In an article on "Product Development Performance: Strategy, Management and Organization in the World Auto Industry," K. B. Clark and R. Fujimoto[2] report that

· It takes American manufacturers 60 months on average to design a car from initial concept to start of production.
· In Japan it takes 43 months due to more advanced use of technology.

There are not only national differences but differences among companies in the effectiveness of CAD. In the late 1980s, the study of Microvax II and Vax 8800 demanded 1.6 calendar years each because of the expert systems used in design. A couple of years earlier the study of Vax 8600 absorbed 4 calendar years.

---

2   Harvard Business School Press, Boston, 1991.

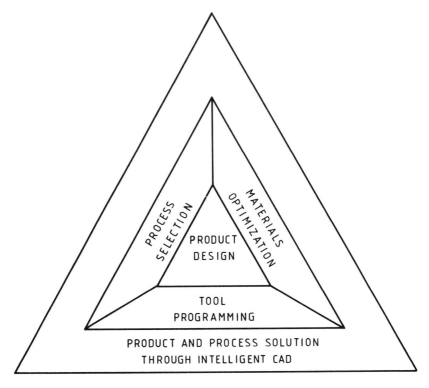

Figure 2   Enriched through knowledge engineering, CAD underpins agile product and process solutions.

As this and other examples help document, there is a significant difference in terms of design productivity due to knowledge engineering enriched CAD. In the case of DEC, the reference is applicable to

· Microprocessor design
· Circuit simulation

Other companies in the mechanical, electrical, and chemical engineering domain also had similar experiences. With accelerating competition, cutting the lead time is vital to profits and survival.

A knowledge simulation approach allows engineers to visually follow the physical process and experiment with it. It also makes it feasible to identify problems that exist in the design in process. Enriching simulation with artificial intelligence is synonymous with increasing the expertise we have had.

As Figure 2 suggests, intelligent CAD extends product design to a wider area of process specification involving

- Process selection
- Tool programming
- Materials optimization

But tools alone will not make miracles. Learning to use technology is an ongoing process that goes beyond one-shot courses in hardware and software basic operations.

Lifelong, ongoing learning is very important in the effective use of computers, and the quality of user support is a key factor in many aspects. Handholding does not need to be manual. It can be effectively assisted through interactive helps and prompts, not only good documentation — though first class documentation is also a *must*.

Ideally, system documentation should be interactively stored in engineering databases and looked at as an integral part of the user support infrastructure. There is clearly more to design than mere CAD tools. As engineering designers become more sophisticated users of CAD, they increase their demands on the features the system should have.

Coordinating the tools used by vendors and their clients is also an issue. In Japan, for instance, it is common for suppliers to have the same CAD system as their major customer, directly accessing the customer engineering database for their design work. This makes the company more effective in

- Managing the overall design process, which includes both people and machines, rather than being narrowly focused on running the technical system, and this only at local level.

The interactive access to engineering databases helps the user organization in getting more milage per unit of technology than its competitors, leading to a significant advantage.

The same is true about the use of networked CAD workstations for communications purposes, among the workstations themselves and with file servers. Companies that use computer aided communications have fewer engineering changes late in the design process than those that do not use CAD in this way.

Communications-intense engineering requires a significant amount of integrative work. Toyota is known to have one of the most highly integrated CAD aggregates for automotive design.

- Body stylists, structural engineers, and die designers all work from the same engineering database.
- This is the result of a policy of strategically designing CAD systems to fit corporate needs, rather than applying discrete island solutions to design and manufacturing tasks.

The goal of this and similar projects is to have a paperless engineering design and manufacturing organization where all departments can share the same database. This is a prime goal in manufacturing, provided that we can make the different heterogeneous databases work together as one system.

Modeling Through an Intelligent CAD Solution

As we saw in the Introduction and in the first section, over the years there has been a significant development both in the concepts and in the tools used by computer aided design. A good deal of these advances have come through expert systems, which have been the first business and industrial implementation of artificial intelligence.[3]

We are still a long way from expert advisers — artifacts able to see, hear, talk, and think, communicating via worldwide electronic nets. But we are presently able to implement a very meaningful set of knowledge engineering approaches in computer aided design. Starting with the fundamentals, four sorts of operations are performed by an intelligent CAD system:

· Abstraction
· Specification
· Optimization
· Testing

Abstraction is a fundamental activity not only in engineering design but also in any creative task. We have known this for centuries, and for over 50 years we have appreciated the assistance to the human mind offered through scale models, wind tunnels, and differential analyzers.

We can abstract, hence simplify, and make concrete at the same time. Concrete thoughts and design plans are created through *modeling*. "By model," said Dr. John von Neumann, "is meant a mathematical construct which, with the addition of certain verbal interpretations, describes observed phenomena. The justification of such a mathematical construct is solely and precisely that it is expected to work."

By working analogies we simulate. Simulation can be significant in helping to abstract, and therefore it has attracted considerable attention in engineering. Successively we have moved

· From analog simulation to digital simulation

---

3 Practical examples on the implementation of expert systems in manufacturing are presented in Chapter 4.

For instance, three-dimensional modeling is required today in many applications, from architectural design and computer animation to the design of motors, autos, airplanes, and a host of other manufactured products.

- Traditionally, 3-D model entry involved a laborious manual process based on two-dimensional input devices such as tablets. But the recent advent of interactive 3-D input techniques and automatic shape acquisition using 3-D active rangefingers alleviates some of the problems in reference.[4]

Today modern shape acquisition techniques based on regular video images are available to industry. They will most likely become widely applicable as video technology gets embedded in workstations. Also, algorithms can construct the object from the resulting image sequence, leading to a variety of 3-D manipulation techniques.

While in the past simulation basically concerned physical characteristics, knowledge engineering tools can now simulate logical processes. This is a new dimension in abstraction of which the design engineer must be aware in order to appreciate it and use it appropriately.

The merging of CAD and knowledge engineering has opened an exciting field of research in a discipline that has come to be known as *cognitive engineering*. It lies at an overlap point between psychology and mathematics, where the theoretical and the arcane come together to produce practical applications.

In an era of increasingly complex engineering and manufacturing projects, there is every reason why artificial intelligence tools are necessary for technological progress. At the same time, their creation gives a rare opportunity for real life experiments with models of the complex cognitive processes involved in design.

Often it is not sufficiently appreciated how important nontechnological considerations are in engineering design. Even if we pay close attention to algorithmic processes, knowledge representation, and control structures, our project could fail in a real life application if we don't assure able human interfaces and other sensitivity factors.

Careful consideration must be given to how the system is introduced to its users and how it will affect their work patterns. To help the enduser act in familiar ways, visualization should support a wide range of representations, such as

- Interactive development of 2-D and 3-D images
- 2-D and 3-D contour and surface models

---

4 Ingrid Carlbom, William M. Hsu, Gudrun Klinker, Richard Szelishi, Keith Waters, "Modeling and Analysis of Emperical Data in Collaborative Environments," Communications of the ACM, June 1992, Vol. 35, No. 6.

· 3-D volumetric representations
· Consistent color patterns

Visualization should not be twisted due to incompatible internal data representation. The designer should be in a position to visually correlate parts of different information elements in many different ways, use overlays, and point in multiple windows.

The modeling and visualization approach should include a knowledge enriched image and data reconstruction techniques. A variety of registration and segmentation approaches have been developed for that purpose.

Modeling and idealization have often been one man's work. They must now be promoted to the level of concurrent engineering with model integration and interactive manipulation being two of the goals. This can have a dramatic aftermath on time to market.

Advantages Gained Through Interactive Specification and Optimization

Specification involves a negotiation between different parties concerned with a product's features and what constitutes a valid solution. The designer has a concept that might be more or less clear, but marketing may wish some different features. Manufacturing is concerned with tools and processes, and top management thinks of processes and costs.

There is give and take in any design situation, but this cannot take years or even months. It has to be done very fast. An intelligent CAD engine is asked to present specifications that are formal, verifiable, and capable of developing a properly functioning product with market appeal.

The use of knowledge engineering in this negotiation process is promoted by the fact that expert system techniques are more rapidly accepted among designers. This is especially true of those endusers who have viewed computers as "useful, but ... they can't solve my conceptual problems," the given reason typically being that conceptual problems involve a lot of judgment.

Based on a project of a leading lamp manufacturing firm, Figure 3 brings into perspective a specification oriented view of an engineering design all the way to an integrated product layout and the construction of manufacturing engineering specs. Notice the feedback necessary between product and process.

In the specifications level of engineering design, expert systems provide the ability to arrive at an interactive solution while trying a number of alternatives in compressed time scales. They also make the duplication of expertise easier.

Working within this context, an expert system would allow the designer to experiment, contributing his imaginative approaches to the development of successive stages depending on

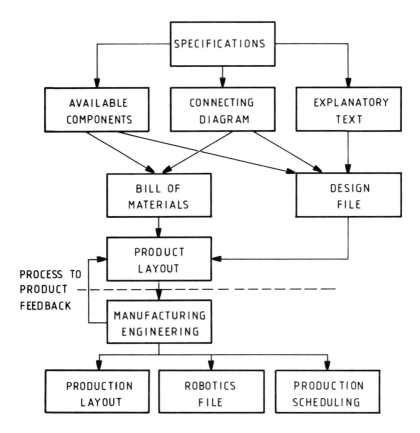

Figure 3   A specification view of design from product layout to manufacturing engineering.

·   The representation appropriate to the product or application
·   The relative compatibility of this representation within the larger system to which the object of the design belongs

Knowledge enriched CAD solutions facilitate this intervention and also see to it that as much use as possible is made of past designs in the generation of new models.

In the background of this reference is the fact that endusers and computer-based processes are no longer two distinct issues but integral parts of the same problem. Artificial intelligence tools provided by modern technology help bring them close together, with expert systems assuring the connectivity help.

As investments in new products and processes are running into the billions of dollars, cognizant management appreciates that a far looking approach to fundamental design requirement is vital in terms of competitive advantages. At the same time, competitive pressures see to it that value added features have to be part of further refinements in CAD implementation.

With time and experience, off-the-shelf knowledge banks will appear with thousands of rules; while until recently applications typically used a few hundred rules. Chip vendors are working to develop these larger building blocks of expert systems, which will become transportable and marketable compared to books and software:

- They will represent design knowledge in an organized but adaptable manner
- They will support product-specific knowledge in terms familiar to endusers
- They will employ user-friendly interface functions, exploiting different kinds of reasoning.

For any product, and for any process, the initial specification and the resulting criteria for a successful design are essentially responses to market needs and reflect ever changing values. Given an adequate specification and the means to modify it according to requirements, there is no reason why intelligent CAD tools should not be developed for all areas of engineering design.

Therefore, there is no wonder the U.S. Department of Defense has identified artificial intelligence as one of the critical technologies for national defense and for continued economic leadership in the 1990s. The industrialization of knowledge is a competitive leading edge.

Optimization is a more complex process than specification. If done automatically, there is an advantage in that simulated data is generated and experimentation takes place to optimize a product, process, or system that was already found to be feasible. Knowledge engineering can play a key role in optimization for two good reasons:

1. It brings into play the way the real expert works in optimizing product characteristics, making this knowledge widely available to other engineers.
2. It helps in structuring and formalizing the methodology to be used, thus making feasible a homogeneous approach throughout the work group.

Logical methods supported through AI enable us to employ and control upward-propagating constraints. This gives the designer the opportunity of doing with expert systems what is done in classical design: feeding back information. But it also provides the designer the added facility of studying difficulties in implementation details and bringing them to higher levels of representation, which can than be adjusted or modified.

Looking carefully at problems of constraints regarding novelty, functionality, costs, and other variables — including their contradictions — the designer is naturally led to the identification of areas about which not enough is known. Many questions need to be answered:

· How can algorithmic and heuristic knowledge be combined?
· How do we elicit the knowledge needed for building artifacts for optimization reasons?
· How can we access heterogeneous databases on which reside the products and processes we are working on?
· What kind of formal language should we use for representation of schemata and methods?

Representation has an important influence on logical problem solving. The wrong representation can make even the most competent problem solver inefficient. (If you don't believe this, try doing multiplication with ancient Greek numerals). By contrast, a good representation can lead to problem solving — it can also extend the power of a problem-solving strategy into new domains.

Through a good representation, an expert system may be able to learn to do more than what a single designer could achieve. The bottom line is that there is more than one way of acquiring knowledge from the expert — more than just asking direct questions. Methods of inducing rules from examples are being developed, and rules established by this method have been found to be quite efficient in performance.

Particularly in the fields of optimization and testing, representation by example can make previously obscure domain knowledge explicit, coherent, and logical. This deepens and extends our grasp of the domain and also leads to meaningful testing processes.

Using Knowledge Engineering for Quality Testing

Quality testing is not just the final phase in every product design; it is much more than that. It is a philosophy of design that embeds quality testing since the very early conceptual stages and whatever comes afterwards.

For instance, the evaluation of optimized plans can be subjected to tests produced by expert systems with a number of features can dominate:

· Simplicity
· Functionality
· Low cost
· Homogeneity
· Consistency

One of the main aims in developing intelligent testing systems should be to evaluate criteria for a good design, both in isolation and in synergy. Topmost issues, for instance, reliability and the need for a supportive crash-proof solution, must be brought into perspective. Another criterion at the top of the list may be agile man-machine interfaces.

- Through expert systems CAD can be placed in a context in which the values used to produce judgments about what makes a good product are more evident.
- This enables the designer to identify salient problems and address himself to them in an effective manner, instead of being lost in the details.

As experience in the implementation of expert systems in engineering design steadily grows, we will be able to address aggregate issues that the simple manipulation of electronic or mechanical parts of a given system cannot ameliorate. Typically, such problems are logical in nature and require new techniques for their solution, such as

- The incorporation of knowledge expressed in rules

and/or

- The expression of interrelationships in fuzzy engineering terms[5]

The provision of advice through an expert consultant program assists in the analysis of the design and reveals the influence of logical processes in any manmade system. It can also assist in the social organization of the design team and on the way the design task is partitioned.

Valid system testing results can be obtained by matching technical solutions to practical problems. One of the key questions in a recent implementation was: "What can be efficiently automated and what cannot?"[6] This leads to the consideration of some fundamental issues of formalism and representation.

To appreciate the benefits obtained from a dual qualitative and quantitative approach to system testing, we must recall that design has long been considered an ill-structured problem that is difficult to handle through software. But research into the possibilities presented by AI has revealed the importance of using logical representation of the problem as a key to making critical evaluations of alternative solutions.

- This finds its counterpart in the way that a good notation in mathematics makes thinking about mathematical concepts easier.
- A little appreciated fact is that the language which we use forms our mind, which talks volumes of knowledge engineering and simulation.

---

5 See also D. N. Chorafas, *The New Information Technology — A Practitioner' Guide,* Van Nostrand Reinhold, New York, 1992.

6 A question asked in regard to the grand design of an integrated computer and communications system.

Through CAD algorithms and heuristics we now can have at our disposal formal mathematical methods for automating not only design but testing procedures. With expert systems we should aim at capturing informal knowledge, which is the concept of an *expert consultant* approach to CAD through artificial intelligence.

Since results along this line of reference are already apparent, in the coming years advanced CAD equipment will incorporate embedded, second-generation expert systems, particularly

· Fuzzy engineering
· Neural networks

Once advanced computer-based methodology moves into the domain of the designer, it will be employed in a growing range of tasks. At the same time, sophisticated expert systems facilities will become major sales features in an increasingly competitive market:

· They will allow us to describe many types of products and their behavior.
· They will tackle issues that do not readily admit to algorithmic or state-change representations.
· They will incorporate qualitative as well as quantitative relationships.
· They will support deductive inference and associated analysis.
· They will promote logical problem-solving methods and testing procedures.

Online, interactive access to distributed heterogeneous databases will provide the framework for integrating models of physical processes and human behavior, subject to various constraints. And it will do so with goal-seeking capabilities.

Within the next 10 years, we can expect engineering design knowledge to create engines capable of handling tens of thousands of inference rules and millions of objects. While not yet realized in hardware, such machine architectures are generally viewed as comprising an essential feature both of the new generation of computers and of knowledge engineering at large.

A Quality Function Deployment (QFD): Application of Knowledge Engineering in CAD

A practical application of knowledge engineering in industry is synonymous to the seamless access to engineering databases where crucial, multimedia information on products and processes lies. That is why Part II is fully devoted to the ways and means necessary to overcome the problems presented with incompatible databases, and Part III presents case studies with solutions adopted by successful organizations.

A basic problem encountered by many manufacturing companies is that over many years of design, practice applications have been made in a discrete islands approach with little thought given to integration. As we will see in Part II, we now have to find or remedy for this situation, a remedy that can be applied without delay.

The more sophisticated the design artifacts we develop, the more we need interactive access to distributed, largely heterogeneous databases. Projects promoted today by leading manufacturing companies have to keep this fact in mind, while at the same time bringing more knowledge-intense approaches into computer aided design.

Many industries are keen on having at their disposal tools that permit integrative access to different, heterogeneous design files, bringing marketing requirements into play as they develop. An example is the quality function deployment (QFD) tool for designing autos.

Originally developed by the Japanese, QFD has become very popular in America and in parts of Europe. It allows design as a function of

- Customer desires
- Marketing findings

After receiving this dual input, QFD translates it into technical requirements to integrate into CAD an approach that greatly helps in concurrent engineering. Toyota says that, through it, the lead time has been reduced by 65%.

Developed by Ford and Inference Corporation, the Technical Information Engineering System (TIES) is a computer assisted methodology to help achieve significant improvements in product quality, production cycle time, and market share. It is being used to support concurrent design processes in applications varying from specific automobile compoments to a completely new vehicle.

TIES builds upon the Quality Function Deployment method assuring that customer demands are accurately translated into appropriate technical requirements, and thereafter into actions.

- As a design tool, it provides a framework in which cross-functional product and process design teams can collect and store relevant engineering information, as well as knowledge.

This common framework enables separate groups to design components or elements while maintaining consistency with the designs of other groups. Emphasis is placed on

- Product quality
- Design cycle time

Both design cycle time and product quality are critical factors in achieving customer satisfaction by seeing to it that the market desires are timely and accurately translated into appropriate technical requirements.

QFD provided the basis for the planning and process methodology TIES has adopted. It helps to identify the most important product characteristics, necessary control issues, as well as best tools and techniques to use. When employed throughout the product development cycle, it provides a comprehensive tracking tool and communication medium.

The working framework of QFD is a chart called the House of Quality. In it, matrices display interrelationships between customer wants and technical know-how, providing information about weighing factors, comparative data, and correlations.

A basic concept behind the House of Quality is that products should be designed and developed to reflect customer tastes and desires. Marketing people, design engineers, and manufacturing personnel must all work closely together from initial ideas to product delivery.

In QFD this process is facilitated by cascading through chains of related houses as shown in Figure 4. This process is linking customer requirements to engineering characteristics and then to manufacturing. Shown in the figure are:

1. Customer House, translating requirements to engineering specs
2. Deployment of parts and subassemblies
3. Identification of process planning stages
4. Translation into production planning and scheduling

Through this approach, professionals with different responsibilities and problems can explore alternative designs and priorities, but at the same time the structural information included in the context defines a collection of data structures — entities, relations, and matrices together comprising the houses in the cascade.

Entities are user-defined tree structures. They are mapped into the rows and columns of matrices and houses, including the associated labels.

   ·   Matrices are defined by entities of rows and columns.
   ·   Relations are dynamic, user-changeable mappings from pairs of entity nodes (row and column) to values.
   ·   There is a TIES relation for storing cell values corresponding to pairs of entity nodes.

Row and column entities are structured hierarchically with more abstract entities spawning more specific entities, as filials. The knowledge engineering component of TIES enables users to perform various QFD functions at multiple levels of abstraction.

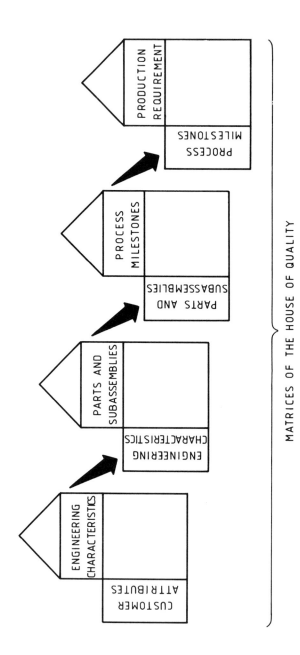

Figure 4   Cascading houses in the quality function deployment method.

Knowledge engineering embedded into TIES provides an analysis of which elements of a house would be impacted by changes to other elements. Two entities interact with one another if there is a relation between them, hence direct impact, or if there is a defined chain of relations.

Requirements for and Benefits from Ford's TIES Project

As the previous section demonstrated, at the Ford Motor Company the TIES project combined engineering methodology, product design, and knowledge engineering to produce a new tool capable of supporting automobile design. Since its conception, TIES has proven itself within the user base and therefore is in steady integration into Ford's design and development processes.

Project management and coordination of TIES applications has been performed by Ford's Research Staff. Software experts were added to the team to

- Support quality assurance testing of the alpha and beta versions
- Complete the production version including documentation

After the concept of a prototype stabilized, users involved in the TIES project began building knowledgebanks that immediately helped enhance their own operational efficiency. There were immediate productivity improvements — but there were also requirements to fulfill.

From the viewpoint of the design engineer, requirements and benefits were tightly knit. The designer was able to input his knowledge directly, making use of user-defined knowledge representation capabilities.

Essentially, in the implementation of TIES it was the designer who decided how to represent his own knowledge within the structured framework of QFD. This definition included

- Entity structures
- Relations
- Contexts

TIES presented the user with a symbolic spreadsheet capability. This permitted designers to define inference rules to propagate qualitative and quantitative information within and across matrices. It also assured a common language and knowledge structure.

One of the challenges in real life application has been the decomposition of design tasks and the merging of partial designs. TIES provided the infrastructure for designers to work on components and their characteristics separately, combining their work in a concurrent engineering sense.

As every engineering manager should appreciate, this capability can be precious — and is particularly desirable in cases where design expertise is scattered among many experts. It helps assure

· Consistency and coordination of parts, assemblies, and whole vehicle programs
· Faster development time for new parts, assemblies, and vehicle programs
· Better spread expertise, particularly valuable to newly hired engineers

In fact, as we will see in Chapter 4, one of the most important benefits from the industrialization of knowledge is the impact it has in terms of day-to-day results. Companies that resist the introduction and usage of expert systems, for whatever curious reasons they may have, should think twice about the benefits they are missing.

As the Inference Corporation suggested during a meeting in Los Angeles, the single most important factor for the success of TIES was that it was driven by the needs of the user community. The project had enthusiastic support from users from the outset and continues to evolve as the number of users expands. Users are providing feedback on improvements and extensions.

Also from a technical perspective, TIES is quite successful due to the flexibility it provides in its employment. In building knowledgebanks, users define their own structures, each through his own terminology. Graphically, they

· View global designs or focus on local, limited issues

QFD and TIES take stock of such user behavior, providing an infrastructure that permits it to flourish. This is one of the key reasons for the system's success.

In terms of development effort, during the alpha and beta tests of TIES, approximately 60 engineers working for Ford collaborated in the U.S. and Europe. They used the artifact to support applications varying

· From the design of vehicle components to the modeling of a complete, new vehicle.

Today, new automobiles at Ford, as well as their parts and components, are produced from TIES-assisted designs. As a result, management anticipates reductions in life cycle times as well as improvements in product quality. Another payoff has been the assistance given to preventing problematic designs and determining how those designs were developed in the first place.

In this and many other implementations of knowledge engineering in CAD, parallel benefits come from documenting, preserving, and internally distributing expert knowledge about customer concerns, design choices, and engineering tradeoffs. The net result is a significant competitive advantage manufacturing companies must be careful not to miss.

4

Practical Applications with Expert Systems

Introduction

Automation has been the key to a remarkable growth in the manufacturing industry. In the process, industries including petroleum, chemicals, petrochemicals, power production, catalytic cracking, and atomic power would be economically unfeasible — if not physically impossible — without the use of the modern automatic control equipment.

In the discrete items manufacturing industries of today there is a high degree of automation in the plant as well as in the office. Automation at the factory floor would have been impossible without an understanding of the encountered control problems, from numerical control equipment to robotics.

· Behind the understanding of the processes and machines that exist in the plant, there is know-how that should be steadily enhanced.
· Know-how is needed for planning and control activities, and this too gets obsolete as technology advances.

Factory scheduling is an example. There are a large number of possible situations comprising all machines in the floor, the partial completions of previously scheduled orders, and many combinations of order types including their deadlines. There are also a correspondingly large number of possible schedules as new orders arrive. Schedules often have to be revised and optimized.

Computers have been used in factory scheduling for decades, but it typically has been done in a rather unsophisticated manner. Such applications required an extremely large amount of data and a relatively small number of computations.

Practically the opposite is happening with knowledge-based solutions encountered among the most advanced industries. At the manufacturing floor, expert systems have been put to work in a range of implementations areas: computer aided manufacturing (CAM), robotics, production planning and control, inventory management, quality assurance, and other fields.

Outside the technical domain, expert systems assist in the activities associated with marketing and sales, as well as a wide range of maintenance operations starting with diagnostics. There is also a wealth of administrative applications valid in a cross-industry manner, including

·   Finance
·   Controllership
·   Taxation
·   Legal procedures

The most impressive applications of expert systems in industry are those working on line. Some artifacts are complex, others (a lot of them) are simpler. By exploiting information in manufacturing databases, they provide significant assistance to managers and professionals, as we will see in this chapter.

Du Pont Automates Package Design Through Knowledge Engineering

As we saw in Chapter 3, engineering design has been a fruitful domain for AI artifacts — and not only in regard to mechanical and electrical engineering projects. Taken from a different domain, the example in this section regards the use of knowledge engineering in plastic food package design.

This specific application comes from Du Pont. When the company entered the high-growth barrier resin market, it encountered well-established competition. To gain a competitive advantage, it responded with an expert system that

·   Educates customers about the Du Pont product line while automating the complex process of rigid food package design.

The *Packaging Advisor* can evaluate optimal specifications for a rigid container in a few minutes. It calculates its cost of production all the way to profit margins and presents a comprehensive answer to its user.

The knowledge engineering artifact eliminates the tedious effort of calculating the benefits of possible alternative combinations of resin products. The expert system evaluations encompass products from both Du Pont and its competitors, providing marketing with instantaneous information on which to bid.

The concept embedded in the Packaging Advisor rests on the fact that food packages typically consist of multiple layers of barrier resins (needed to guard against spoilage through oxygen infiltration) and lower cost, structural resins. For reasons of optimization, design engineers must choose

- The most appropriate of several hundred possible combinations
- These involve some 20 different types of barrier resins and a corresponding number of structural elements.

It takes an hour or so to manually calculate a single resin combination. Therefore, design engineers tend to favor a smaller range of materials (ones they are familiar with), sometimes missing cost-effective solutions.

Automating the design and optimization process helps eliminate this limitation. The Packaging Advisor sweeps through a large database, assessing multiple product combinations by using the knowledge embedded into the system.

The AI artifact also determines the amount and cost of barrier resins needed to keep oxygen permeation at a given level during the shelf life of a package:

- It ranks alternatives by cost
- It lists competitive materials that are more cost-effective
- It evaluates products of competitors against what Du Pont has to offer.

Users can modify tables in the database to reflect their own resin costs and process economics. They do so interactively, in contrast to old data processing which was massive, monolithic, and inflexible. Expert systems are agile, knowledgeable, and user friendly, serving the new perspectives in manufacturing.

These qualities of the knowledge-based artifacts have been exploited since the development phase of the Packaging Advisor. The project started with the simplest plausible prototype. The first goal was to identify critical design factors and learn from the use of a model, which reduced the problem to its fundamentals.

- Newer, more sophisticated releases came by level, creating successive prototypes.
- While the sophistication increased, ease of use remained a steady goal.

In day-to-day implementation, package designers work on different hypotheses, for instance, the maximum temperature a package will experience. The expert system helps in this process by responding to English language queries. A typical session includes questions regarding

- Package dimensions
- Fabrication process to be used
- Desired shelf life
- Maximum allowable oxygen infiltration
- Wanted optical properties and other primary design parameters

The artifact infers information for secondary parameters. Data and inferences are presented on an interactive screen, the Package Requirement Summary. Cost-affecting inferences concerning scrap material and recycling rates can be adjusted at this point.

Du Pont is expanding the capabilities of the expert system to address flexible and rigid packaging, as well as to improve the handling of factors relating to high-temperature sterilization processing which can affect container shelf life. Du Pont is also focusing on stress resistance analysis to automate testing.

The logical concept behind this and other knowledge engineering constructs is explained in Figure 1. At the right side are definitions, constraints, assumptions, and facts. These are nicely reflected into the knowledgebank of the expert system. At the opposite side is human behavior, including an expert's response to a situation developed in his domain of work. The two are linked together through a first order logic construct, which may reside in the human brain or in a metal shell that contains the computer memory.

First order logic may work by default, and it often does so. At a higher level of sophistication, the artifact may emulate behavior by means of fuzzy engineering which permits manipulation on a higher order logic. The Du Pont plastic food package design construct does not use fuzzy engineering; it is a rule-based system. Even so, its qualities saw to it that

· The Packaging Advisor appealed to many Du Pont customers regarding its usage for their own needs.
· This expert system is now employed by nearly 80% of Du Pont's barrier resin customers for the work they are doing in their shops.

In conclusion, the Packaging Advisor has met Du Pont's goals of establishing itself as a technology leader, demonstrating the value of its barrier products, and increasing resin sales. Since producing and fielding the Packaging Advisor in 1988, Du Pont has become one of the top four barrier resin suppliers, which is a telling example of the benefits derived from expert systems in the manufacturing industry.

An Expert Approach to the Screening of Warranty Claims

Innovative solutions do not need to be revolutions against past database practices. They can very well be evolutionary, integrating with and significantly upgrading what already exists.

But as I will never tire repeating, the implementation of high technology in the manufacturing industry should focus on the cross-database problem, i.e., the input and reference files to the application. The following case of a financial expert system done by Ford Motor Company with the assistance of Inference Corporation helps document this point.

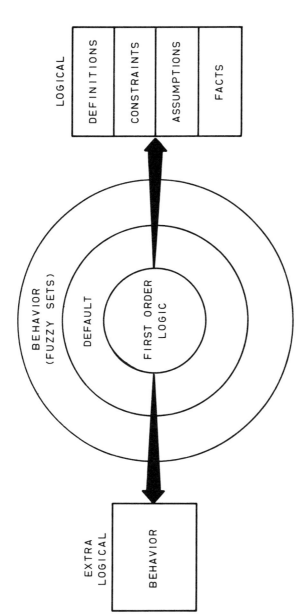

Figure 1 The logical concept behind the development and use of knowledge engineering constructs.

This application concerns warranty claims. Ford receives thousands of them every night. It is part and parcel of the normal procedure; changes need to be done often, which is cumbersome with the monolithic computer programs that have been used so far. This process is too slow and too costly with Cobol code.

The newly developed expert system for Claims Authorization and Processing (ESCAPE) is used by Ford Parts and Service Division for the validation process regarding warranty claims.

·   The program checks each incoming claim and attaches an error code to those that are not valid.
·   It does so by replacing a portion of an existing Cobol code, which served the same function but in a cumbersome manner.

Due to the complexity of the old programs, the maintenance group was finding it increasingly difficult to implement changes in warranty policy with sufficient speed to respond to the evolution in automotive market conditions and requirements.

The new approach started with the fundamentals. The warranty claims are submitted by Ford dealerships throughout the world (Ford and Lincoln-Mercury Divisions). Policies include:

·   Normal warranty coverage
·   Extended warranty coverage
·   Special warranty programs
·   Company recalls

By submitting the claim, the dealer is requesting reimbursement from Ford to cover the cost of the parts and labor needed to perform the repair. Each claim is verified with appropriate disposition made within 24 hours.

The expert system verifies the vehicle type, production date, mileage, part and labor costs, as well as other information appropriate for the warranty coverage, indicated by the submitting dealer. The claim cannot be validated if

·   The mileage is too high
·   The vehicle line is not eligible for a specific policy
·   Other error conditions are identified

When control is passed to ESCAPE, it asserts needed data as facts, processes the incoming claim, returns codes for any errors that it detects, retracts all of the facts asserted from the current claim, and finally returns control to the Cobol program. Then, the AI artifact hibernates until a claim problem is submitted to it. This symbiosis is shown in Figure 2.

Unvalidated claims are returned to either the Claims Review Activity or the dealership with an appropriate error message explaining why reimbursement was denied.

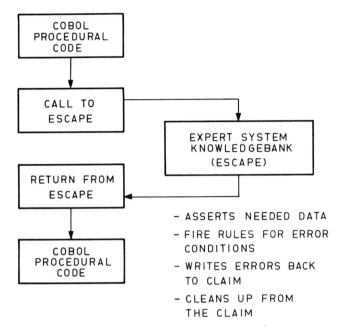

Figure 2   Improving the performance of an old code through knowledge engineering.

- This application closely resembles a myriad of other filtering and testing actions that are vital to industry.
- It also exemplifies how, through an escape mechanism, new solutions can work very closely with the old, providing a perfect synergy.

The core of ESCAPE consists almost entirely of actual warranty claim validation tests, but as a whole the artifact also performs interfacing functions. Interface rules are needed to allocate the necessary buffers for data transmission, to write error codes back to the original claim, and to clean up data (garbage collection) at the end of each claim.

- Validation rules are separated into sets called *edits*.
- An edit is simply the rules which make up the validation tests for a warranty policy.
- The number of these rules varies, depending on the scope of coverage, for the warranty policy the edit describes.

Inspection rules flag errors with the incoming claim, firing only when a problem is detected. The objective is to filter out the invalid claims and allow the correct ones to pass through. Since the majority of the incoming claims are correct, the program was structured to act by exception.

Program design reflects one-to-one mapping between the expert system rules and warranty policy rules. This mapping enables the maintenance personnel to quickly and correctly identify the criteria for any warranty policy, update existing rules when warranty policy changes occur, and validate the processing accuracy of incoming claims.

ESCAPE provided savings in several areas. First and foremost is the reduction of maintenance for the special warranty validation process. Second is the contribution provided in terms of smart database access. Third is the demonstration that hybrid solutions do work.

After nearly 30 years of visionless developments in computer software for manufacturing and other industries, it is rewarding to see the results of new, imaginative departures. The worst enemy of profitability is inertia, and this is true whether we talk about computer applications or any other domain.

A Top Role for Domain Expertise Through PROFILE

Given the results obtained through ESCAPE, another expert system called PRO-FILE has been developed at Ford. Its goal is to automatically determine under which one of the eligible warranty programs a claim should be paid. As a matter of principle,

·   Warranty policy coverage is not mutually exclusive, thus leading to a complex decision process.

For this reason, a single claim could be eligible under multiple warranty programs at the same time. There is a common procedure for sorting-out different cases:

·   Develop hierarchy of relationships between warranty programs, helping to resolve these issues when they occur.

This is precisely what PROFILE is doing.

Work is also under way to develop a translator tool that can support more effective communication between the warranty policy administrators, the database, and systems programmers. Management correctly views this approach as critical in getting the policy administrators more directly involved in the implementation of warranty policy.

These and similar applications go beyond the concept of conventional database management, though they do provide access to current databases without altering their structure. The point is that the solutions of the 1960s and 1970s, and to certain measure those of the 1980s, are incapable of dealing with the more logically complex notions in database interactivity, and warranty claims need plenty of it.

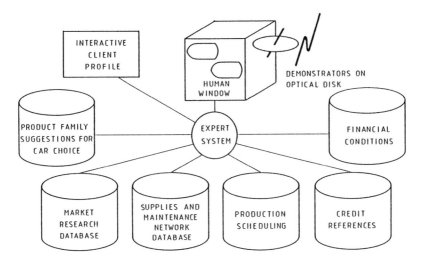

Figure 3   Self-actuated expert system for marketing motor vehicles.

As we will see in Part II, solutions to the multidatabase problem, which in the general case involves totally heterogeneous structures, are both vital and urgent. If this is true of claims warranties, it is even more so with cross-departmental applications.

Along a similar frame of reference, Figure 3 presents the example of an expert system for marketing motor vehicles, developed by a different vendor. One of the most important modules of the artifact is an interactive client profile analyzer, which permits salesmen to more accurately detect client drives and desires.

In terms of system design and operation, seven different databases are accessed and manipulated by this artifact. Each one plays a key role in total performance.

1. A product family database facilitates car and component choices for the expert system.
2. Demonstrators stored on optical disk present virtually real-life experience to the buyer.
3. The financial conditions database not only provides pricing information, but online assistance to salesmen for integrating client requests as well.
4. Distributed databases channel credit references toward acceptance procedures.

These databases are accessed during a sales contact negotiation. There are others that will support the client relationship further:

5. The production planning database provides the client with the exact schedule prior to delivery.

6. The supplies and maintenance database network helps during servicing.
7. Market research databases must be updated on a steady basis, not only through market research proper but online from the profile analyzer to maintenance action.

Every single one of these domains can be served through expert systems. But even the best expert systems support will be of little avail unless there is a first class infrastructure of databases.

Whether for warranty claims, profiling, or other reasons, the knowledge that engineering constructs provide is a degree of expertise unavailable through classical programming approaches. This expertise encompasses the client's (and the product's)

- Characteristics
- Qualification
- Implication
- Causality

The obtained information will be databased and enriched with text and data already existing in the enterprise, which is interactively available from other sources like transaction processing.

It is no longer enough to deal with information about a small world containing a fixed number of entities and relationships that cannot be expanded because the technology is lacking. No database contents are immutable. The cutting edge of the marketplace requires dynamic approaches and should squarely reflect the way we project, operate, and maintain our corporate database.

Knowledge Engineering at the Lawrence Livermore National Laboratory

As the previous examples have demonstrated, the capable management of distributed database facilities has become not only a major competitive advantage but also the cornerstone to effective implementation of information technology. But over the years, and this is true of many organizations, the importance of databases got somewhat forgotten — with the necessary streamlining taking the backseat.

Quite often, management has been throwing money at the problem rather than searching for solutions. Nowhere can this counterproductive policy best be documented than through the indiscriminate buying of DBMSs of several vendors rather than developing imaginative solutions like IDA,[1] custom-made to the problem on hand.

---

1   IDA, by General Telephone and Electronics (GTE), is presented in Chapter 13, Part III.

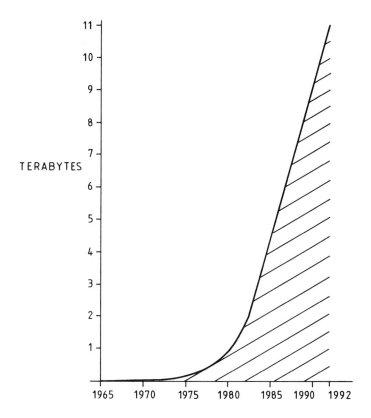

Figure 4   Rapid database growth at the Lawrence Livermore National Laboratory.

Companies that forget this principle are those failing to acquire the necessary skills, and with time they fall further behind in their ability to deal with their sprawling databases. This can be deadly:

·   A good example of how fast databases can grow is offered by the Lawrence Livermore National Laboratory (LLNL) and is shown in Figure 4.
·   LLNL is also a leader in technology, with a significant inventory of expert system applications closely connected to database usage.

The first example from LLNL is the qualitative reasoning and symbolic analysis artifact for engineering design. This is a workstation package that gives the engineer, at an early stage, insight into the behavior of his design. The LLNL method uses graphs to organize knowledge about the dynamics of the physical system.

State variables are inferred from these graphs. The designer can reason about the system in qualitative terms, such as positive or negative values of a state variable. This approach is integrated with traditional numerical and symbolic engineering design methods.

Another imaginative implementation at LLNL, which also depends on database access, is an expert system for monitoring and interpreting security alarms. Its goal is to identify security incidents by

· Associating
· Classifying
· Prioritizing

monitored sensor events. Interfacing a variety of monitoring and access control devices, the artifact is creating a dynamic representation of the state of laboratory security in the form of a map-based user interface that provides the operator with a comprehensive view of security hazards and their locations.

An even better example of database usage in conjunction with knowledge engineering implementation is offered by the expert systems developed by LLNL for treaty verification. Seismic verification of a Low-Yield Threshold Test Ban Treaty or a Comprehensive Test Ban Treaty requires the ability to

· Detect
· Characterize
· Identify

the nature of a large number of seismic events. LLNL has developed rule-based expert systems to aid in the verification of treaties by automating the task of data interpretation for various seismic monitoring systems.

Another application at LLNL, which offers a good example of what can be done as well by private research laboratories, is an expert system for triple quadrupole mass spectrometry. Known as TQMSTUNE, this artifact is a combination of rules, frames, and Lisp code, a good part of its contribution being the tuning of an instrument.

As engineering laboratories know by experience, tuning a sophisticated chemical measurement instrument like the triple quadrupole mass spectrometer is a complex task. The use of the expert system resulted in large gains in instrument sensitivity, and it is an approach applicable to the tuning of other sophisticated instruments such as accelerators and laser systems.

Another tuning expert system at LLNL addresses itself to particle beam accelerators. It is designed to function as an intelligent assistant for an operator, implementing strategems and reasoning in steering the beam through the transport section of the Advanced Test Accelerator. This artifact uses the Monitored Decision Script, LLNL has developed.

There is also an expert system to control a fusion energy experiment. It is a rule-based expert system that automates the critical process of conditioning new or rebuilt neutral beam sources by encoding the behavior of several experts as a set of IF-THEN rules.

Some of the expert systems projects done at LLNL find their counterpart in industry, for instance, the fault finder developed by ICL to audit the design of its new mainframes and flash out conceptual and/or implementation faults.

Martin Marietta Aerospace has designed the fault isolation expert system (FIES), a rule-based detection program projected for space station power subsystems. It isolates the fault and performs or recommends appropriate correction.

Another artifact by Martin Marietta, the energy management expert system (EMES), manages the allocation of power to various electrical components of a spacecraft. It also permits graceful degradation of critical system components. A third, is a fault handling expert system for satellite propulsion. A fourth, Automatic Task Automation (ATA), is designed for robotic inspection tasks. It integrates robotics, computer vision, path planning, and task scheduling.

As the span of these examples helps identify, there is significant potential in the use of knowledge engineering in industry. This potential is further increased through the implementation of second generation expert systems methodologies as we will see in the next section.

Japan's Fuzzy Adaptive Control System[2]

Systems control based on fuzzy engineering is a very successful application. Developed by LIFE, this artifact uses fuzzy sets to encode knowledge for adaptive control by means of representing pairs of a reference model.

To realize a robust control system, this fuzzy engineering construct focuses on the usage of control gains by means of process reference models, which are given in fuzzy rules:

- The *Learning Vector Quantization* (LVQ) helps to directly evaluate a process output, connecting it with the main model through fuzzy rules.
- LQV can automatically create membership functions of fuzzy sets in cooperation with the *Fuzzy Associative Memory Organizing Units System* (FAMOUS).

This solution has been found useful for connecting reference models with their controllers for different processes. Neural networks have been used for lower level functions.

FAMOUS has three features. The first is fuzzy knowledge representation by means of causal relations. The second, a hierarchical knowledge realization by

2 Based on the work done by the Laboratory for International Fuzzy Engineering (LIFE) and Chiba University.

means of associative memories. The third, fuzzy inference through association. The main features of the fuzzy adaptive control system are

1. Membership functions created by LVQ in fuzzy rules
2. Fuzzy inference by means of associative memory
3. Fuzzy knowledge representation using relations interpreted from fuzzy rules

In subsystem 1 (the IF-part), LVQ networks evaluate process output and show the distances between output response patterns for process and for the reference models. This is done through fuzzy sets. In the fuzzy IF-THEN rule part (subsystem 2), an associative memory system connects reference models for processes with their controllers. The controllers' structure is given in the THEN-part (subsystem 3).

Since, in the IF-part, LVQ networks are used for evaluating process output, LVQ clusters the input space which consists of output response patterns for the controlled process. This is accomplished by means of unsupervised learning by LVQ.

For instance, LVQ can show the distance between an output response pattern for a given process and for the suitable reference model. It does so by using the pattern's ability to automatically create membership functions of fuzzy rules.

While fuzzy engineering addresses the higher-up cognitive functions, a neural network associated to this process handles the lower functions. The neural net has three layers:

· The first layer is for input
· The second helps in creating membership functions of fuzzy rules
· The third evaluates a truth value of each rule.

The first layer input is a time response pattern for controlled process. The second layer receives an input vector from the first and maps it to a neuron plane. Each neuron of the second layer has an activation function inversely proportional to the distance between the synapse weight vector and the input vector. In this second layer, membership functions are trained by LVQ through a fast learning algorithm able to realize a continuous mapping according to the relative distance between two vectors.

The third layer has linear neurons whose number is equal to that needed by the fuzzy rules. After training the second layer, the activation patterns can be regarded as the membership functions of fuzzy rules. The model connects the second layer to the third layer with the weights, which are proportional to these activation values.

In actual implementation, the weights are scaled so that the third layer activation values should be in an established range. After the connection, the third layer activation values stand for the fuzzy rule truth values.

To represent pairs of a reference model for a given controlled process and its controller, the LIFE project used fuzzy-type representation:

· The IF-part shows characteristics of the process reference model.
· The THEN-part connects to controller activity.

A fuzzy controller, which maps an observed output response pattern to a parameter space and synthesizes the control gain, has been designed to control a nonlinear system with parametric variance. Online learning by LVQ is used for a fuzzy clustering of the parameter space. It employs a representation scheme.

Using the associative memory system FAMOUS, the researchers connected these reference models to their respective controllers, enriching analogical reasoning with fuzzy rules. The model uses an entropy feature to control increasing system fuzziness.

Associative fuzzy inference improves one of the weak points of logical inference: increasing fuzziness of inference output. A reason for the fuzzy controller's high stability has been LVQ's continuous mapping in parameter variance space. The system proved to be very useful for the control of nonlinear processes with parametric variance.

Starting with the Simpler Steps to Learn the Method

The sophistication of a fuzzy engineering implementation, such as the one with LVQ and FAMOUS in the previous section, may bring the wrong message — that only complex expert systems are useful. This is not true. It took a couple of hours of steady work to create a simple factory planning system containing a dozen rules, with at least two conditions attached to each rule:

· To create the expert system, the designer started by listing all of the possible equipment this type of factory might need.
· The list was entered into the computer as a protocol of alternatives, with two or three types outlined per required piece of equipment.

The options available for each alternative were at the center of the logic trails mapped into the computer. Subsequently, through the use of this simple expert system, factory personnel obtained answers to a series of queries, with choices based on the type of products to be made.

Each response moves the system into a logic chain, leading to the selection of a machine tool. At any point, the user can ask to see the rule upon which the program is basing its questions and answers. The user can also ask to see all of the conclusions to get a personal opinion of the results.

Planning expert systems are a growing breed in business and industry. At American Airlines, for example, knowledge engineering modules working in conjunction with SABRE, the carrier's legendary reservation system, handle most backoffice and inventory management functions that used to be done on paper by or through batch. This allows inventory to be managed more efficiently, speeding up restocking with huge inventory savings.

Other artifacts have been designed to drastically reduce overlaps and allow managers to compare performance. This is no different than applications in manufacturing plants where the master scheduler expert system is given a list of tasks that must be completed for any given day.

- · The master scheduler must consider many objectives when assigning workers to tasks.
- · These objectives take the form of constraints and preferences, handled through heuristics.

Preferences include allowing employees choices for partners and crews and providing variety in the assigned task. The heuristics are rules of thumb for producing good schedules quickly.

- · Constraints include the list of skills available during a given shift and their qualifications or certifications.

One specific expert system implementation for scheduling chores reads three different files as input then acts on the information elements contained in these files:

1. The list of tasks that must be assigned to employees on the current day
2. Data about the tasks and their associated priorities
3. Reference to the database of employees, including their names, qualifications, and previous task assignments

After the knowledgebank has processed the data, it produces a worker task assignment. Notice however that the more challenging part of this application was not the IF-THEN rules and heuristics but the cross database access. A sophisticated approach was necessary because the files in reference resided in different heterogeneous databases.

While expert systems are an easy and natural way to solve the problem of resource allocation, as we will see in Part II the implementation of cross-database access is not necessarily straightforward. Hence, the wisdom of planning ahead for efficient database access solutions can overcome incompatibilities.

Steady database access is needed because any knowledge-based scheduler worth its salt utilizes a wealth of realtime plant information to generate programs that

- · Observe factory resource constraints while taking advantage of the possible flexibility

A scheduling system built along these lines by a leading manufacturing firm uses heuristics developed by an experienced factory scheduler, along with a deterministic simulation concept necessary to project on decision points.

As this project has shown, knowledge engineering and simulation share many concepts. Hence, the two disciplines can be used synergistically. This implementation also demonstrated the ability to control the flow of entities through the production system using conditional probabilities.

- Heuristics rules fit problems with part dispatching, determining which order will be scheduled next from a lot of candidates.
- By contrast, conditional probabilities assist in the definition of quantities on the basis of customer orders and batch sizing considerations.

Optimization concerns machine selection, determining which machine among a group of candidates will be used to process the selected part order. Another problem regards interval selection, i.e., which time interval in the window of time considered on the selected machine is most suitable to process the selected order.

Trade-offs are evidently necessary and can be handled through expert systems. An example of a trade-off is machine setup vs. just-in-time inventory management — also coordinating preventive maintenance and other events affecting production.

As these examples help demonstrate, there is plenty of specific information that must be incorporated into the model. This can be done effectively using knowledge technology. But while there is considerable experience with problems connected to handling production clones today, those relative to database interoperability pose the more challenging requirements.

5

Organizational Prerequisites to Computer Integrated Manufacturing

Introduction

Today, it is no secret that manufacturing needs systems that support design, production, marketing, and field maintenance through integration. There is a significant shift occurring in the way products are made, as well as the policies followed in this regard.

Total quality, just-in-time inventories, flexible manufacturing cells, quality assurance, and real time monitoring require integration of manufacturing processes. They also call for reliable execution of product and process design and implementation.

As leading-edge manufacturing companies know from their own experience, concurrent engineering and computer integrated manufacturing are not only competitive tools but also realities in the workplace which change the way engineering and manufacturing are organized and managed. Knowledge engineering can be instrumental in supporting this restructuring effort.

The U.S. government is sponsoring standard representations of intelligent product descriptions. This effort is known as Production Description Exchange/STEP. Using STEP (PDES) is expected to provide a key to successful implementation of concurrent engineering and CIM.

But government-promoted processes are only part of the story. The point laggard manufacturing organizations are missing is that traditional computer software, as well as hierarchical, Codasyl, or even relational databases, cannot handle the

- · Complexity
- · Polyvalence

·   Distributed manner
·   Performance

required for concurrent engineering and computer integrated manufacturing. They simply fall short of providing the necessary capabilities to effectively support the evolving requirements.

The now classical computer solutions and the system software they employ — which essentially means those developed during the 1960s, 1970s, and the first half of the 1980s — are not able to address complex, interrelated engineering and manufacturing issues. Performance with integrated automation systems requires improvements over past practices by a factor of 10 times, to 100 times or more.

Policies Regarding an Intelligent CIM Technology

Team product and process design necessitates shared, distributed databases as well as integration and coordination among departments. Though the latter is an organizational requirement, it has technical prerequisites as well, such as a seamless approach to databases and flexibility in systems structure.

Any company that plans for survival has to continually improve manufacturing efficiency by shortening the manufacturing cycle, from component purchases to product sales. This requires a significant amount of coordination which cannot be supported by the old, inflexible mainframe-based approaches.

Precisely for these reasons, as we saw in Chapters 1 and 2, the Japanese Ministry of International Trade and Industry (MITI) has instituted the Intelligent Manufacturing System project. It uses knowledge engineering to integrate software, hardware, and robotics. The algorithm is

$$IMS = CIM + AI$$

The Intelligent Manufacturing System goes beyond CIM because it tackles very advanced computer technology. Since the new solution has many unknowns it is projected to take about 10 years in terms of development, while producing intermediate results that can be used for manufacturing automation purposes.

Such intermediate results require breakthroughs in CIM technology, and breakthroughs do not come by chance. They need

·   Strong leadership
·   Sound investments
·   Rich databases
·   Industrialization expertise
·   Tremendous patience

The goal should be the development and implementation of a knowledge enriched integrative architecture, which presents a standard level of reference in software

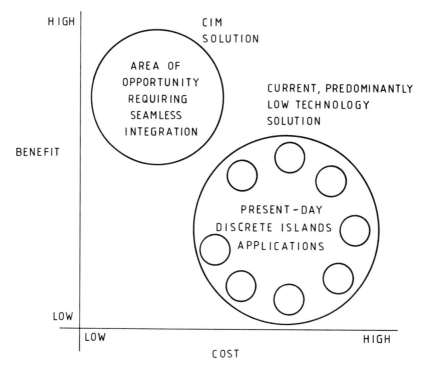

Figure 1   The goal of high technology implementation in manufacturing.

terms. We have to enhance program portability and the cross-database exchange of information elements.

Virtual database integration tackles a wide range of subtle, technical interactions among the various components and subsystems of a manufacturing company. Figure 1 helps clarify this reference by contrasting the benefit obtained from technology-based services against the costs these represent.

It is not surprising that only the leaders have discovered how this relationship works. The majority of manufacturing companies continue spending big money for only minor results, attested to by their inability to unstick themselves from Cobol and the mainframes.

One of the major aims sought out by the leading manufacturing companies is to be able to integrate all of their divisions into one functional system, each division with its own niche of expertise.

· This makes the exploitation of complementary skills and increasing overall performance feasible.

· It capitalizes on the fact that many operating units are expert in a given domain, but lack specific bits and pieces of knowledge other units possess.

As we have seen in earlier chapters, a sound approach along this integrative line of reference must first take a macroscopic view in order to establish the proper perspective. Then it should look at the physical level of resources, progressing toward the higher-up conceptual level.

The databases have to be analyzed, and with them the programming languages provided by (or at least supported by) the database management system (DBMS) and used by the running processes. This is what a complete CIM-oriented work will demand.

Precisely for this reason, companies that have put their priorities right are well advanced in terms of new approaches to manufacturing automation. The McDonnell Douglas Corporation, for example, uses an object-oriented database management system, Ontos, to integrate features-based and rules-based tools. This involves

- Part features
- Manufacturing rules
- Process standards and machines
- Tool and material attributes

All of them are handled as objects. The integration sought after is essentially concurrent engineering. An intelligent CAD/CAM prototype shares a common object representation assisted through knowledge-based artifacts.

Unless process design is associated with an analysis that shows it to be compatible with the evolving requirements of the company's products and processes, factory automation as a whole, and the production lines in particular, will not work that well.

- Throwing money at the problem never solves it.
- In many cases, the problem amplifies and becomes worse.

Nothing short of a rigorous systems approach to the entire issue of factory automation can serve in reaching effective, lasting solutions — and intelligence-enriched approaches are key to this reference.

A good methodology that establishes the profile of operations starts with a bill of materials of all processes running on the company's computers, including programs down to the module level, whether they are on mainframes, minis, LAN servers, or workstations. This should include the identification of all files and records these processes address.

In my professional practice I have found that such analysis is a prerequisite to any meaningful work on integration. The bill of materials of the analytical study should include

- Operating systems (OS)
- Teleprocessing monitors (TPM)
- Database management systems (DBMS)

While the old traditional record-keeping applications have changed, becoming more sophisticated, lack of the proverbial long hard look sees to it that users keep on receiving a low quality service. Throughout the manufacturing industry, poor performance characterizes all short-sighted approaches.

However, computer literate users now demand the support of new and increasingly complex features, and this cannot be done effectively through old concepts and worn out tools. Buying off-the-shelf software is more cost-effective than writing new routines. Quite often, however, not enough attention is paid to *homogeneity,* and the company ends up with incompatible solutions it can ill afford.

Organizations that know how to use technology to their advantage, don't let themselves get into that trap. Different efforts have been set-up to help companies get off of the beaten path, some private and other cooperative on an industry basis.

For instance, the South Carolina Research Authority (SCRA) and American Manufacturing Research Consortium (AMRC) are designing a CIM system with the objective of delivering a part within 30 days of the order, even if the part has never been manufactured before. This design integrates

- Production planning
- Shop floor control
- Automated, semi-automated, and manual manufacturing equipment

The project generates online manufacturing process plans, employs object-oriented technology, and cuts new ground on how CIM challenges should be confronted. It aims to optimize planning operations, improve productivity, favorably affect outgoing product quality, and reduce maintenance effort.

CIM, Object Orientation, and Product Lifecycle

In Chapter 3, on computer aided design, it was said that the reason why concurrent engineering is so competitive is that it yields product and process designs capable of promoting time and cost reduction through the product lifecycle. This permits, but does not guarantee, the realization of major savings.

New and improved technology must be employed for efficient manufacturing and for quality results. Intelligent approaches to CIM should be instrumental in integrating new solutions with existing investments, and in this regard object orientation can be very helpful.[1] Object database management systems provide some fundamental strengths:

---

1   See also D. N. Chorafas and H. Steinmann, *An Introduction to Object-Oriented Databases,* Prentice-Hall, Englewood Cliffs, NJ, 1993.

- They make cooperation with existing investments in relational databases, regarding CAD/CAM and marketing solutions feasible.
- They ease online access to manufacturing data, which may be spread in many locations and incompatible systems.
- They help create flexible processing routines for online execution, as well as in their maintenance.
- They assist, in a lifecycle sense, the engineering, manufacturing and field service information regarding *our* services and products.

Object-oriented implementation leads to this result, starting at the concurrent engineering level where the CIM effort should begin. Let's always recall that product lifecycle is initiated with the product definition.

Intelligence-enriched approaches, the alter ego of object solutions, help product representation in a way that fully describes that product, its features, and constituent parts, as well as the manufacturing processes it uses. But as it cannot be repeated too often, intelligent CIM rests on two pillars:

- Knowledge-based solutions
- Seamless access to databases

Many manufacturing applications today are not properly supported by databases. Others are unfeasible because the needed databases are not effectively linked together.

In a number of cases, the applications interfaces are substandard and/or data transfer is done in a rather primitive manner. Yet, a rational manufacturing system architecture should provide cooperation between

- Multimedia (text, data, graphics, images, voice) storage managers distributed in a network-wide sense
- Applications that preserve their proper autonomy and functionality, but cooperate within the global environment

Such an approach is fundamental to the management of processes and products. Through knowledge engineering and object orientation we can model system-specific gateways to encapsulate the details of particular underlying computer implementations, making change control in a heterogeneous environment possible.

But what is really meant by *object orientation?* The characteristtics of the object-oriented approach are centered around the concept of abstraction, but they go well beyond that level.

- Objects are abstract data types that ignore details of usage but have associated operations and constraints.

· In this way, both dynamic and static aspects of the database can be represented declaratively.

An object is a named, encapsulated entity which typically includes information elements (IE) and commands. An *object* is an instance of a class and a basic run time entity. A *class* is the abstraction of shared characteristics exhibiting

1. Inheritance
2. Equilibration
3. Metarules and constraints
4. Distributed concurrency
5. Extensibility and interoperability
6. Network-wide behavior monitoring
7. Referential integrity (within a context)
8. Message orientation or operations orientation
9. Query relevance
10. Reusability

The user community, and most particularly the foremost manufacturing organizations, increasingly recognize that without an object approach parochial databases will dominate in a way similar to that described in Figure 2, and we will not have the means for their functional integration. Hence, it is looking for ways to effectively implement a distributed architecture that supports multiple applications written in multiple languages.

The aim is to provide gateways into distributed databases at all times — our own gateways as well those of our business partners, clients, and suppliers. The whole computing environment needs to be revamped in order to respond to these requirements in an effective manner.

· Centralization of computing resources is by far the worst possible solution.
· The technical answer which fits concurrent engineering and CIM requirements in the *client/server* model of networked workstations and databases.[2]

Even if centralization of our computing resources was a workable proposition, it would have meant very little in terms of global functionality because the computers of our clients are a de facto distributed heterogeneous landscape. This often tends to be forgotten by the proponents of centralization.

The aim of any serious solution should be that of supporting an open, distributed, multiclient and multiserver architecture. Such a solution should allow multiple

---

2 Beware of computer manufacturers who call their obsolete mainframes "servers".

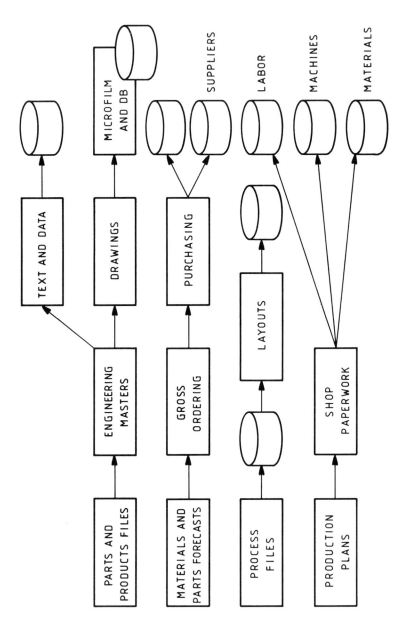

Figure 2   Discrete islands of databases that must work together in a seamless manner.

client applications to share the same information elements through remote data access and to update multiple servers.

The approach to be followed should be able to deliver paths for development of new applications, migration of existing applications, and integration with existing systems. Just as important is a fast track to systems development, including interactive reporting and visualization tools.

The aim of this technological strategy is not one of reaching a permanent equilibrium in manufacturing activities or in a product lifecycle. The goal is to provide able management in a state of flux. "When you reach an equilibrium in biology, you are dead," suggests Arnold Mandell. The same is true in business and industry.

Supporting Management's Policies Through Technology

Successful management has vision. Vision takes imagination, foresight, and guts. Successful management is also relentlessly cost cutting and pushing for productivity gains; that is why it is interested in computer integrated manufacturing.

Successful management sees to it that with a dose of discipline and a good deal of high technology the company can profit and survive.

·   Working in a disciplined manner is a personal philosophy, it is not just going by the rule book.
·   Using high technology is a far seeing policy that drives for innovation before obsolescence.

Invariably we are talking about solutions that integrate product-and-process technology as documented in the previous section. And in a lifecycle sense, product technology is not just an internal company affair. If anything this subject is more extrovert than introvert.

An article in *Business Week*[3] said that "(Thomas Graham) has instituted what became known at USX as his monthly 'prayer meetings'. These are sessions during which Graham grills midlevel managers. He also is getting to know customers one on one. That's how he gathers intelligence about his own company and prevents senior managers from trying to snow him."

Is this computer integrated manufacturing? Of course it is — and it is paying off. CIM is not just the electronics of the system, it is first and foremost a culture that has organizational prerequisites, e.g.,

·   Self-discipline
·   Orderly handling of issues
·   Ability to focus

---

3   "This Barracuda is Still on the Attack," January 20, 1992, pp. 58–59.

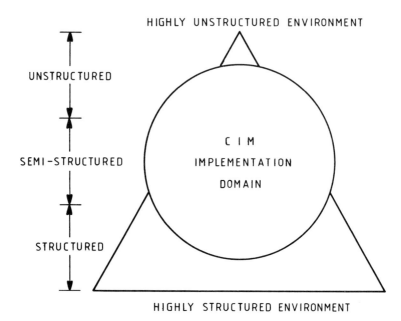

HIGHLY UNSTRUCTURED ENVIRONMENT

UNSTRUCTURED

SEMI-STRUCTURED

C I M
IMPLEMENTATION
DOMAIN

STRUCTURED

HIGHLY STRUCTURED ENVIRONMENT

Figure 3   Any manufacturing environment has structured and unstructured components; CIM tries to integrate both.

Throughout his career as a senior executive in the steel industry, *Business Week* suggests, Graham applied unrelenting pressure to *improve quality* and *cut costs* in the mills. He does not buy the widely held notion that things will improve when prices rise — a rise he is not even sure will happen. Instead, he thinks steel companies should make money even in a downturn by lowering breakeven levels. That is true of any company.

Technology, CIM evidently included, will not have any miracles in lowering breakeven levels unless management has decided to do that much. But technology can help see that the various problems associated with each management category are classified along a complexity spectrum ranging from structured to unstructured.

As Figure 3 suggests, the most unstructured problems tend to be at the top management level. Here fuzzy engineering could be of assistance, and its implementation will increasingly be seen as part of CIM.

By contrast, highly structured problems are at the bottom level of the pyramid, where data processing addresses its services. An example is general accounting. Knowledge engineering uses this layer as an infrastructure for data collection, but its real impact is on problems that lie above that level, e.g., the Internal Accounting Management Information System (IAMIS).

- Structured problems are those associated with well defined, rigid, and routine decisions whose solution procedures and decision rules are legislated and understood.
- Unstructured problems typically have ambiguous or fuzzy solution procedures, as well as an incompletely specified input — but require analysis and management decision.

An example of an operational system that is unstructured is Treasury operations, involving not only cash management but also currency risk and interest rate risk. Other examples are research and development and product planning, all the way to quality assurance when examined at early design stages.

While heuristics can serve management purposes, it is still human ingenuity that makes the difference. Therefore, Graham is right when he blasts industry members for rushing out to buy expensive technology in the hope they solve their problems. Inland Steel Co. has poured nearly $2 billion into its high-tech mills but is still losing money. Throwing money at the problem will not solve it; it will only make it worse.

Even if it could be implemented in bureaucratic environments — and it can not — computer integrated manufacturing will solve nothing as long as management permits red tape to persist. CIM has a chance only when top management has no patience for corporate bureaucracy and its procrastination.

Paper shuffling and CIM are incompatible. The main role of paper shuffling is to hide the fact that current management ran a high cost, unprofitable operation, masking a sense of impending doom until the doom takes place.[4] "The purpose of a report is not to inform the reader but to protect the writer," Dean Acheson once said.

CIM is a means, not an end in itself. Other means are the management policies being implemented. Said *Business Week* in regard to the policies Thomas Graham has followed: "In his drive to increase productivity, he slashed U.S. Steel's work force by 73 percent, lowering the number of hours per employee it took to produce a ton of steel by 60 percent."

CIM is not going to do that job, management has to do it. Bloated payroll is a company's worst enemy in its struggle for survival, yet it is a subject most companies approach half-heartedly, always pushing the fateful day further off.

The message is that while technology can be friend or foe, even as a friend it is not going to substitute for good management. The investments we make in technology should support management's policies all the way, provided such policies exist — they are a complement, not an alternative.

---

4   Just think of the communist bureaucracy in the former Soviet Union.

Strategic Prerequisites to Computer Integrated Systems

There are strategic and structural prerequisites to computer integrated manufacturing that many companies tend to forget. When these prerequisites are not observed, the systems being developed turn out to be much less valuable than they cost to create.

For instance, automobiles are an industry whose customers are accustomed to shopping for price rather than value, but this is often forgotten. In 1991, Ford and General Motors sold just over 1.6 million cars each in Western Europe.

- While GM had record net profits from its European operations,[5] Ford of Europe had only red ink to show for its efforts.

Ford's European problems seem to be rather deep-seated. The company is confronting severe structural challenges, as it seeks not only to recover the ground lost to its rivals but also to prepare for the Japanese onslaught.

Industry analysts don't buy the Ford of Europe executives' argument that points to the failure to forecast the depth of the British recession. The president of the company said "The market fell away from us so fast we had excess stocks. Each month the industry was falling away faster than our forecasts." The Ford of Britain CEO advises: "We were building vehicles for a market that did not exist."[6]

There will always be exceptional circumstances. One of the tasks confronting management is that of liquidating the bloated auto inventories. This led to a very expensive price war in the U.K. In 1 year in Britain, marketing costs jumped to the shocking level of 24% of revenues from 14% in 1990; they ranged from discounts and low cost finance to special fleet deals.

- As marketing costs escalated, production had to fall to bring inventories under control, meaning the company came under the burden of fixed costs.
- Production cuts and production booms can be very costly indeed.

There were other reasons that had to do with foresight. The Ford U.K. factory that fared best was the one equipped to manufacture lefthand drive cars for Continental Europe, where exports soared. The imbalance between market demand and product availability seems to have been exacerbated by a shortage of the right mixture of engines and gearboxes.

In 1991, one of the Ford factories in Britain was left with having to push brown engines to unwilling customers in Germany because of the lack of green engines equipped with catalytic converters. This did little to improve the international competitiveness of U.K. operations.

---

5 Nevertheless dwarfed by GM's huge losses in the U.S.
6 *Financial Times,* February 17, 1992.

These references help document what was said in the previous section, that tough management policies and organizational perspectives make the difference. Ford of Europe has good technology, and in preceding chapters we have seen concrete examples of knowledge constructs at work at Ford. But though necessary for competitive purposes, technology alone is not the answer.

The management of Ford of Europe believes that part of the current lack of competitiveness stems from its supplier structure. This is important to an industry where about 50% of the costs of a car are brought in from outside sources. As a result, the number of suppliers is now being cut radically, and remaining suppliers will have to shoulder much more of the research and development burden.

· The number of suppliers has been cut by 15% to 900 since 1988.
· Ford plans to shrink the total by another 33% to 600 by 1995 — practically half what it was in the late 1980s.

The company is also aiming at a 25% cut in its investment spending by 1997, without reducing the quality of investments. This could be done by

1. Involving component suppliers early on in the product development cycle
2. Getting designers and engineers to work simultaneously
3. Asking consumers what they want sooner than it is now done

Every one of these steps have been endorsed in this book. All of them represent tough management decisions and, on the technological side, call for cross-data-base access throughout the domain of business partners.

At the same time, Ford of Europe seeks to reduce the complexity of its model range. It also has the ambition of reducing new model development times from the 72 months of the recent past to only 36 months by adopting the radically different Japanese style for rapid development.

Another major goal is to make an independent business unit out of each major car product line. Management admits that Ford has been very compartmentalized with a vertical structure:

· Sales and marketing
· Manufacturing
· Product development
· Finance and human resources

All reporting upwards. Now it is seeking a *horizontal structure* with decision-making responsibility pushed down in the organization. The ultimate aim is to become a low cost producer.

"I know that most men, including those at ease with problems of the greatest complexity, will seldom accept even the simplest and most obvious truth if it be such that would oblige them to admit the falsity of conclusions," Leo Tolstoy once suggested. Many manufacturing executives have reached the wrong conclusion — that CIM is *the* answer to their problems. The fact is that CIM is one of their tools. The answer is new management policies.

Caring for Merchandising Requirements at an Early Time

There was a time when most manufacturing industries cared only for their own products and processes. They were not particularly interested about what was coming before or what could happen after a sale was made. The times have changed.

Large stocks of raw materials, semi-manufactured products, and other supplies buffered the manufacturing company from its suppliers. Today, just-in-time inventory has cut these stocks to the bone. Feeding the production cycle is hand to mouth. That is why CIM and online access to supplier databases are so important.

Something similar of course has happened at the other end of the cycle, which concerns products being sold. The merchandiser had his profit and loss (P+L) to look after. Now he appreciates that the bottom line requires considerable fine tuning of the relationship not only with customers but also with suppliers:

- Computer integrated manufacturing will be castrated without including the buyer's business perspectives.
- Access to heterogeneous databases is the cornerstone to online handholding positions with any and every business partner.

Even military procurement is focusing on such a relationship with the explicit aim of reducing stocks. The U.S. Navy, for instance, is in the middle of a program to cut down manufactured parts acquisition from the current 300 days to a maximum of 30 days. In addition to accurately representing the part data, the Navy is after a system that could improve performance many times over.

By now 30 days is a long time for manufacturing and merchandising firms who have been able to increase inventory turnaround from 12 to 18 times or more per year. To do so, however, they need advanced computers and communications solutions which many companies call computer integrated business (CIB). Here is an example:

After Federated Department Stores emerged from bankruptcy protection in early 1990, management decided to enter the information processing business. Through its Sabre Group,[7] Federated is selling to other retailers the computerized

---

7   Not related to American Airlines Sabre reservation system.

inventory management and back office record keeping service it uses in its own stores.

Throughout the U.S., department stores are finding that technology can help identify what products are selling and warn management of those that may be drifting toward the clearance bins. This is not a one-time example.

· Sabre tracks inventory from the time a purchase order is placed, through the delivery and distribution process, until a sale is made.
· Sabre keeps track of payments through an accounts payable system, tells a user when and where a delivery was made, and records each and every sale.

By accounting for the inventory before it enters the system right up until it leaves it, the company is able to keep less inventory on hand and mark down less merchandise.

The whole concept works online, using databases on the fact that the most informative data comes straight out of the cash register when a sale is made. By looking at sales information, a buyer knows what is hot and what is not early enough in the season. Hence, he can reorder merchandise and mark down slow selling goods accordingly.

Sabre also establishes direct links to manufacturers and suppliers. Orders used to be written out and posted, then entered once again into the manufacturers' computers. With the online system, the exchange of order information goes directly from computer to computer. It is fast, accurate, and reasonably error-free.

As a supplier of goods to mass distribution channels, the manufacturing industry has to be quite sensitive to these merchandising requirements, which can best be handled through real time algorithmic and heuristic approaches, that permit

· *Planning and analysis,* typified by the study of trends and exceptions involving "what-ifs" and modeling
· *Monitoring and control,* including exception reporting and dealing with large volumes of incoming data
· *Operational support,* with frequent high-volume, time-critical, event-responsive events such as transactions and messages

These examples go well beyond the classical confines of industrial automation, with its robots, monitors, controllers, and planning/control nodes. It includes messaging through electronic mail and other notification systems, as well as answering complex queries.

As shown in Figure 4, a whole network of databases is involved in this operation, many among them heterogeneous and incompatible. Efficient cross-database solutions are needed, and they can be provided as we will see in Part II.

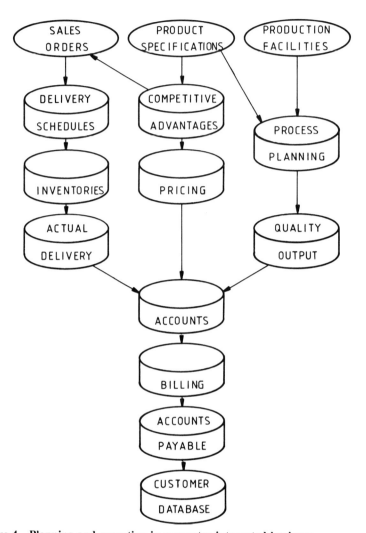

Figure 4   **Planning and execution in computer integrated business.**

Is There an Easy Road to Integration?

Satisfied customers mean a profitable business. As we all know, customers are satisfied through greater functionality, more convenience, higher quality, and lower cost.

These are not contradictory aims. Functionality, convenience, and quality do not necessarily mean higher costs, provided they are built into the product from the beginning and not pushed into the process at late stages.

The best approach to quality is getting it right the first time. It starts with identifying what a customer wants, then making sure the customer gets it. The same is true of functionality and ease of use.

These are the first targets a manufacturing system should fulfill. If we aim at computer integrated solutions we do so because we wish to bring together online cross-departmental functions and information. Often these stop at organizational barriers and stay there, creating discontinuities in the process of management.

As I will never tire repeating, the first and foremost mission in CIM is organization. A personal example helps explaining the meaning of this reference better. Some years ago, as consultant to the board of a major manufacturing company, I advised a computer integrated solution.

- The *grand design* called for bringing the systems used by three different engineering departments together, which was not without its technical challenges.
- By far the major hurdle was one of organization and structure, hence of *careers* and *personalities* — that was the stumbling block.

The three engineering departments greatly overlapped in their work, which cost the company money in terms of duplication of effort. It also led to incompatibilities. However, the department heads always found a good reason for continuing this inconsistency. The integrative technology changed this perspective because it documented the long standing overlaps — and with this came an organizational explosion.

It is therefore a purely theoretical diatribe to say that designing a CIM system has to be done according to integrative approaches or to explain that an integrative approach consists of connecting and facilitating communication between systems that already exist.

Not only are such statements vague and missing their target, but they only tend to suggest that there are only technical issues which, once solved, will bring a new epoch to the enterprise. There is nothing more untrue.

Supposing, however, that careers, personalities, and organizational and structural problems have been successfully attacked,[8] there will come a need for valid technical solutions. Simplifying, and up to a point generalizing, there will be two alternatives:

1. The creation of a new system whose functions sit on top of those performed by its subsystems or even replace many of them
2. The elaboration of a solution that unifies the functions performed by its subsystems, making the latter transparent to the user

It would be superflous to suggest that each approach seems to have advantages and disadvantages, but I should not fail to mention that alternative 1 is rather unrealistic.

---

8 Which is the exception rather than the rule. Such problems are never "solved" in the literary sense of the word, but they have to be faced.

Slowly, and very carefully, we can replace part of the old system of operation in a manufacturing environment, but this will not necessarily assure an integrative architecture. Hence, the grand design has to come first, and therefore the best strategy — if not the only one — is alternative 2.

A fully renewed manufacturing system, end to end, is like an unidentified flying object in one sense: a lot of people have reported seeing one, but none of them can agree on what it looks like. Manufacturing systems evolve over time, and the development timetable should be fast, but they cannot be replaced overnight. A grand design for CIM

- Rests on an architectural choice
- Identifies interfaces and protocols
- Defines software that monitors various devices
- Brings together into one functional aggregate a broad range of processes and products

The most critical of these processes and products in a CIM environment are databases. On the surface, database integration is a straightforward network application running on hardware and supported through software. But as we will see in Parts II and III real life solutions are much more involved. The best approach goes back to the fundamentals.

II

Multidatabase Challenges and Solutions

6

What Can Be Done with Heterogeneous Databases in Multivendor Environments?[1]

Introduction

Part I has shown the reason for incompatible databases. Databases traditionally have been called heterogeneous when they feature different data models. Yet, one of the most difficult issues to overcome is semantic heterogeneity, which exists even if all the data resources in a centralized or distributed environment follow a common model and language.

Few people pay necessary attention to semantic heterogeneity and even fewer try to do something about it. The classically observed aspects of heterogeneity include

· Differences in data representations
· Incompatibilities in names
· Schematic discrepancies (see the section on linguistic support in this chapter)

There are significant differences in normalization, as it happens with relational databases. Schematic discrepancy is a less addressed problem which appears when the data values of one database correspond to *metadata*[2] in others. Such schematic discrepancies can be frequent and pose complex problems.

---

1   This is a slightly technical chapter. Some readers may choose to skip it, but careful readers will go through it even if every issue is not 100% comprehended. Chapter 7 returns to predominantly managerial viewpoints.

2   Data about data, or schema elements. *Schemata* are discussed and defined in the section on linguistic support.

A great deal of the database integration issues with which we are confronted today stem from the fact that schematically diverse databases may have similar purposes, even if they don't deal with the same application. The effect of discrepancies is accentuated by the growing need for cross-database access. The A, B, and C of this problem can be put in the following terms:

A. We are given a group of databases containing similar or complementary information.
B. We would like to obtain and present an integrative view of all the collective data.
C. Such presentation should be done in the same style(s) in which the users view their own local databases.

The homogeneity we are after has many levels of reference. Presentation is one of them, to be executed locally at the workstation. Access to and fetching of incompatible data structures is another. There is synergy between these two references.

A typical need characterizing the users of a *multidatabase*[3] is transparency achieved through a unified view. Users want an interactive ability to formulate and pose ad hoc queries to each database they have to access in their work. Preferably, they would like to do so by

· Spanning over several heterogeneous databases accessible online
· Employing the same formal expression in spite of different schemata (conceptual views)

An able solution to such requirements will permit the enduser to see all the databases in a network *as if* they conform to the schema he knows. This helps provide an integration transparency through customized views. But we said that different databases have incompatible characteristics. Are we better off through centralized approaches?

Are We Better Off Through Centralized Solutions?

To answer this query in one sentence: Given the manufacturing industry's complexity and need for competitiveness, a centralized database solution today is an obcenity. But this response may not convince some readers without supporting examples. Therefore, let's look at the examples.

When 30 years ago manufacturing applications on digital computers were small and limited and computer storage was expensive, all we had available was a centralized file management. As applications spread in the factory and in the

---

3   A term that will be used interchangeably with distributed heterogeneous databases.

office, different areas of implementation got their own machines, rarely connected to one another. This has created the problem of

- Discrete islands of computer implementation in "this" or "that" division
- Heterogeneity in database structures, even if each little environment was practically centralized

When they became aware of this fact, some companies (with mainframe mentality) stumbled backwards toward the future. They tried their hand at total centralization — and they landed in lots of troubles.

There is an evolution in the databases of the manufacturing industry of which it is wise to take notice. Figure 1 describes the main stages of developments that have taken place over three decades: 1960s, 1970s, and 1980s. The 1990s have gone well beyond the distributed database environment of the 1980s, as examples we will see in this chapter help document.

One of the issues the proponents of centralized databases have forgotten is that to maintain their growing structures they have to manage a horde of necessary pointers and indices.

- Nothing is simple in implementing overbig centralized structures.
- By contrast, housekeeping is more manageable when databases work as a network.

Database centralization often masks certain facts that make lot of difference on how well we run our system. For instance, it is not unusual in mainframe environments to see two or three DBMS running on the same machine, for instance, IMS and DB2 with some of the files under VSAM.

- This is a heterogeneous and incompatible database environment, even if it is over-centralized.
- The different DBMS compete with each other and with the applications for scarce machine cycles on one computer.

Eventually, the systems software (operating system [OS], different DBMS, and transaction processing monitor), eat up the available — and expensive — mainframe cycles. What is more, the database incompatibility problem has not been solved.

By contrast, what we would really like to have for our service is a distributed database management able to support an integrated view of multiple preexisting databases, even if they are heterogeneous. This will provide *database consolidation,* while avoiding messy incompatible software running on the same machine.

As if the technical ills of database centralization were not enough, over the last few years centralized database solutions have led to organizational upheaval, as they failed to deliver the promised homogenization and database integration.

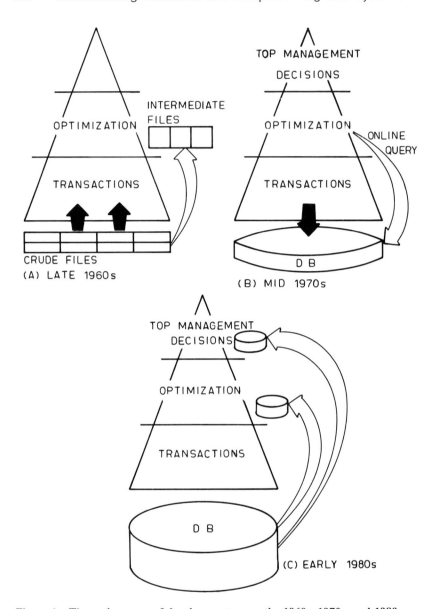

Figure 1   The main stages of developments over the 1960s, 1970s, and 1980s.

· The goal of homogenization is to overcome differences in software at the same or different sites.
· Database integration should resolve differences in semantic relationships among multiple preexisting files and records.

Whether centralized or distributed, preexisting databases often exhibit conflicts in their contents or schemata. Hence, the solutions we provide should offer a means for resolving such conflicts without physical modification of the databases.

Heterogeneity in manufacturing databases is not only due to different hardware and software platforms. The structures with which we work may also differ in regard to

· Data models
· Query languages
· Message processing capabilities
· Transaction models
· Other systems programs

Not only can databases have data conflicts, they may feature metadata conflicts, where similar information is defined and structured differently. It is a nontrivial task to match corresponding records when they have fundamental differences.

As a result, whether centralized or distributed solutions are adopted, users organizations are faced with multiple target platforms, incompatible standards, the need for integration with previous commitments in data structures, and DBMS incompatibilities. Organizations are also faced with the goal of hiding complexity from the endusers.

In a research and development organization, for instance, the endusers may be distributed in different departments, each with its own CAD and scientific or engineering database. All of them use data as corporate resources, and as shown in Figure 2, they should be in a position designed to interoperate, even if these engineering databases happen to be heterogeneous.

"We have to live in a heterogeneous world," said the chief technology officer of an American corporation, "therefore, our aim is to provide efficient bridges among distributed database resources, so as to increase the availability and interoperability of our applications across different hardware platforms, incompatible operating systems, and the diverse DBMS we are using."

A Federalist Approach to Heterogeneous Databases

The examples presented so far leave little doubt that the challenge of the 1990s is to provide a comprehensive, flexible and efficient solution to the problem of interoperating heterogeneous databases. Solutions are needed to support the growing use of computers and communications resources in the business world.

As many manufacturing companies know by experience, the design and implementation of ad hoc solutions is a major undertaking, often necessary at user organization level because major vendors failed to address the problem of integration

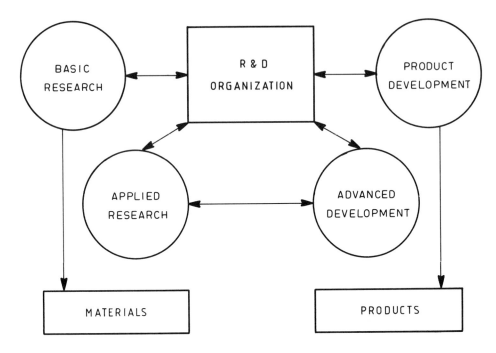

Figure 2   In an R & D operation, scientific and engineering databases should interoperate.

in a capable manner. There are several issues that must be studied before robust heterogeneous cross-database management becomes possible:

· Mapping the views of existing applications into various database structures
· Resolving the semantic heterogeneity in multidatabases
· Distinguishing equal but logically different objects stored in the database
· Consolidating different representations of the same object
· Maintaining consist information elements in the presence of distributed concurrent transactions

Efficient solutions must define relationships across the manufacturing database landscape, address the forementioned problems in a network-wide sense, and resolve domain mismatch by providing real time conversion capabilities. They must also assure data integration by generalizing common functions and views.

Along the lines of this approach, the last 7 years have seen several projects provide effective integration of incompatible DBMS and data structures. In the mid-1980s, such efforts centered around the ability to define a unified *schema*,[4]

---

4   See the section on linguistic support.

translating local schemata into it. This approach led to blind alleys and it has been dropped.

As no up and running solutions have been provided after some years of effort in the provision of universal schemata, it became evident that a schema integration provided the required answers.

· Success in schema integration depends on understanding the semantics of schema components (attributes, relations, entity sets, and relationship sets).

This *might* have been feasible in a stable environment where the involved DBMS are pre-established and fixed over long time periods. But it serves precious little in ad hoc situations, which characterize the relation between the manufacturing company and its business partners.

Major technical difficulties have been found in making the unique schema idea work, and these have been instrumental in leading to its demise.

· Technical difficulties have to do with the ability to reason with and effectively handle multiple semantics.

For some time, researchers have been led toward explicit representation of attribute relationships and schema interrelationships by means of advanced knowledge and data modeling. Others found that case-based reasoning can assist in nearly semi-automating the schema integration process, but not in the sense of a highly flexible, ad hoc, fully automated integration.

Evidently these findings had an impact on the organizations sponsoring the cross-database projects in reference, as well as on others that observed the results prior to making up their mind. Slowly, the concept that arose is that, in a distributed database environment, we can have *global* and *local* qualities at the same time.

· Some transactions and some queries are global — they may be few, but they are very demanding.
· Many transactions and queries are local, and they are not bothered by database heterogeneity.

This led to the concept of *federated* databases, which can act alone in a local manner and in unison when global transactions and complex queries refer to the contents of many databases. The two conditions are not incompatible. With proper care they can have a nice symbiosis.

There are, of course, trade-offs associated with the exploitation of federated techniques instead of the more conventional database monoliths. Such trade-offs can be illustrated in terms of a design approach that combines both knowledge of the ways a distributed database system is put into use and conventional database management approaches. Such efforts aim to obtain the advantages of both.

Let's start with the principle that federalism is not just another word for decentralization. The conceptual differences between the two are quite important.

· Decentralization implies that the center *delegates* certain tasks or duties to the outlying units while the center remains in overall control.

The center does the delegating, the initiating, and the directing, whether delegation regards government authority, company chores, or database management.

· Federalism is different — the center's powers are given to it by the outlying groups, in a sort of *reverse delegation.*

The center, therefore, coordinates, advises, influences, suggests — but it does not order. The center may be a little "more equal" than the other participants of the federation, but has no hierarchical authority over them.

This is precisely what is meant when we say that in a federated databases solution each local unit works autonomously; it handles its own local transactions and queries. But it is always ready to collaborate in global events.

· This concept of "less than 100% control" is widespread enough in business.
· It is fairly alien to many technologists, and most particularly data processors.
· It is a powerful approach that merits a great deal of attention.

In a way, federalism is how the board of management works in central European companies. The members of the board are equal or semiequal, and the chairman practically acts as the speaker of the board, reigning by consensus. There is no president or chief executive officer with 100% control.

Facing the Application Challenges Through Standardization?

It is no secret that the increasingly widespread use of computers has led to an ever broadening scope of their applications. But as we saw in the preceding sections, to link computers from different vendors into a single system we need effective cross-database solutions, able to offer the broadest possible range of services. Short of this, manufacturing organizations face

· A never ending challenge of interconnection
· A low level of portability for their application programs
· Difficulty in interworking different software modules
· A variety of incompatible operating methods, depending on the different computers being used

Many problems stem from vendor-specific differences in interfaces, which are of direct concern to user organizations. Other problems are embedded in the work done by software developers, network system designers, workstation endusers, and more generally by computer-literate people.

On the one hand, in recent years the heterogeneity of systems, and most particularly of databases, has multiplied. On the other, in the computer industry international standards have been around for 35 years and cover a number of issues, among which are programming language specifications and communication protocols.

The old example of how language specifications can be blown to pieces is Cobol. Theoretically, this language got standardized by Codasyl in 1958. Practically, 15 years later, there were some 200 different Cobol dialects. These were incompatible with one another. The American National Standards Institute (ANSI) also standardized Cobol. Again in 1973 I had found 7 incompatible ANSI Cobols.

· Converting from IBM's ANSI Cobol to Honeywell's ANSI Cobol (and vice versa) practically meant paying some 30% of the cost of the original investment once more. Therefore, in the particular major project I have in mind, it ended up being less costly to change equipment and align to one vendor than continue programming for both of them.[5]

ANSI also standardized SQL in 1986/87. Two years later they found it lacked established norms. Thus came the improved 1989 version of ANSI SQL. But ANSI SQL 1989 (also known as SQL 1) could not handle transactions. Therefore, in 1992 SQL 2 which corrects this gap, was published. Since SQL 2 does not cover graphics and object-oriented processing, SQL 3 is now in the works, with norms expected around 1995. It would be superfluous to add that SQL 1, SQL 2, and SQL 3 are not necessarily compatible.

Besides all this, while standards are welcome, in general, they are not produced. Lack of production often makes their implementation questionable, in the sense that each vendor interprets them in his own way. Even two different divisions of the same vendor can end up producing two incompatible versions, for instance,

· SQL of DB2 under the operating system MVS and SQL/DS under VM — both on the same mainframe.

It could be added that from the user's viewpoint, many areas still lack standardization despite an obvious need for it. Since many standards are compromises,

---

5   This particular project concerned a common system for three financial institutions, of which one had IBM computers and two had Honeywell.

depending on different opinions and on the vendor's understanding of what ANSI and ISO[6] specifications mean, software reusability is relatively low.

However, user organizations with big buying power have the muscle to push through what they would like to see as a standard. In America, this happens with the Department of Defense.[7] In Japan, an effort undertaken to respond to the requirements of software portability and database interoperability is the multivendor integration architecture (MIA), which was first discussed in Chapter 2 as an exemplary systems initiative taken by management.

The MIA project has been initiated and managed by Nippon Telephone and Telegraph (NTT), with partners DEC, IBM, Hitachi, Fujitsu, and NEC.

· Released in February 1991, MIA Version 1 defines interfaces, taking into consideration not only international standardization and the present state of technology, but also users' needs.

The object of MIA is not to provide a sort of common denominator of currently available standards and/or interfaces already implemented by vendors, but rather to set a flat earth systems software reference.

· MIA is based on international standards that are stable and already in practice, but it extends such standards and adopts some de facto norms.

For interfaces for which there is no appropriate international or de facto standard, MIA has established specifications through joint research among its partners on currently projected technological developments.

The concept is projected that MIA specifications will be revised depending on progress in standardization, the development of technology, and the expansion of application areas. Norms will also be modified to keep pace with international standards and with de facto standards, as well as to eliminate possible unclear descriptions and errors.

Goals of the Multivendor Integration Architecture

An explanation of the technical issues characterizing MIA is important not because one has to implement it absolutely, but because it is a thoroughly thought-out effort that describes a valid method of program portability and system integration. This is the best lesson to be learned from the study of MIA.[8]

---

6   International Standards Organization.
7   Particularly for Unix and the TCP/IP protocol.
8   For technical details, see D. N. Chorafas and H. Steinmann, *Networked Databases*, Academic Press, New York, 1993.

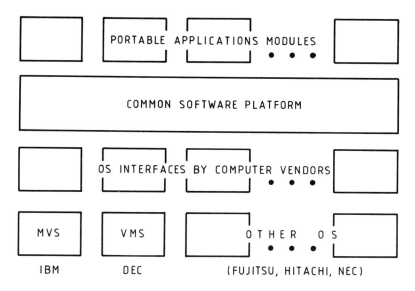

Figure 3   The MIA concept provides a software reference platform on which applications and OS functionality meet.

The subject of the multivendor integration architecture was introduced in Chapter 2, but no technical details were given. As shown in Figure 3, one way of thinking of MIA, NTT suggests, is that it is like a standard software wire to which different operating systems and the applications running on them will be attached.

DEC for VMS, IBM for MVS, and the Japanese computer vendors for their respective OS have written the necessary software to fill the gap between

·   The functionality and primitives of these operating systems and the standard software wire MIA Version 1 has defined

MIA Version 1 specifications will be revised periodically to help system managers, system designers, application designers, and endusers capitalize on advancements in technology. This is written with a full understanding that, as with ANSI SQL, there will be successive and probably not so compatible versions of MIA. Specifications defined by Version 1 focus on

·   Application programming interface (API)
·   Systems interconnecting interface (SII)
·   Human interface (HUI) in the execution environment

The API function is fundamental in a database sense and will be increasingly critical in the coming years, not just in connection to MIA but throughout the computer industry. API can interface the data dictionary, file access requirements, and in cases, program guidelines when vendor-specific interface specifications are included in the API.

SII defines lower layer protocols corresponding to open system interconnection (OSI) layers 1 to 4, and upper layer protocols corresponding to layers 5 to 7. It also addresses itself to needed services for protocol implementation.

Based on a network, lower layer protocols are used for data transfer to assure correct data exchange between computers, irrespective of the prevailing data structure. Upper layer protocols are required to share resources and distribute processing chores among computers, including file and mail transfer.

Human interface (HUI) specifications define display and operation interfaces provided by system software. The display interface addresses the structure, shapes, and other features of windows and similar components on the workstations.

·   The key point is to provide a means for maintaining compatibility among multiple human interfaces.
·   MIA focuses on the interchange of information between development and execution environments and the porting of data and applications between computers.

A basic assumption is that this is done by portable media or, preferably, by telecommunications lines. Specification define the formats common to all interchanged information, including syntax and semantics, as well as programs ported within the execution environment.

Hardware characteristics and internal system software interfaces, which have no important bearing on users, have not been included in the scope of the MIA Version 1 definition. Three levels constitute the basic reference:

·   Level 1 — addresses itself to the forementioned interface specifications, API, SII, and HUI
·   Level 2 — defines minimum function and management requirements that hardware and system software must meet
·   Level 3 — regards users' guides that supplement L1 and L2, as above, to assure application portability and interoperability

The three sets of L1 specifications, API, SII, and HUI, form the nucleus of MIA Version 1. L2 requirements for system definition in MIA Version 1 are meant to complement API and SII specifications. L2 functions specify properties in application execution and other parameters required for transaction processing.

Multivendor systems consisting of computers conforming to MIA Version 1 specifications can provide a standardized application development workflow. Using computer aided system engineering (CASE) tools, database and screen definitions can be developed up to a point on a common vendor basis. However,

- Vendor-specific methods may have to be used to move development information to and from the execution environment.
- System definitions and operator commands will also have to be generated and submitted in vendor-specific ways.

Functions required for streamlining online applications include database access, communication protocols, and user authorization. These are provided by system software, file access being typically supported by a programming language.

For remote database access, MIA has chosen the Remote Data Access (RDA) protocol by ISO and ANSI. RDA is produced by the SQL Access Group, a Silicon Valley cooperative outfit with 42 members — mainly American and Japanese. Practically all computer vendors (except IBM), and a good deal of user organizations, are members of the SQL Access Group.

Federated Solutions in a Multivendor Environment

Technical solutions, like the multivendor integration architecture and approaches along the line of federated databases, have become necessary because recent years have witnessed a dual phenomenon: the aging of operating systems and the proliferation of database management systems.

As we saw through examples, the proliferating DBMS concepts, methods, and tools reflect different data models and their associated languages. Each aims to do better than its predecessors, but they also increase the already existing heterogeneity. This proliferation has been prompted by

- An evolving technology aimed at replacing traditional file management applications with the latest DBMS concepts
- The support for new and expanding applications such as office automation, computer aided design, and knowledge engineering

The irony of the evolution which took place during the last 20 years is that, in the typical large organization, most corporate information is found in heterogeneous environments. However, current DBMS do not make their databases accessible to users who do not write transactions based on the specific language of a DBMS. Even if there was no other adverse reason, this inhibits data sharing among databases and their users.

- As the proliferation of incompatible DBMS accelerates, the number of separate supporting hardware, software, and personnel is also multiplying.
- As a result, the cost and complexity in maintaining and supporting the growing heterogeneous DBMS and databases increases.

· This is even more pronounced when we try to establish a strict network-wide discipline through attempts to support a global schema.

But high costs and growing complexity in information technology run contrary to corporate goals. Every organization would like to minimize cost and complexity by simplifying its operating environment.

Here comes the advantage of federated solutions, which provide for simplification without compromising the local autonomy of the individual databases, their security and integrity requirements, or their application perspectives. This is the message which was given previously with the practical example of MIA Version 1.

Federated information systems solutions and principles underpinning the MIA effort, for example, complement one another. They also derive strength from traditional goals, which are now being fulfilled:

· Multivendor architecture, means an open vendor policy permitting multisourcing in the procurement of computers and communications equipment.
· Federated principles in database implementation rest on a concept that existed long before, adapting a known organizational solution to information technology.

Whether we talk of the management of states, companies, or databases, federated organizations are reverse thrust organizations. The initiative, the drive, and the energy come mostly from the periphery, the distributed units, with the center acting as the long term influencing force. By their nature, federated organizations are loosely coupled, to use a technological jargon.

This is the concept of federated databases that any database architect, administrator, or designer will be well advised to learn in its details. As we have seen, there are alternatives, however, the concept of a strict global schema has been tried, and it failed where simple *passthrough* has its place mainly as an intermediate solution for query purposes.

What is meant by a simple passthrough is a facility offered through 1991 and 1992 announcements, which accesses heterogeneous databases for query purposes but not for the handling transactions:

· In 1991, Lotus Development introduced DataLens which works in conjunction with its 1,2,3 spreadsheet.

DataLens can address 20 incompatible databases, extract from them information elements, translate this data when necessary, and feed it into the spreadsheet.

· At about the same time Apple Computers introduced DAL, which has roughly the same functionality.

A limitation of DataLens and DAL is that they work only with products of the vendor who launched them. But at least they run on personal computers. Similar passthrough functionality is supported by IBM.

· Developed by Information Builders and announced in 1992, EDA/SQL[9] extracts information elements from incompatible databases in response to queries.

EDA/SQL does about what DataLens is doing but at a much higher cost. It runs on mainframes only, under MVS, and is typically sold in conjunction with the IBM Information Warehouse, which is essentially a query facility.

With this, we can regroup what we have said in terms of costs and effectiveness, in the structure shown in Figure 4.

· One key distinction concerns the level of *functionality.*

Handling transactions, particularly complex ones addressing multiple databases, stands at a much higher level than serving queries.

· The other major distinction is *cost.*

Let's face it. Some solutions cost many times that of others. Using a mainframe for passthrough would cost a few million dollars, but the PC will only cost a few thousand dollars.

Finally, the different levels of coupling federated databases should be appreciated. The tighter the coupling, the better the response to transactional requirements, but also the more complex the resulting system.

Linguistic Support for Database Interoperability

Whenever the discussion focuses on interoperability requirements, a number of queries come up, for instance: Under what conditions do an integrative schema exist? What are the correct criteria? How does yet another database merge into the schema? Does this integrative schema have some unique features?

Starting with the fundamentals, an *integrative schema* should not be confused with the *global schema.* The latter aims to be unique throughout the networked databases; the former reflects the different participating schemata within the distributed database environment.

No answer to the questions asked in the first paragraph of this chapter can be meaningful without first defining what is meant by a *schema.* In logic, a schema is a syllogistic figure. It is also diagrammatic representation, a scheme, an outline.

---

9   EDA stands for Enterprise Data Access.

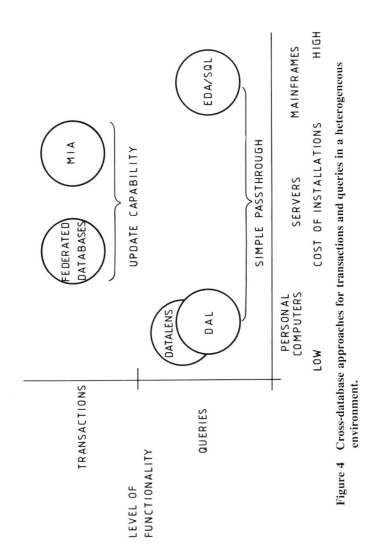

Figure 4   Cross-database approaches for transactions and queries in a heterogeneous environment.

- The philosopher Immanuel Kant (1724–1804) looked at schemata as mediating factors, making the application of categories to phenomena possible.
- The mathematician Gottfried Wilhelm Leibniz (1646–1716) considered a schema the principle essential to each monad (unit), constituting its peculiar characteristics.

With computers and databases, we look at a *schema* as a conceptual framework that defines the components of a database and their relationship. This contrasts to a *method,* which is the code determining object behavior, such as the calculation of a manufactured good's cost or price.

In terms of the design characteristics mapped into it, each DBMS has its schema. Hence, adding more DBMS to the network increases the magnitude of the solution necessary for interoperability purposes.

Interoperability essentially necessitates a mapping procedure in regard to database schemata whose usefulness depends on the richness of the view definitions. Linguistic constructs supported by the DBMS help to

- Define the different views
- Support appropriate methods
- Provide the operability primitives

However, when DBMS interoperability comes into the picture, the requirements posed on linguistic constructs exceed the traditional relational capabilities, even if the goal is only to assure connectivity between relational databases.

Ideally, the syntax and semantics of query expressions should be developed recursively in an object-oriented manner.[10] For instance, a query expression may correspond to each kind of object. This approach must be powerful enough to

- Overcome schematic discrepancies
- Reconcile linguistic differences

Such a feat is not necessarily feasible at a relational level of reference, and cannot be done without appropriate modeling. An example of schematic discrepancies is the way Reuters, Telerate, Telekurs, and Quotron structure and present their data streams while acting as information providers — and in spite of the fact they more or less appeal to the same market.

The reconciliation of linguistic differences is fundamental in the migration towards transparency in a cross-database sense. What is more, it must be done in a way that keeps the application running, in spite of differences in schemata and linguistics, among the different databases in the network.

---

10   As discussed in Chapter 5.

The message is that we need language features that deal with schematic and linguistic discrepancies. The drive towards integration transparency poses the problem of providing a consistent view, in spite of a change in schematic representation in one of the networked databases.

· The challenge is to make homogeneous the presentation of defined information elements within a heterogeneous database environment.

This goes beyond the passthrough database access made for response to queries, of which we saw different alternatives in the previous section. It demands:

· It demands a high level language[11] approach that translates higher order semantics to first order formulas.

An example of a higher order query is: "Did any stock close above 2% from yesterday's price?" A metadata approach can be helpful, but to treat metadata and data synonymously we must use nested objects and expressions that lead to complex structures.

What is more, since we increasingly deal with complex queries positioned against a federated schema, the latter must be decomposable into simple queries, each against component schema.

· Each information element in the heterogeneous database environment must be traceable to the component repository it comes from.
· Therefore, software must be available to sort the networked databases into more homogeneous groups, with a driver per heterogeneous database.

This is a type of functionality no SQL version today can provide. Hence, the SQL characterization made by the Electrotechnical Laboratory in Japan — "naive SQL". There are many other problems like faithful query translation and the virtual integration capability regarding heterogeneous databases.

In conclusion, to provide the appropriate linguistic support for the manipulation of databases through high level artifacts, our goal should be to

· Understand the function of the real world objects
· Develop languages to execute these function effectively
· Handle them at shell level, letting object code compilation up to the machine

---

11   Many people, and some books, call Cobol, PL/1, Fortran, et al. "high level languages". That is false. These were high level languages 35 years ago because everything else was lower. Today, they are very low level languages, and low technology too.

Performance requires a blending of concepts from a number of disciplines: knowledge engineering, object orientation, database design, communications, human windows, and associated sensitivity.

Linguistic solutions should address problems related to agile enduser interfaces as well, making it possible to deal with multimedia entities such as images and vector graphics, voice and other sound recordings, a variety of text forms, as well as classical data. In essence, this means the online manipulation of compound electronic documents. Chapter 7 tells how leading companies approached this subject.

7

Solutions with Integrated Object-Oriented Databases in Manufacturing

Introduction

Practically everyone today agrees that the key issue for future competitiveness in manufacturing is product *quality* and leadership in *software*, which both underpins advanced products and links a number of resources into one system. The more classical mechanical and electrical manufacturing industries today are the ideal field for application of a variety of advanced technologies:

· Product design and prototyping through concurrent engineering[1]
· Manufacturing automation and robotics, including new materials and lasers
· Just-in-time inventory management and cost control
· Environmental protection and energy conservation, including emissions, combustion control, and fuel additives

Over the last 10 years, the auto industry, for example, has experienced significant hardware innovations for emission control, a number of technical advances in engine design, and breakthroughs in testing issues. Some of these developments were prompted by legislative and regulatory policies, but all of them affect motor vehicle design.

Keeping with the automotive example, we can appreciate the acceleration in the renovation of older concepts and components, e.g., intelligence-enriched vehicle highway systems solutions. Contributions to motor vehicle performance come from diverse industries, many concern formerly stand-alone products which must now be integrated together into one well-knit aggregate.

---

1 As we have seen in Chapter 3.

One of the new fields of interest is *mechatronics*, and it stands for the use of electronic equipment in the car itself and in its manufacturing process. Today, electronic systems supervise and control motor management with the goal of

· Increasing the motor life cycle
· Providing a preventive fault detection
· Improving the economics of operation

Future cars will be software guided to make driving more comfortable and safer. Some vendors are developing fuzzy engineering solutions to promote

· Comfort
· Safety

Sophisticated software and databases will relieve the man behind the wheel from monotonous actions and assist him during extreme traffic situations.

There is no doubt that these considerations are applicable to all the domains of manufacturing industry, from heavy equipment to home appliances. But their implementation requires a new corporate culture, as the following examples document.

Return on Investment and Systems Solutions

In the course of the last 30 years, computer-based automation processes promised to deliver improved manufacturing competitiveness in terms of *quality, productivity,* and *costs*. In reality, at least in the majority of cases, the manufacturing industry only got islands of automation and, therefore, return on investment (ROI) has not been what was expected.

As we have seen in Chapter 5, we now know better and appreciate that islands of automation are not the solution. Computer-based applications such as computer aided design, production scheduling, materials planning, and general accounting chores should not be done independently of one another.

If islands of automation is the policy, then we should not be surprised when the competitive position of our manufacturing enterprise rises only little or not at all, in spite of major expenses in computers and other automation equipment — as well as software. Islands of automation have been typically the result of

· Short-sighted management directives or none at all
· A lack of underlying technology that enables these islands to effectively communicate with each other and share databases
· The complex nature of manufacturing products and processes — from design to quality inspection — which in many cases has eluded an integrated solution

· Traditionalist culture that has been more concerned in doing something with minimal effort than using brains and inventiveness.

Yet, we all know that designing, manufacturing, and marketing world class products requires precise coordination and integration of all company resources.

As Chapter 6 has demonstrated, it is not enough to have several separate databases for design, inventory management, accounting, and marketing. The information elements contained in all these structures have to be interlinked into one, at least virtually, homogeneous system.

This can be done effectively if we have a concept, a methodology, and software. But we must properly appreciate that traditional approaches to software development and the implementation of computer technologies do not adequately deal with

· Complex product lifecycles
· Market-pull evaluations
· Development of new manufacturing processes
· The observance of tough quality standards
· Complex human interactions

Only the leaders of industry have understood that in the design and development of competitive products, there is need for flexibility to meet customer requirements, reduce production time, and better the output quality. To achieve these objectives, more and more intelligence enriched solutions have to be used in conjunction with a policy of cultural change.

In practically all manufacturing strategies, there is an urgent need for supervising and monitoring the production flow from subassembly up to final assembly, thus assuring flexible production according to the customers' specifications. A parallel need is the incorporation of better fault diagnostics to increase maintenance efficiency.

· Results along these lines of reference require a great deal of experimentation, hence algorithmic and heuristic mathematical models
· They also pose severe databasing requirements, an issue that will become much more critical by the mid to late 1990s.

Interdisciplinary results will not be forthcoming unless we are able to access, in real time and in a seamless manner, a number of distributed heterogeneous databases, as we have seen through a significant number of practical examples. Clear-eyed companies are therefore on the lookout for integrative technologies that promote rapid design and time to market. This is helped by concurrent engineering and manufacturing automation — but the bottomline is management culture.

The goal successful manufacturing companies pursue is to simultaneously raise product quality and deliver lower cost products, along with significant productivity improvements. Part of this mission is to allow systems development to deal with complex manufacturing applications in a way not yet feasible. This concept is exemplified by the NEC case study.

An Integrative Manufacturing Policy by Nippon Electric Company (NEC)

The solution better organized companies are after is not based on just the idea of totaling all information elements but on integrating manufacturing technologies and robotics with design, production planning, inventory management, and quality control. This requires

- Proper architecture systems services and methodologies, providing a virtually unified distributed database, which is remotely accessible

The latter can be composed of many heterogeneous data structures, incompatible DBMS, diverse operating systems, and multiple equipment sourcing. This is the real life situation prevailing in business and industry today, and it is useless to deny it.

A solution along this integrative frame of reference is possible in a system-wide sense. It has been achieved by Nippon Electric Company (NEC) and can be seen in Figure 1. The NEC Nonstop Production System at Niigata, Japan[2] has been implemented on a wide area value added network (VAN). It includes not only NEC operations but also material and parts vendors, Japanese subcontracting companies, and overseas suppliers.

The concept of NEC Niigata is to coordinate and integrate all activities involving general administration, finance, engineering design, purchasing, production planning and quality control. The goal is an intelligent, knowledge-enriched manufacturing system. To realize this concept NEC top management incubated the following specific aims:

- Develop a total system that covers everything from booking to shipment
- Improve quality by a significant ratio, with improvements continuing year after year
- Double the productivity within each section through office automation (OA) and factory automation
- Shorten production lead time by 50% or better

---

2 NEC Niigata is a 100% owned NEC subsidiary in Kashiwazaki, Japan, established in 1974 as a major manufacturing plant for office automation products, e.g., personal computers and printers.

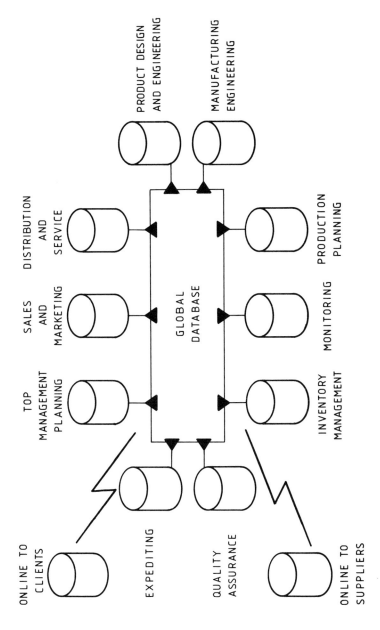

Figure 1   A solution to database integration by Nippon Electric.

To achieve the latter goals, NEC focuses on policies, systems, and procedures which make small lot-sized products and flexible manufacturing. It also expanded its intelligent network and the databases attached to it for overseas factory support.

To reach its goal, NEC has used insight and foresight in connection with the wider scope of the manufacturing process. It has employed open technologies and stable, proven standards whenever possible. But it has also provided for interactive processing extensions so that the current solution can be improved:

· New technology becomes available
· Still more cost-effective approaches are possible

Three lessons can be derived from the NEC case study. First and foremost, it is top management which has taken the initiative and led the company to a new, more advanced frame of reference in terms of computer integrated manufacturing. Second, the proverbial long hard look dominated top management's decision. Not only did this close the computer-management gap that prevails in many companies, but it gave the message way down the line that everybody had to move. Third, NEC used high technology to reach its integrative goals and made it known that norms would change as technology advances. Top management could be satisfied only with the best.

Placing Emphasis on Knowledge Engineering

As we have seen in Part I, concurrent engineering includes several phases: basic design, functional design, detailed design, and prototyping. This scenario is just as valid for products as it is for processes, tools, and the workplace as a whole.

Any integrative approach in manufacturing has to pay attention to all phases of concurrent engineering, progressing toward the production floor. This is what NEC has done, and this is also true of other manufacturing companies that live with their time.

American companies, for example, suggest that emphasis in concurrent engineering is placed not only on technical planning and design proper, but also on providing knowledge engineering enriched tools for

· Design to production control interfaces
· Implementation of monitoring processes
· Real time cost analysis
· Quality planning programs

In NEC's case, online interactive connection is provided to databases holding every aspect of production information. Integration has been seen as a prerequisite, all the way from product planning and requirements planning to manufacturing scheduling, purchase management, warehouse control, and steady cost supervision.

Not only concurrent engineering as such, but also programs for process monitoring, order tracking, and dispatching are based on online access to databases — and the same is true of quality control. The latter focuses on

· Product quality from design to field service
· Equipment diagnostics and maintenance
· Mold and tools control, as well as standards

Tough cost supervision has become a management policy and, therefore, a key point in NEC's systems solutions. Most importantly, there is a policy of steadily updating standards as more robotics get introduced into the production system.

This is a solid way of looking at computer integrated manufacturing processes. The approach, which has seen real life implementation within the NEC operating environment, is typified by the CIM network at Niigata and shown in Figure 2.

In all domains of manufacturing, generic approaches like this are necessary as companies, even the more mighty, face the challenges of a steadily more demanding market, whose drive is amplified by the globalization of manufacturing. These challenges concern

· Costs
· Quality
· Time to market
· Competitive pressures

Among the topmost corporations, that is those who have decided to survive, the challenges in reference are being addressed by new design and manufacturing techniques. We have spoken of the means in Part I: concurrent engineering, total quality management, and computer integrated manufacturing — but let me repeat that these are the tools, not the goal.

Increasingly, the new manufacturing techniques are based on using knowledge-enriched processes to support the entire product lifecycle. This spans diverse processes and disciplines including

· Conceptualization
· Product analysis and design
· Process planning
· Materials management
· Fabrication and assembly
· Testing and quality assurance
· Financial management
· Marketing and sales
· After sales service
· Retirement and disposal

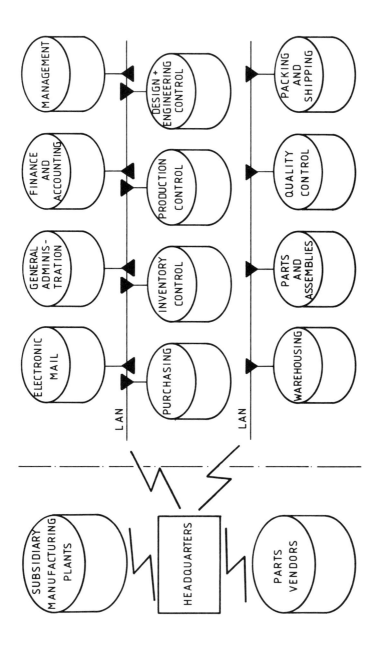

Figure 2   A CIM network of manufacturing databases at NEC Niigata.

Products are not made to live forever. Eventually they die. So do the machines used to make them. Factories also die when they outlive their purpose — a fact many companies find difficult to comprehend.

Through each of the aforementioned phases, the appropriate software technology must enhance the whole product and process lifecycle. Also, systems solutions should promote the concept of integration of group work, avoiding the discrete islands of which we spoke in the Introduction.

As NEC aptly underlined during a meeting in Tokyo, while improving total quality we must be able to reduce total lifecycle cost — even when confronted with a shrinking product lifecycle. It is because of these reasons that flexible integrated manufacturing solutions are becoming the main production system in the mechanical, electrical, and electronic industries.

Besides supporting quality and costs, knowledge enriched solutions must account for the demand from customers regarding many product aspects, including their function and design. For instance, there is a need for solutions to

·   Reduce the total lead time from design to manufacturing
·   Deal with the fluctuations of demand and supply
·   Help answer the growing customer requirements

References to fast product development and time to market, as well as the dynamic aspects characterizing production processes, underline flexibility as the key factor in systems design. A flexible approach, NEC suggested, demands

·   CAD enriched through knowledge engineering
·   Intelligent manufacturing equipment
·   Expert control systems for shop floor management

Robots and machine controllers can substitute human workers in automated manufacturing lines. The next demand is for *intelligence,* the ability to substitute for eyes, ears, and brains of human workers.

·   The new generation of automatic manufacturing cells and stations will be realized with intelligent manufacturing equipment in mind.
·   This will be achieved in the near future with advanced technologies in sensing and artificial intelligence.

With flexible shop floor control systems, it will be possible to produce many different products in the same shop. To operate these investments efficienctly, we need excellent supervisors who know the abilities of their shops and can solve various problems from the management viewpoint. These professionals will be assisted in their work through expert systems.

Decision support artifacts enriched with knowledge engineering are the answer to the task of intelligent supervision. But even the newest solutions will not last for long. They must be steadily improved with multimedia technologies, using the tools of the second generation of knowledge constructs such as fuzzy engineering and neural networks.[3]

AXIS by Japan's Electrotechnical Laboratory

The implementation of the advanced solutions Nippon Electric and other manufacturing companies are after requires new and more powerful tools than those we have had so far available. Effective networking capabilities, object orientation, and knowledge engineering are in the background of the generation of logical tools now coming to the market or in advanced stages of development.

In this section we will study one of the better examples. Designed in Japan, its goal is one of providing a much more agile DBMS than those currently available, particularly one that can serve networked workstations.

Japan's Electrotechnical Laboratory is developing the prototype of a product with extensible DBMS functionality, called AXIS. It is projected and designed to operate in an environment of distributed workstations and servers, supporting a variety of multimedia database applications.

One of the basic premises with the AXIS project is that the multimedia applications of the 1990s require many kinds of data structures and must be flexible enough to adapt to a variety of usages. A modern DBMS should be highly extensible and customizable:

- Internal functions of the database management system, such as file structures and query processing strategies, should cover performance and function variation.
- Knowledge engineering constructs should be employed to promote the concept of an intelligent distributed database.
- Query languages should answer ad hoc requirements supported through a multilingual environment, under an open architecture.
- Supported functions must be managed through an object-oriented implementation, interoperating in a network-wide sense.

The basic module of AXIS is a database kernel with programming interfaces. These permit a set of functions to cooperate in a networked environment with other subsystems, doing so in a flexible manner.

With AXIS, all information elements, including program codes, are stored in the database server whose configuration can be modified by the system users. Multiple servers with different configuration are allowed within the supported network environment.

---

3 See also D. N. Chorafas, *Expert Systems in Manufacturing,* Van Nostrand Reinhold, New York, 1992.

In real life operations, to customize and extend the kernel of the system they are employing, users often write application-specific database functions, e.g.,

· Image-join
· Voice filtering

With AXIS, all functions of the database kernel have common programming interface based on remote procedure call (RPC). These kernel functions can be used as a database toolkit and are callable from any programming language supporting RPC, which is essentially a network protocol.

Several applications can be served through the toolkit, among them a graphical user interface. Since all information is managed by AXIS on a distributed basis, users can share their environments. The database operation definitions of a given user can be reemployed by another user without copying the original definition.

Other organizations, too, are following this approach and the more advanced enrich it through object orientation. Citibank, for example, has used an object methodology to reengineer the retail banking business. Switzerland's Ciba-Geigy did the same in revamping chemicals for the agribusiness.

According to the opinion of the Electromechanical Laboratory, "naive" SQL cannot satisfy the expanding and revolving user requirements. For this reason, the Japanese researchers extended the query language to enhance interactivity, as well as the ability to customize. This extension, called XSQL, is based on

· Object orientation covering extensible abstract object types and inheritance as useful tools for database customization
· Database constraints to specify the integrity and checking procedures invoked with every update on a type
· Set operations approximately provided to the object types and views.
· Interfaces to other programming languages, assured by some of the SQL extensions

Since different applications may require various query processing strategies or different concurrency control mechanisms, care has been taken to assure that customization provides for the necessary adaptation.

Object definition functions and corresponding file operations have been included in this project. Tools for inheritance and complex object handling are also supported. Users can customize the definition to extend the basic object database model.

Users can write method programs, including header files. Such programs are compiled by the system and no preprocessor for database procedures is required. XSQL dynamically calls the object codes corresponding to the query, including the methods.

Database models can be controlled by means of an associated toolkit. Users are not required to specify the details of the network control through RPC. Lock and commit functions are provided.

A hash based file is used as an internal file access function of XSQL. The key of this file is the identifier of the objects that can be automatically generated and maintained by the system. Since, in an object-oriented database, it is indispensable to traverse an identifier chain to access some complex objects, the toolkit is extended to cover this kind of access as well.

ATLAS by the Bristol Laboratories of Hewlett-Packard

The Hewlett-Packard factory in Bristol, U.K., has developed ATLAS. This is a prototype of an object infrastructure, addressing itself to objects in a distributed manufacturing environment. It features heterogeneous databases operating in a network of thousands of computers over a wide area.

The immediate goal of the project has been to integrate different databases with an already existing infrastructure and representation. Associated to this objective was the provision of seamless access, at least from the enduser viewpoint.

- The infrastructure is based on the IRIS Object DBMS, of the same vendor.[4]
- There is a knowledgebank management system (KBMS) and knowledge engineering tool.
- The programming languages have been Prolog, object SQL (OSQL), and C++.

Figure 3 shows the interdependencies between these systems components. Another goal of ATLAS has been to provide a solution able to break down the wall between office automation applications in the factory. In this sense, it has been implemented mainly as a vehicle for experimenting with distributed office information systems.

- An application will typically be a collection of objects that use method invocation as their primary means of communication.
- There is dynamic creation, deletion, and migration of persistent and nonpersistent objects.
- The solution, which has been reached, supports fine-granularity objects in a clientserver networking model.

This implementation helps demonstrate that object-oriented technology and knowledge engineering are appropriate tools for the integration of heterogeneous sources of information and associated processing facilities.

The choice of object DBMS, KBMS, and object-oriented programming languages has been promoted by the advantages presented by object solutions.

---

4 IRIS was the prototype. In early 1992 the product was released and is known as *Open ODB*.

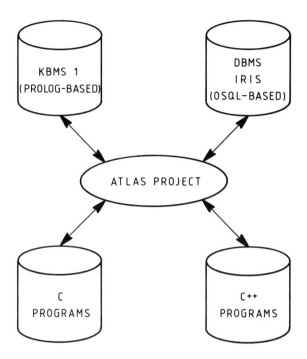

Figure 3   Object DBMS, KBMS, and languages in the ATLAS project.

· Every object communicates uniformly with other objects executing in different environments.
· Crucial in their access and usage are the interfaces being provided.

Implementation takes place behind an interface. All ATLAS objects are instances of a class.[5] In the case of ATLAS, this strategy is designed for the support of distributed heterogeneous networks.

An ATLAS object can invoke methods on another ATLAS object that resides in a different environment. Through this approach the Hewlett-Packard researchers were able to show that the object paradigm is appropriate for breaking down the traditional barriers between

· Office automation and different types of data processing

The project made it possible to have different kinds of databases available as integral parts of office automation systems by simplifying the access to each of

5   See also D. N. Chorafas and H. Steinmann, *An Introduction to Object-Oriented Databases,* Prentice-Hall, Englewood Cliffs, NJ, 1993.

them. Accessing has been achieved uniformly from any ATLAS object, whether it is implemented in the primary database itself or is executed outside of it.

Objects implemented in one DBMS can invoke methods on objects implemented in another DBMS. However, in real time cases, this implies a lower level of interoperability between the two databases. "Very fast interoperability is not the goal. The goal is the ability to provide the lowest common denominator between databases and the knowledge bases," the Hewlett-Packard researchers suggested.

All ATLAS objects have a unique identifier. Global reference is feasible through the ATLAS library. This library is the language dependent part of ATLAS, linked with every object process. It is the library's responsibility to present all modes of the local processes.

Nodes are networked and there is a single core process on each node in the network. This core process has been specifically designed to handle

- · Object location and routing of methods across security zones
- · Intermachine deliveries of method invocations

The core process also assures that the object process to which the object belongs is executing when a method invocation is delivered to that object. This means getting involved in object migration and providing services that require persistent information. Figure 4 demonstrates the structural connection.

Hewlett-Packard suggests that a structural connection is important as objects execute in object processes. It also helps in terms of implementing better security conditions, as all objects in the same object process belong to the same security zone.

The basic means of interobject communication is method invocation. Mappings are necessary to enable invocation of methods from and to ATLAS objects, implemented in one of the supported programming languages. Such invocation consists of three parts:

- · Object identifier (OID)
- · Method (function) identifier (MID)
- · A set of parameters

Mappings from IRIS object identifiers to MID and vice versa are maintained in a table. Another table contains the mapping from IRIS object identifiers to OID, with proxies used to represent remote ATLAS objects in IRIS.

A proxy supports methods corresponding to those in ATLAS objects. Invoking a method on a proxy causes function invocation to be sent to the corresponding object. This is transparent to the programmer, who only sees references to IRIS objects and associated functions.

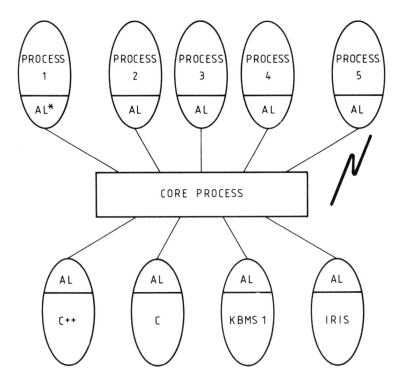

Figure 4   Structural connection through the ATLAS core process.

The Consolidated Product Database

ATLAS was an experimental project undertaken to demonstrate the practicality of an object solution involving heterogeneous databases. Its implementation was limited within the Bristol factory of Hewlett-Packard. Other companies too have experimented with real life applications, e.g., General Dynamics.

Over the last few years, object-oriented approaches and DBMS have permitted General Dynamics to develop a consolidated product database (CPDB). It provides product definition views able to support concurrent engineering. Information elements include parts attributes, assembly structures, and the like.

·   Product information is represented at the most detailed, individual part level.
·   Aggregation of component parts into various assemblies is managed by the object database.[6]

---

6   Through the Ontos DBMS by Ontologic.

Prior to this implementation, multiple bills of materials (BOM), with parts represented only by identification numbers, led to overlaps and sometimes to confusion. The object-oriented system did away with such problems. It also facilitated storage and retrieval of drawings, including their descriptions in the same database.

Like all state-of-the-art companies, General Dynamics appreciates that BOM is an activity that requires a database flexible enough to permit changes as a product moves from prototype to production. Object-oriented solutions have the functionality and performance needed to allow access to diverse information, such as engineering drawings and BOM, stored in a variety of heterogeneous distributed databases.

With this background in mind, we can integrate the CPDB and ATLAS results emulating an object implementation environment able of extending the internal applications to two directions preached in Chapter 5:

- Customers
- Suppliers

Such an extension will require interoperability within a much more heterogeneous environment, linked at the macroscopic level through wide area networks (WAN) and at the local level through local area networks (LAN).

Next to interconnection in a communications sense, the challenge is one of programming for interoperability. In this emulated solution, we will proceed by using the facilities described at the end of the previous section.

Through the explained approach, the programmers will be able to invoke generic functions, which can be handled in different ways in various environments. For their part, the information systems of customers, suppliers, and the manufacturing company itself will be able to retain their original characteristics and functionality.

This solution can be carried all the way through concurrent engineering to BOM, production schedules, and the management of inventories of ready products. It will permit

- The identification of basic aspects of implementation and their interfaces
- Strong notation of object identity throughout the network of heterogeneous systems
- Location transparency but *not* failure transparency[7]
- Isolation of language dependencies within each information technology environment

Support for different languages can be introduced by incorporating appropriate compilers. To integrate knowledge engineering functionality, an object model

---

7   Which cannot be successfully supported by most of today's systems.

similar to ATLAS can be added. This is helped by the services supported by objects and in turn permits the handling of methods.

Extending the ATLAS and CPDB experiences within the client/manufacturer/supplier landscape, objects can be built on top of knowledge structuring mechanisms, which include methods and metamethods, e.g.,

- An object's state can be effectively held in a method in the KBMS.
- All instances of a particular class share this method, with rules implemented as predicates.

BOM that originate in diverse databases can integrate into the system being described. Knowledge engineering would help provide the necessary format translation, data structure changes, or other needed services.

The KBMS would maintain a mapping between an object identifier and the method state of the corresponding object. It will also map from method identifier to linguistic predicates. Such mappings enable invocations on objects to be executed by evaluating a given predicate.

Transaction models must be given particular attention within this implementation perspective. The system should be designed to support efficient communication among loosely coupled objects in heterogeneous networks. Individual objects or groups of objects can thus be applied to provide high-level execution guarantees like failure atomicity.

In terms of distributed transactions it is important to support global identifiers. These are immutable identifiers that focus on one, and only one, thread of control, and are assigned through an explicit fork or an asynchronous method invocation.

Assuring an Effectively Working Database Environment

The importance of the emulated implementation example shown in the previous section rests on the fact that networked heterogeneous databases are a high point in the 1990s — at the same time the world of communications is undergoing a far-reaching transformation. These two issues are dependent upon one another, as they are both due to the fusing of information processing, telecommunications, and database technologies.

The message this chapter has tried to convey is that knowledge engineering and object orientation are playing a locomotive role in the process of integration in the manufacturing industry by helping develop state-of-the art solutions. But projects undertaken in this direction must work closely with the different players, deploying a strategy that provides effective response to pivotal challenges:

- Technological advances have made networks with unparalleled intelligence possible. This, in turn, has spawned a host of diversified products and services.

· Databases have outgrown the confines of central computer installations and find themselves under every desk, wherever there is a workstation.
· User organizations are moving out of system architectures proprietary to "this" or "that" computer vendor and towards open systems aiming to integrate diverse technologies.
· The changing regulatory environment makes open architectures a necessary framework within which have to fit diverse and often incompatible applications.

New strategies are necessary and they seem to be taking a tangible form through various initiatives, in particular the progressive emergence of a modern infrastructure comprising interconnected networks and databases. In this connection we have seen examples from three continents:

· America
· Asia (Japan)
· Europe (England)

As this chapter has shown, equally important is the development of technologies to support future requirements for networked databases. Therefore, we should continue to promote advanced technology in order to support the company's own interests, i.e., its competitiveness in the market.

Manufacturing companies simply cannot get away from the fact that today many independent information resources exist. Both for historical reasons and because these resources must serve the needs of various applications, there are many different types of database management systems and data structures that have to be integrated.

There are also many different types of processing routines: classical programs written back in the 1960s, teleprocessing routines and decision support modules from the 1970s, expert systems with their knowledgebanks from the 1980s.

Diversity and incompatibility in information resources is a perverse issue which is not confined to protocols and data structures. It includes language compilers, application generators, report generators, and spreadsheets. Different types of resources are largely incompatible with each other in syntax, formal semantics, and more.

Most incompatibilities and heterogeneities arise due to different hardware and operating systems, as well as different formats used to represent information at

· Physical level — block or page
· Conceptual level — object-oriented, relational, Codasyl, or hierarchical
· Data structures of the database
· Programming languages, featured by the database management system.

Though they work together as business partners, different organizations are having informal and largely incompatible semantics about the real world. These may differ due to culture or language, but most often they differ due to management rules and, not unlikely, to chance.

What this means is that the solutions we are after are not easy, and they have to be established while the environment itself is changing. As the knowledge revolution affects literally every area of our lives, communications systems will spread such novelties as distance learning, distance working, tight client/supplier linkages, even remote health care. But the prerequisite is virtual compatibility.

Knowledge, information, and communication technologies naturally propagate as they progressively become part of the economic and social fabric and bring about a general change in the very nature of society. To survive, the manufacturing enterprise must concretely demonstrate that it can keep pace — the "how" has been shown by the previous examples.

8

Interoperability in Distributed Manufacturing Operations

Introduction

The first step towards the integration of distributed heterogeneous resources in a manufacturing industry is to recognize the domain in which database interpretation and process interoperability are relevant. Part of this approach is the appreciation of opportunities federated solutions can provide. Other essential concepts are

- · Understanding the tradeoffs between issues associated with remote data access
- · Differentiating among possible alternative solutions
- · Determining which solution is most appropriate to *our* situation in terms of cost and functionality

Interoperability, also known as cooperative processing, allows the applications and the DBMS to be decoupled. Information elements stored under heterogeneous DBMS are viewed as a common commodity. A wide variety of applications is expected to access the information in these databases regardless of hardware, OS, and DBMS heterogeneity.

In this chapter we will see what the dynamics of interoperability involve. After this issue has been examined, the phase of the mechanics starts. They begin with proper identification, by location of the distributed database and nodes in the network, and involve

- · Examination of the contents of repositories with emphasis on both data and metadata
- · Decision on whether data transfers will be done on a scheduled basis or on demand

· Evaluation of whether or not there are reasons for replication of information elements

The best way to approach the interoperability problem is by first identifying the global system and then elaborating a nucleus solution. This could be subsequently expanded to other platforms to protect our investment in existing data structures.

A sound policy will see to it that preservation of investment will not inhibit sustenance of high performance in cross-database access. This is true of ad hoc, real time queries, as well as of the distributed transaction environment. Essentially:

· We are looking for payoffs by going beyond the limitations implied by current systems.
· We want to use database optimization as such technology becomes available.
· We like to provide for a cross-database access using standards, as long as the job is manageable through established norms.

Throughout this work we must appreciate that it is very difficult to provide *static* integration — besides what is really needed is *dynamic* solutions. The latter require a good understanding of the components entering our system and their tuning.

While we may not need to know all the fine print of the heterogeneous database environment prevailing in the manufacturing enterprise, we have to know what is preestablished, inflexible, noninteroperable, or static. We also need to know which sort of public or homemade standards have been followed. Only then will we be able to come up with a rewarding solution.

Is There a Unique Meaning of Integration?

The answer to the query posed by the subtitle is NO! Practically everybody has a different definition, and some of these definitions are contradictory. But we can put together a concept toward which many definitions tend to converge.

Integration is at the same time the means, methodology, and practice of combining (through interfacing) component parts of a system and aggregating them into a cohesive set. Such work is typically done by understanding and preserving the *interrelationships* and *interactions* of the various components.

Integration goals provide access to the broader landscape, which includes heterogeneous parts, trying to convert them into a well-knit aggregate. For instance, in the case of databases, we wish to obtain seamless access to information that is

· Stored in different forms
· Managed by different systems

Our aim is to do so while preserving constraints and dependencies between various chunks of this distributed information resource, all the way from update to query. An associated goal is to make the programs that create or manipulate the information interoperable, able to invoke joint services.

Take for example a company with five factories in different parts of the U.S. Each one of them has a quality control function, and usually the associated information processing is done at the local plant on platforms which, plant-by-plant, can be heterogeneous.

To simplify things, say that all plants observe a procedure that is normalized throughout the company as shown in Figure 1. But the OS, DBMS, data structures and so on being used are incompatible.

- Quality assurance function at headquarters likes to access quality information in a cross-factory sense.
- This is wanted not just in an end-of-the day batch form, but analytically and in an ad hoc manner.
- Access must take place online at any one of the databases shown in Figure 1, from incoming inspection to testing, losses, and rejects.

This is not what is offered today by the different computer vendors, with their obsolete information center ideas, where data is dumped overnight through batch processing. What we are talking about is dynamic access to transactional databases, which may be incompatible among themselves but workable in the job.

The aim of the distributed heterogeneous databases is to allow users (people, workstations, hosts, and applications) to combine information elements from multiple sources and create applications in which various procedures can cooperate. This requires understanding and documenting the relationships and dependencies existing among data and procedures.

The definition of dependencies and relationships can be difficult when the information elements are stored in heterogeneous databases and managed by incompatible DBMS. Starting with the premise that the main vendors are way behind in providing software for interrelationships and interactions, to serve the user organization in the best possible manner, many manufacturing companies have developed their own solutions.

Most of these efforts took place in the 1980s as the cross-database problems to which we make reference became acute. Table 1 presents a birds eye view of the most significant efforts. We will examine a couple of them in greater detail in Part III.

While the projects to which reference is made are significantly different from one another, they also have similarities. The most significant is that the integration services hide or remove heterogeneities among databases and procedures:

- Providing means to assure that dependencies are supported and constraints enforced

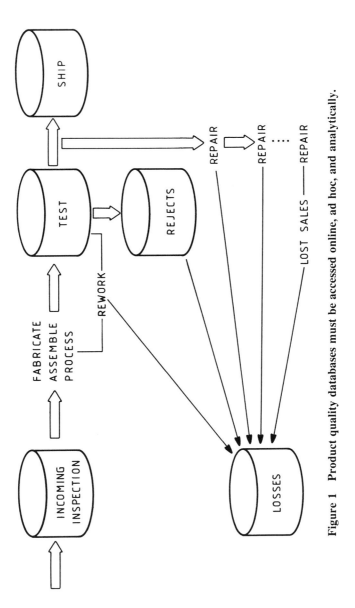

Figure 1   Product quality databases must be accessed online, ad hoc, and analytically.

Table 1   Cross-databases solutions worked out by user organizations

1. ADDS, 1986 — Extended relational approach, addressing hierarchical and relational files; tightly coupled, limited updates, inhouse use of the prototype system
2. CALIDA, 1988 — Relational approach, addressing relational and relational-like files; inhouse use
3. DAPLEX/MULTIBASE — Addressing network and relational databases; tightly coupled, schema integration, auxiliary schema service, global query optimization, number of component DBMS integrated in various prototypes
4. DDTS, 1987 — Relational, addressing Codasyl and relational databases; tightly coupled architecture, constraint checking, local query optimization, use of local and long haul communication
5. DQS, 1988 — Relational, addressing hierarchical, network, and relational databases; tightly coupled, primarily within an IBM environment
6. IISS, 1986 — Entity relationship oriented, addressing network and relational databases; more or less tightly coupled, queries must be compiled, forms-based user interface
7. MERMAID, 1987 — Relational, addressing relational databases with partial integration of text
8. MRDSM, 1985 — Relational for relational databases; loosely coupled architecture, multidatabase language, dealing with multiple semantic interpretations
9. OMNIBASE, 1989 — Extended relational for relational databases; loosely coupled, DEC environment, query processing in distributed DBMS
10. Other, earlier, cross-database efforts: SIRUS-DELTA, 1982 — Relational for network and relational databases; SCOOP, 1982 — Entity relationship for hierarchical, network, and relational databases

- Invoking mappings with consistent names, values, formats, descriptions, and calling sequences

The core issue is to make logical heterogeneity transparent. In other terms, the user should not be aware of the fact that the various databases have been designed independently, and therefore the same entity may have been modeled in different ways.

As all these efforts to cross-database operations have found out, no solution is made in the abstract. An approach must not only provide seamless access but also be thrifty in

- User time
- System time

User time is the amount of time the process spent executing nonprivileged instructions. These include arithmetic calculations, but are mainly connected to database access, sorting, searching, calling user-level functions, and so on. *System time* is the time the process spent executing privileged instructions, i.e., kernel commands such as system calls and some system level overhead like context switching between processes.

The *elapsed time* is often more than the sum of the user and system times. The difference is spent waiting for input/output operations to complete and waiting for a signal from another process sleeping or swapped out on disk while another program is running. Everything counts in terms of performance.

Bottom-up and Top-down Views of Information Elements

Two databases may be logically heterogeneous even if the DBMS managing them are homogeneous. Relevant work in this area includes concepts relative to schema integration in the way discussed in Chapter 6, in the section on linguistic support. Such an approach is, up to a point, facilitated if the data model used to describe the integrated schema is semantically rich.

Practitioners in the database management field suggest that there are two different viable approaches when we talk about integration in the context of a heterogeneous environment.

· *Bottom-up* requires that the local schema of an existing participating data-base is transformed into the modeling language of the multidatabase system.

Subsets are created from such transformed schema, known as *export schemata,* to be integrated into one or multiple common schemata. The latter, let's again repeat, do not have claims of being global or unique.

· *Top-down* is essentially view integration, with external schemata of cooperating applications combined into federated common schemata to be connected.

Notice that both approaches aim at schema integration but take different roads. Contrary to what might superficially look like the case, bottom-up leads to more tightly coupled systems, top-down to more loosely coupled ones.

Both approaches have a good deal of prerequisites and characteristics in common. In an integrated system, relationships among data and/or applications must be traceable, expressible, and preserved. This should be the case regardless of the heterogeneity of the components that store information elements and manage them.

Such requirements, however, do not exclude that each component database may support specific internal relationships, which are difficult to describe in a network scheme because there are no common facilities for identifying related elements. Besides this,

· Component databases may modify information independently of any notion of central control.
· Information elements updated in one of them may not have a counterpart in another, hence, there are no corresponding changes in cross-database.

The latter reference can best be appreciated if we return to the fundamentals and bring to mind that, even if they belong to a federation, local databases operate autonomously. Only global transactions and global queries address many of them at the same time.

Taking as an example the graph in Figure 2, two designers working through concurrent engineering have a given concept in their mind. The design they project involves A, B, and C parts from databases that are heterogeneous but accessible online.

- The product designers may have different approaches and views shown by the graph at the right of the figure.
- The access mechanism they will employ can be common, and this is described at the left of the figure.

The meaning of interoperability in multidatabase systems is that applications can execute using common information elements created by other applications and stored in a logically global database, which physically may be widely distributed. In such an implementation, an agent mediates all accesses between applications and these local databases.

If all local databases are defined according to a single set of semantic conventions, with the multidatabase in mind, the integrative schema would not be so difficult to construct. Quite often the job is more complex because construction must overcome semantic heterogeneity among information elements in the networked local databases.

To assure consistency across the system, the integrative approach will try to make the heterogeneity of the underlying components, and of their information contents, transparent to the user. This means making them look *as if* they were homogeneous by hiding their incompatibilities.

Given the many aspects of heterogeneity and the constraints that must be overcome, the level of integration is bound to be quite variable. The higher goal is a basis for cross-vendor interoperability. But as we have seen in Table 1, many projects undertaken by user organizations have addressed only subsets of that objective.

Existing studies and surveys compare integration levels, but there are really no standards for doing such comparisons, much less proceeding with a benchmark. A cross-database project will, however, be well-advised to define a multidimensional design space for integration, which includes

- Inclusion of different forms of data structures
- Access to heterogeneous DBMS and data models
- Transparency by endusers
- Program interoperability
- Mappings and relationships
- Dependencies and constraints

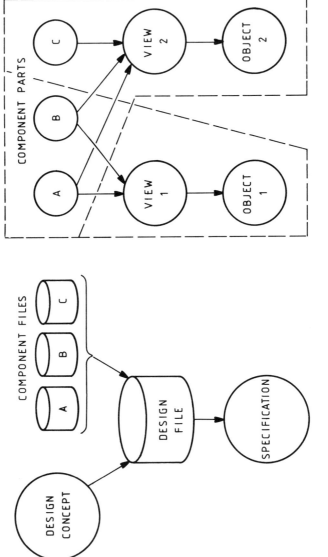

Figure 2   A different view or version of a product can be developed through concurrent engineering using the same cross-database solution.

Constraint analysis includes logic-based representation of database semantics, specifications of database operations, updatable user views, and generated rules for integrity maintenance. We will look more closely into this subject in the next section.

Constraint Analysis and Object Orientation

Constraint analysis can be applied to the study of database views and associated operations, identifying side effects due to the execution of global updates. Such a process helps refine the scope of a global view based on the transactions and queries to be performed.

The aim of constraint analysis is to help provide a formal basis for representing operations associated with semantic data models. In turn, this assures a way of explaining database semantics, the specification of database operations and the translation of constraints to integrity maintenance rules.

Put at the service of the enduser, cross-database transparency is subject to a number of constraints. The main dimensions affecting a transparent solution are the

- *Data model* and its primitives
- *Database schema(ta),* descriptive of the databases and their information elements
- *Data sources,* including locations and derivations
- *Dependencies* and relationships, including their semantics
- *Time and cost* for the provision of an interoperable solution.

Among the key questions in qualifying and quantifying these issues, we distinguish: How are entities and relationships represented? Can behavior be specified, and how? How are aggregates formed? What is the form of the query language? How are constraints expressed?

Solutions should focus on domain modeling in a way that permits behavioral representation leading to explicit specifications. They must provide for schema evolution as well as account for data and knowledge distribution in reasoning about

- Metadata
- Metaknowledge

Valid approaches would typically reflect ways that permit a dual modality — having object transparency and object visibility at the same time.

Knowledge engineering can play a significant role in this process. Figure 3 demonstrates the component parts of a prototype developed to answer cross-database requirements. Though this has been a rule system, experience suggests that fuzzy engineering might give still better results.

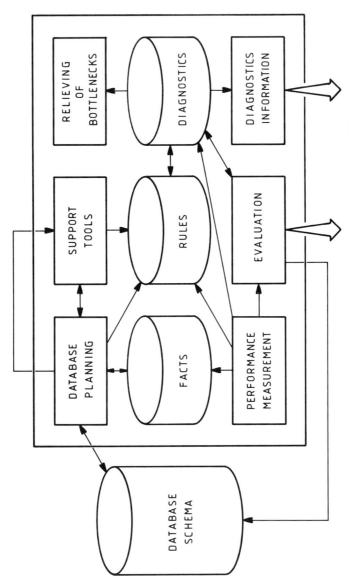

Figure 3   A knowledge engineering artifact for cross-database operability.

A solution that integrates multiple data models must provide mappings between concepts in one model and those in another. This can happen by degrees. When differences between data models are completely hidden, a heterogeneous database landscape looks as if each of the members is defined in terms of the same primitives. The other extreme is that all differences are completely visible.

- When schema disparities are visible the user must provide routines to resolve the differences.
- A midrange solution may allow for seamless queries but not for seamless updates in a cross-database sense.
- The more sophisticated approach assures schema transparency, completely hiding heterogeneity in the structure and semantics of elements.

With every project, it is important to define the degree of transparency of an integrative solution. In general, there will likely be different feasible implementation strategies that produce about the same level of integration.

The object approach assures that process hierarchies remain an effective form of communication between analysts and users as, for instance, entity relationship diagrams effectively show data decomposition. Entity relationship is one of the stepping stones that led to the wider usage of the object paradigm.

Enhanced with knowledge engineering, an object orientation can be instrumental in assisting cross-database activities, though this too can be subject to constraints. In many cases, data and process decompositions occur more or less in parallel, each contributing to the definition of the other.

Entity types may be defined by sets of attributes, relationships, and processes, each of which could be inherited throughout entity-type structures. Multiple inheritance may also be supported, as well as encapsulation by normalization of the process model, providing benefits in the areas of reusability and maintainability.

Technology makes available artifacts that hide certain aspects along different dimensions. Implementation choices are likely to resolve some of the integration issues better than others. In all these cases cost/benefit considerations help define the practical levels of integration.

Cross-Database Access as a Competitive Advantage

The diversity of the solutions through which industry has tried to solve the cross-database dilemma documents the importance this problem has taken since the mid-1980s. Throughout the First World, business and industry feels the need for *accessing* and *correlating* multidatabase information.

While endusers don't wish to be bothered with technical details and are demanding seamless access, technologists must be able to assure *query* and *transaction* models to reflect a variety of existing applications, as well as new ones under development. The solutions to be provided must be

- Semantically rich
- Suitable for increasingly sophisticated applications
- Capable of observing maximum data independence
- Able to serve multimedia requirements
- Capable of integrating different database models: object-oriented, relational networking, and hierarchical

Supported functions must be able to represent attributes and relationships, as well as the computation of objects. They should serve an environment that is increasingly characterized by polymorphism, handling both local and foreign functional needs.

Any integration site must be able to manage with practically the same efficiency as *local* data types and those *imported* from foreign databases. Technically, this has been approached through type abstraction — defining supertypes of existing functions — as well as procedural abstraction.

Procedural abstraction deals with a number of integrative issues, one of them being handling differences in DBMS. Such differences are at times subtle but they are present, e.g.,

- DBMS I handles "Management Payroll" as an *attribute,*
- DBMS II approaches it as an *entity.*

Other differences can center on real life issues with which an application has to deal, e.g., model mapping, involving a variety of incompatible data models; schema mapping of different schemata, to overcome domain and structure mismatch; query translation, query optimization; and execution.

Knowledgeable users list among the benefits obtained from object-oriented database management solutions the ability to develop new, innovative applications faster:

- Direct modeling of information
- Reduced maintenance costs
- Easily extended functionality
- Increased possibility of code reusage

All of this protects existing investments, as well as facilitates the access to existing information elements and code. Provided the proper homework has been done, SQL-like languages can serve, but more powerful constructs will be even better.

As far as the homework is concerned, a vital notion is that of *unique object* identification. Even within a homogeneous database, its handling involves many compromises to avoid conflict situations:

- Dealing with local naming autonomy — but also locating objects through unique object identification (ID)

- Handling both universal and local object ID, assisted by knowledge engineering
- Managing equivalence during query processing in a cross-database sense
- Addressing a range of constraints any distributed environment involves
- Accessing in a seamless manner diverse and incompatible databases as well as operating systems

Such functionality is increasingly necessary given the current market trends. A study among 100 information technology (IT) managers of the Fortune 500 companies[1] identified that 72% use or plan to use computers from multiple vendors, 81% have applications requiring data access from multiple computers, and 62% have implementations requiring data access from multiple vendors' computers.

The same study focused on distributed database environments and found that 63% of installation environments have applications requiring database access from multiple sites. The ratio of IT installations with implementations requiring data access from *multiple databases* or file systems stands at 84%.

While some of the integrative approaches followed so far have not been particularly successful, companies that compared relational and object-oriented solutions comment that the latter provide the possibility to work in a more comprehensive manner. Object-oriented solutions make work easier and faster than relational environments.

The Overriding Demand by User Organizations

As the research which led to this book helps document, wherever an object-oriented methodology has been applied it has provided much greater efficiency than alternative solutions. But, as it cannot be repeated too often, an object orientation will not make up for organizational deficiencies such as

- Failure to properly identify our current and future requirements
- Using a new technology but with a backward mentality from Cobol experience
- Lacking the knowhow on ways and means to protect our past investment in IT

According to references provided during the meeting with Hewlett-Packard, there are many reasons why companies explore object-based solutions. At American President Lines, for example, programming time for one market share report

---

1 By the International Data Group.

Table 2   Maintenance estimates in man-days for four operations in a gas utility

Application Functionality	Old Software	NCS
Listing 200 largest accounts	3	0.5
Implementing online cycle billing	50	19
Expanding account balance	146	88
Supporting rate restructuring	1500	950

was cut from 7 months to 7 weeks. Using a prototype of the Pegasus object-oriented facilities, the company programmers obtained significant results even at the beginning of their learning cycle.

At General Dynamics the Pegasus prototype was used in rocket simulation. They built a user interface that allows noncomputer experts to easily communicate with the system. "You could do it with Fortran, but it is much more difficult," said a company executive.

The new customer system (NCS) application at Brooklyn Union Gas was developed using an object-oriented methodology and a relational database with the assistance of an integrator. The results include increased functionality, reduced code amounts, greater flexibility in responding to regulatory changes, as well as bridging the semantic gap between endusers and analyst programmers. Table 2 gives maintenance estimates in man-days for the old and new software; the difference is significant, ranging from better than 1:1.5 all the way up to 1:6.

At Bell Labs, C programming used 80% of the new code for a given application. Through C++ use only 20% of the code was newly written for that application. After accounting for design and debugging time, the total development time was often decreased by 60%.

Converting a large relational application to an object-oriented DBMS, Hewlett-Packard's own manufacturing facilities managed to reduce the size of the project by over a third. Based on the object paradigm,

· A rich information model was built, including both objects and functions
· A powerful integration mechanism was developed with supertypes and subtypes, as well as local and global object identification

When it comes to object-oriented applications, however, considerable research issues still remain for deeper study. One of them is the service offered by the object approaches to the unification of information schemata, including federated external schemata, data model mapping, and other integration issues.

Another major implementation area is query processing. This involves issues such as query decomposition and translation, query optimization (including new, more powerful factors) as well as the handling of

· Long queries of SQL type
· Multidata queries as opposed to data-based queries only

Precisely because of the possibilities the new methodology offers, the foremost vendors are working on new languages that can support database-wide interactivity, including graphic editors and browsers. Part of the effort is to embed in them existing languages for software portability, which can be effectively done through appropriate programmatic interfaces.

As we have seen in Chapter 6, these are by and large object programming constructs operating over relational databases. The aim is to modernize the system by providing the stage for interoperability leading to effective operational integration. In an object-oriented approach, operational execution corresponds to sending a message to an object:

· How this message will be executed is of no concern to the sender.
· The message will most likely be handled by underlying software.
· In this process, data and operations are treated alike.

Data objects and associated operations reflect the logical structure and semantics from information elements and underlying applications programs. By using an extra layer of metadata, overlaps and other incompatibilities, as well as semantic heterogeneity, can be put on the backburner.

One of the demands of user organizations is that vendors should face the fact that in an expanding implementation environment data objects may have single valued and multivalued attributes.

· The definition of attributes in a class implicitly describes the capability to read and write these attributes.
· A class does not prescribe any implementation or presentation, though associated with a class are different operations.

The top objects of a given hierarchy may be directory-like, the lowest levels corresponding to details. Through reference links, a nonhierarchical structure can be superimposed in a way that objects form a network the user browses and manipulates directly.

Objects can be selected from this network in order to apply operations to them. Results from computational operations can constitute computed attributes so that the network may be manipulated by the user for further access and processing operations. This presents significant flexibility in an implementation sense, and therefore it is valued by most user organizations.

Objects, Knowledge Engineering, and Client-Server Architectures

As we have seen in the preceding sections, knowledge engineering can provide considerable assistance in meeting cross-database access goals. One of the key areas of attention is a knowledge-based retrieval system, including monitors, triggers, and logic inferencing.

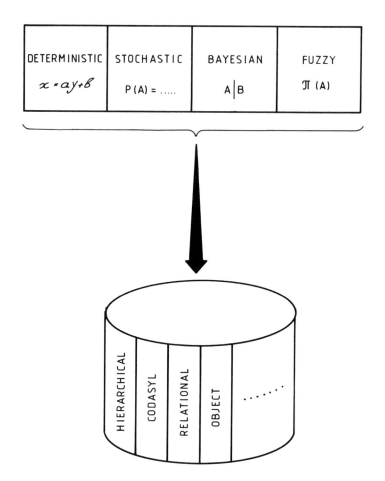

Figure 4   Use of alternative methods in supporting heterogeneous database access.

Database mining capabilities can be enhanced through fuzzy engineering and neural networks. Figure 4 suggests that there are four different ways to explore database contents in a networked environment with heterogeneous structure:

- Algorithmic and therefore procedural, based on a deterministic approach
- Algorithmic but uses a stochastic approach, probability of event A: P(A)
- Bayesian, hence conditional; IF A THEN B
- Heuristic and uses a possibility distribution.[2]

---

2   See D. N. Chorafas, *The New Information Technologies — A Practitioner's Guide,* Van Nostrand Reinhold, New York, 1993.

Based on fuzzy engineering, the last alternative is both the most recent and the most powerful. Experience on how to use it is still being developed, with the Japanese having taken the lead in this domain.

Many of the participants in my seminars ask whether it is knowledge engineering *or* object orientation that would be the preferred approach. The answer is *both*. Knowledge engineering and object orientation work in synergy, and we should capitalize on the strengths and relative advantages of each.

Some of the user organizations that are accumulating experience in the cross-database access field comment that object-oriented languages have been incredibly productive. Because of this, they

· Have changed their reward system for productivity purposes
· Threw out their old project planning and control rules for information technology

These companies are developing new approaches to software planning and control specifically dealing with the new tools that have become available in regard to databases. They aim to provide integration through better knowledge of the semantics of information elements.

This effort is assisted by the fact that the object model of the new generation of DBMS has rich semantic and modeling constructs suitable for such requirements. It also requires a new departure rather than trying to provide dying Cobol procedures with life support.

Invariably, alert IT users find out that object databases are better suited for *multimedia* information. Since multimedia solutions are represented and implemented a myriad of ways in terms of underlying systems technology, experience indicates that the following facts should be kept in mind:

· Multidatabase applications require maximum data independence.
· The object DBMS and its methods shield the applications and allow only semantically correct operations to be applied.
· Integrative object DBMS, like Pegasus, Versant Star, and RDB Star, also incorporate mappings from both relational and nonrelational models.

Such integrative approaches are particularly important in environments where the client/server model dominates, with clients and servers interconnected through a network. Processes cooperate in the form of multimedia access, transaction execution, distributed query handling, and so on.

Object orientation is vital in communications-intense environments. A client requests a service by sending a message to the corresponding server; the server performs the service and responds to the client request. But each server provides more than a response to the networked clients — it aids in upkeeping system-wide functionality. A breakdown in this process will

· Upset the organization as a whole
· Lead to serious disadvantages in its business

Such disaster can befall at any time. It typically hits people and companies that fail to learn from past mistakes, or do unnecessary and marginal things just to find work for the unemployable.

Disasters of this nature are particularly vicious with centralized systems, where a core failure means total blackout. But these references do not mean that we should forget about the risks involved with distributed structures. To the contrary, we should study them.[3]

In conclusion, data independence, applications independence, and integrative approaches are useful in providing interoperability for a wide range of computers. All three are well served through object orientation, knowledge engineering and a distributed architecture. But computers and communications systems both present opportunities and have constraints. We should be careful with our choices.

---

3 For Systems Reliability see D. N. Chorafas, *Handbook of Communications and Computer Networks,* 3rd ed., McGraw-Hill/TAB Books, New York, 1991.

9

Serving the Need for Homogeneity in Database Functions

Introduction

Management readers may wonder if some of the contents of Chapters 6 and 8 were not a little too technical for them. The answer is: May be. But if management does not take a glimpse at the technical side, the computer/management gap that exists today will perpetuate itself to the detriment of the company.

A computer-based solution is *logistics,* and logistics should follow very closely the business goals of the manufacturing firm. This is precisely the role of technology, and when it is not executed in an able manner, operations suffer and they are no longer profitable. The sense of this reference is that

· The need for logistical, and therefore technological, support has been created by industrial expansion.
· It is mainly the advanced business deals that ask for a better technological infrastructure, though once in place such an infrastructure also helps the other operations.

As trade at large, and most particularly world trade, grew during the 1960s and 1970s, companies initially followed the familiar pattern of linear globalization. Operations, including overseas operations, related exclusively to headquarters. This is no longer effective.

Over the years, experience demonstrated that the centralized reporting practice becomes a bottleneck and therefore is impractical. Hence, they substituted it with mesh-type globalization in which individual units operate with increasing autonomy, dealing directly with each other.

The any-to-any communications among distributed corporate entities posed *database* and *networking* problems. Initially, these could be handled the old way, as they were not so complex. But then came the challenge of heterogeneity among the distributed databases as many of them

· Had developed in a manner totally independent from one another
· Featured incompatible protocols, formats, data structures
· Posed rather severe problems in terms of their interconnectivity

Skill in handling these problems was not lacking, but an integrative approach had never been taken prior to the mid-1980s. Furthermore, the general purpose mainframe concept dominated and database computers were not popular.

It is interesting to notice that an exception to the so-called von Neumann architecture, which underpins mainframes, was the Univac file computer. It has been first delivered in 1954, but failed commercially. Thereafter, it took two decades for alternative hardware solutions to show up and another decade before the concept of a database computer got accepted.

What Can Be Accomplished with New Technology?

Both through their day-to-day experience and by means of special studies, the foremost companies have come to the conclusion that the integration of distributed heterogeneous databases is both a high priority project and a significant challenge. This is just as true for manufacturing companies and merchandising concerns as it is for financial institutions.

Often in my seminars people ask: "How did we reach the messy state of incompatibility in which we are?" The answer needs a brief historical background.

Special software, what essentially became the DBMS, was promoted as the handler of database problems. Its evolution has been based on step-by-step developments which led:

· In the mid-1950s to file access routines
· In the mid- to late 1960s to hierarchical and Codasyl DBMS
· In the late 1970s to logic over data approaches
· In the 1980s to the advent of the database computer

This was a slow technological evolution while, as the introductory paragraphs have shown, at the same time changes in industry and commerce posed challenges well beyond what step-by-step approaches could solve.

In logistics terms, the transition is exemplified through the frame set by four major changes described in Figure 1. Among them, these changes saw to it that a virtual integration of the incompatible databases existing in most organizations

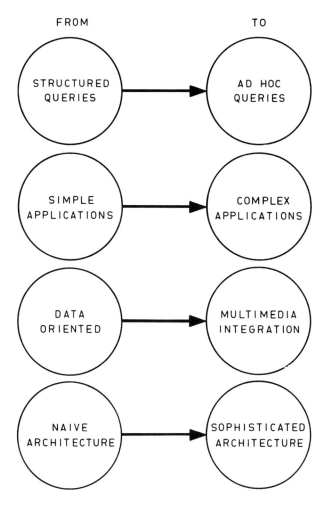

Figure 1   Four moves requiring a comprehensive and universally valid solution.

is necessary as an enabling technology. Indeed, it is a precondition for being competitive.

As we have seen in the preceding chapters, from the mid-1980s — when the need arose — to the early 1990s solutions have necessarily been *ad hoc*, since no vendor of computer equipment had come up with a universal approach able to provide

- · The system architecture
- · The protocols
- · The rich software routines

needed for a valid, corporate-wide implementation of integrative approaches regarding the text and data resources. Vendors, of course, do not admit this. They would rather say that "they have the solution," but what they offer is limited and parochial — though since 1991 some commodity software has started coming to the market.

The reason for new and rigorous departures in handling databases is that the old ones have failed. They have failed because they have not been made for the transitions of which we spoke, nor for transactional and query systems which are awfully complex in their requirements[1] and therefore in the skills and tools they need.

As we will see in Part III, with GTE's excellent reference among others, the best approaches available today are using artificial intelligence to solve the challenge of integrating heterogeneous databases. They also implement object-oriented tools.

- · There is evidence that realistic and timely knowledge engineering projects can provide the results we are after in terms of database integration.
- · At the same time, there are no tangible reasons to believe that this can be successfully achieved without high technology.

This is precisely what led the management of GTE to the virtual integration of its distributed heterogeneous databases through the Intelligent Database Assistant (IDA).[2] General Telephone and Electronics is not the only company to believe and invest in knowledge engineering.

The late Jean Ribout, a former investment banker and chief executive officer of Schlumberger, had this to say on the use of new technology:

> This technical revolution — artificial intelligence — is as important to our future as the surge in oil exploration. It will force us to design new tools, it will change the capabilities of our services. It will multiply the effectiveness of our instruments. It will change the order of magnitude of our business.[3]

The reason why Schlumberger, GTE, and so many other competitive edge companies are interested in using knowledge engineering and in proceeding with database integration is that they are tooling up for the new markets of the 1990s. These markets go well beyond their past basic services and emphasize *value differentiation*.

---

1 It is indeed quite surprising that in spite of the proven advantages of expert systems many companies still shy away from them.
2 See Chapter 13.
3 Ken Auletta, *The Art of Corporate Success — The Story of Schlumberger,* Penguin Books, New York, 1985.

Emphasis on value differentiation means competitiveness. It is the strategy adopted by manufacturing and service industries that know how to survive. GTE identified a telephone company's future business:

- The *basic services* consist of network design, implementation, administration, and maintenance — assisted through AI — as well as high reliability, broadband channels, and efficient protocols.
- The *value added* services are user oriented: health management, electronic publishing, frequent shopper, frequent flyer, and so on, however they require integrative approaches to database management as well as powerful new tools to produce competitive products.

New departures don't always please those are irritated by change. That is how decay starts. Therefore, the role of top management is to overcome resistance to change. And speaking from personal experience, the role of highly-paid consultants is to give advice on the new action course, whether it pleases top management or not.

"It is not an easy thing to vote against the President's wishes," Henry Wallich, a member of the Federal Reserve Board of Governors, said. "But what are we appointed for? Why are we given these long terms in office? Presumably, it is that not only the present but also the *past* and the *future* have some weight in our decisions. In the end, it may be helpful to remind the president that it is not only his present concerns that matter."[4]

Developing New Technology for Database Integration

To integrate heterogeneous databases, we must develop a data model to which each node can provide an interface. A project at Loyola University[5] uses two alternative strategies and the results were convincing:

1. *Shells* for nonfrequent connections across the databases
2. A *direct translation link* for frequent connectivity and database access

The adopted solution provides alternative paths within the chosen integrated approach for transparent cross-database access. It also serves outside this context to increase efficiency in resource utilization.

The user interface module of the multidatabase system developed by Loyola accepts expressions in an object-oriented database language, based on Smalltalk.

---

4   William Greicher, *Secrets of the Temple. How the Federal Reserve Runs the Country,* Touchstone/Simon and Schuster, New York, 1987.
5   New Orleans, LA. This has been one of the more imaginative papers presented at the international symposium on multidatabases, Kyoto, Japan, April 8–9, 1991.

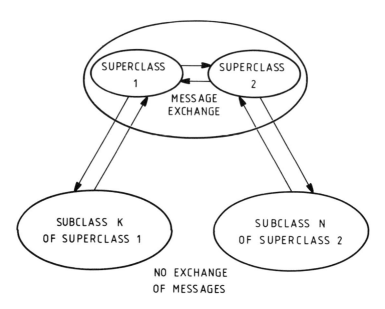

Figure 2   Message exchange mechanism of the Loyola project.

The constructs of the language are Smalltalk classes, instances of classes, and messages. The linguistic artifact that was developed required several extensions to Smalltalk to allow for database operations.

The integration module identifies database requests within a query expression and decomposes the application programs into separate requests to Smalltalk and the DBMS. A two-level schema has been chosen:

· One contains classes and instances
· The other handles the challenge of what to do with the result of certain instantaneous operations

Both levels employ facilities embedded in semantic data models. The project chose the strategy of an interplay between superclasses, classes, and subclasses, as well as aggregate objects.

Superclasses communicate directly among themselves. Subclasses communicate with their superclasses, as shown in Figure 2, but not with subclasses. Message exchange takes place only among the heterogeneous superclasses and between the superclass and its subclasses.

Message exchange is important as it helps to define queries that involve data from more than one database in the distributed environment. The project specified logical links between the different databases by defining messages whose receiver class and result class belong to incompatible structures.

Several situations that may arise when we attempt to link classes from a variety of databases have been examined. Classes can be of incompatible format, but there is an isomorphism, a link, or no link between them.

New classes may be constructed at the multidatabase level using the local database classes. One approach is to define a multidatabase class as a generalization of some specified classes in the local databases. The Loyola project supports this definition, but it also allows further extension through the forementioned superclasses and subclasses.

- The project is imaginative and full of practical ideas.
- It demonstrates how a successful solution to cross-database access should be.

A fundamental assumption in the development of effectively distributed resources is that the system must be built to support pre-existing databases, without requiring conversions of, or major modifications to, their structure and content.

The principle of preservation and support of existing applications and database structures is advanced in recognition of the fact that existing databases have been developed for and maintained by running applications software. Major changes in the databases necessitate significant changes in the software, which may be prohibitively expensive.

Within this perspective, effectively distributed data services require an integrative model based on intrinsic relationships among information elements. This can be achieved through

- A mapping methodology able to relate an instance of the integrative model to the databases that contain the information
- A methodology for controlling dynamic configuration of available segments of the modeled information

There is also a need for a cross-network communications protocol linking distributed information elements, including exchange representations of data operations.

A configuration methodology of the suggested type will assume the existence of an intelligent data dictionary relating the integrative model to specific instances and describing the relationships among the instances. A valid methodology must deal with dynamic situations found in the real world, including conflicting instances and backups — and data dictionary support is always valuable.

Learning from Experience with Conceptually Global Databases

A key approach to the development of a homogeneous environment is the elaboration of a suitable conceptual database schema and the subsequent selection of an appropriate set of relations. These should satisfy, in the best possible way, the information processing requirements of the users, representing a pivot point of reference during the logical design of a global database.

Such an approach, however, requires new departures, as solutions to the database integration problems currently faced by most corporations cannot be reached through minor adjustments in the beaten path of data processing. If we continue to use yesterday's answers to deal with the quite different problems of tomorrow, we will reach practically nothing.

At the same time, knowledgeable information technologists would recognize that it is not wise to try and reinvent the wheel. A more rational approach is to start by studying plausible solutions:

· How companies manage and plan to manage their heterogeneous database problems, including the strengths and weaknesses of their approach.

The idea of learning from what other companies are doing has great merits. It can lead to the identification of solutions that have been achieved by other organizations in terms of heterogeneous database integration or are currently in the works. We should learn from every worthwhile effort rather than trying to do everything ourselves and falling behind.

Model companies should be selected for their avant-garde approaches, but also for incompatible data structures, operating systems, and DBMSs in their information technology operations. With such companies it is also rewarding to study how they face the need for architectural solutions.

The research I am suggesting benefits everyone, those who learn and those who teach. They both gain from the cross-fertilization of ideas. Further to the point, capitalizing on lessons learned, we should then examine

· Ways and means that help provide a uniform, virtual integration solution without disrupting the old systems currently in operation.

A solution will be based both on practical grounds and on the necessary theoretical infrastructure regarding the integration and management of heterogeneous databases. But the greatest benefit will come from learning from failures rather than successes.

Past failures have another advantage. They help forecast future pitfalls. Any effort done in this direction should reflect on the future information technology requirements of the manufacturing company. These will, by all likelihood, revolve around the decision-making structure of the firm.

The decision-making organizational structure can be centralized or distributed, but both require distributed, globally accessible database resources for reasons of efficiency and competitiveness. And when the overcentralized corporation is replaced, for competitive reasons, by autonomous subsidiaries, the database system will be in place to serve the new structure.

The concept of global operations through independent business units will evidently have other far-reaching aftermaths. It will not only impact corporate structure and the logistics at its disposition, but also see to it that many jobs fundamentally change:

- The hierarchical core at headquarters will be getting smaller, which is a positive development as it cuts down on red tape.
- The complexity of business will be put under control, giving autonomous subsidiaries as well as talented employees responsibility for action and *accountability*.

The message these references aim to convey is that the technological infrastructure, current and future, can in no way be distinct and separate from the organizational solutions being adopted. And it is better to have modular technological solutions rather than monolithic ones.

The changing structure of business has its allure in many ways. The need for interactive knowledge and information requirements increase as professionalism is promoted. The steady path of advancement in a hierarchical sense may become a relic, supplanted by a horizontal fast track that provides valued employees an array of work experiences.

It may not sound at first sight that the Loyola project on database technology and what is said in this section on organization and structure are connected. Yet, this is precisely the meaning of the foregoing references,

- Not only do they support organizational structure and technology interleave, but they also support one another.
- Short of this, the solutions we provide are very partial, and they contribute to the computer/management gap rather than closing it.

The contents of databases designed to serve global business systems are used to maintain connection between management and the sources of information. Global contents, no matter where they reside, must be visualized through graphic interfaces.

- Objects may be presented as icons or graphs, rather than tables, with their behavior specifying changes to the iconic representation, e.g., color changes.

Many process control applications work this way, and not only process control. Leading-edge banks have learned from industry and iconic representation enriched with color and set into operations such as foreign exchange and securities trading.

- Links between objects may also be shown in highlighting details and/or alternative courses of action.

The development and evaluation of these alternatives can be assisted through modeling and knowledgebanks. Expert systems are not only used to help interconnect heterogeneous databases, but also for information maintenance and display.

Knowledge-based solutions can provide analytic and diagnostic information or other forms of inference, going beyond the spreadsheet's "what-ifs" to the analysis of effects. This contributes to corporate performance, provided the facts are available in databases to back up the deeds.

Solving Complexity and Planning for Parallelism

A careful study of the transitions that have so far taken place in database management provides the evidence that new technology is rarely used to displace the current ones already embedded in applications. Instead, the emerging, more powerful solutions are used to develop and deploy new applications, i.e., applications that would be difficult or impossible to build using the previous, aging technology.

For instance, in the migration to relational databases it is rare to find existing Codasyl or IMS applications that were rewritten. Instead, new applications with

- Improved flexibility
- Direct enduser access
- Higher programmer productivity

were executed through relational solutions. Something similar is happening with the transition from relational to object-oriented database management, which is now taking place. Quite often with new technology, we aim to reduce the complexity of current systems besides planning for new solutions.

At the factory floor, planning and scheduling are examples where object-oriented techniques are the only successful way of developing less complex interactive applications. The old procedural step-by-step techniques do not simplify productive planning chores but add to complexity.

Precisely because of the facilities new, interactive technology provides, the consequences will be wide-ranging, from man–machine interfacing aspects to the answer of distributed databasing and communications requirements. This will be quite important to society as a whole by the end of this century as more people will be working at home, while at the same time people with better educations (including computer literacy) will be aggressively sought after.

It may sound strange indeed to bring *social aspects* into the middle of a discussion on technology, but it is important to ask the question: "Is technology developed to serve people, or vice versa?"

While all of us are in the middle of a business and technical environment characterized by huge change, few people take notice of it or even seem to want

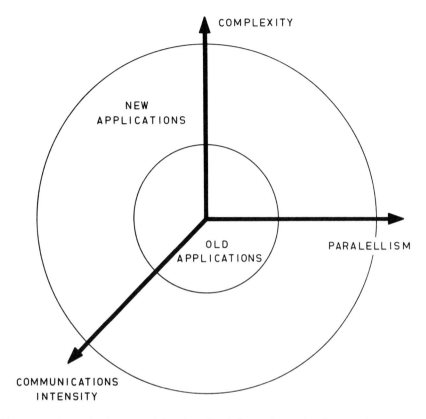

Figure 3   **Axes of reference of the changing information technology environment.**

it. Yet, the wave of change is here. More and more it impacts society in a significant manner and, through it, the way database solutions have to be made. It is particularly important to pay attention to the three axes of reference shown in Figure 3.

Complexity

Given their large number of cooperating components, the distributed applications of a manufacturing environment have a complex overall structure. This is necessary because explicit facilities for polyvalent management are required to handle operations from marketing, to design, manufacturing, testing, inventory management, and back to marketing.

Let's never forget that databases are not being developed in an abstract way or for the fun of it. They are made to serve business and societal needs. As complexity increases, the system becomes less manageable; hence the wisdom is to reduce complexity through the approaches we saw in the last two sections.

Parallelism

The mechanism developed for database access and the requirements posed by distributed, concurrently operating processes have to be supported within an expanding topology and its communication infrastructure. The fine grain of such requirements is often quite irregular and therefore difficult to understand and analyze. But development effort can be enriched through knowledge engineering and supercomputers.

Parallelism in database access from a growing range of applications was virtually unknown in the first three decades of computer usage. It surfaced in the 1980s and now it has such momentum that companies that forget about the competitiveness it offers are condemned to develop moribund systems. In a few years, they will have to be thrown out, together with the money and effort that went into building them.

Intensive Communications

The different components of an expanding applications environment communicate intensively. Hence, very efficient networks are essential and must be supported through a significant degree of parallelism.

When we plan solutions for the 1990s we must account for the future user requirements not for the past. Since the now developing long transactions and complex queries pose totally different implementation perspectives than those to which we have been accustomed, planning for the future is practically synonymous to *cultural change*.

In any dynamic enterprise, these three features: complexity, parallelism, and intensive communications, make the analysis of overall control flow most challenging. And it is wise to appreciate that solutions are much more difficult in centralized sequential applications, the way we have known them for decades.

Fully distributed approaches are the best strategy. Such strategy underlines the need for database integration and virtual homogeneity. The same strategy also suggests the interest in having a methodology that can lead to

- The analysis of database requirements into manageable portions (see the four quadrant approach in the next section)
- Knowledge engineering and object-oriented tools to improve the quality of integrative database schema design
- Parallel computation to increase the efficiency of database access, as well as number crunching capabilities, and avoid bottlenecks

When we do a global information technology study, it is helpful to consider the organization as a set of interacting subsystems coordinated to achieve a set of goals. All specific actions to be performed by the system have to be thoroughly described using a computer assisted development database.

Such actions should be assigned to corresponding components which operate in parallel and communicate with one another. The relationships among functional subsystems must be established, and the path to be taken should not lead to a situation where each organizational unit operates as a watertight technology department.

The more independent the different operational units become, from the center and from one another, the more they need interactive communication and database sharing. While this may sound like a contradiction, it is in fact the basis of an effective solution for technological breakthroughs where authority is delegated but control is not lost.

A Four Quadrant System for Dataflow Analysis

When it comes to the definition of database functionality from the viewpoint of an expanding applications environment, the existence of a metalevel mechanism can be of significant assistance. It will concentrate on conceptual design and predicates, which command the flow, storage, and retrieval of information elements.

The metalevel incorporated into an enhanced *four quadrant* model,[6] which we study in this section, employs a methodology that draws its strength from the functional and informational aspects of business operations. However, certain prerequisites must be observed:

1. The appropriate descriptions have to be developed not in the abstract, but against the precise functional model of the user organization and its business line.
2. The derived functionality must be validated and extended towards both the existing information elements and those being defined for new implementations.
3. The various component parts mapped into the quadrant have to be combined with qualitative, quantitative, and configuration references to generate an operational aggregate.

The best way to study *qualitative descriptions*, and integrate them with quantitative ones, is by means of fuzzy engineering. This is a new advance in computer applications, including database design, on which we have to capitalize.

The high technology reference also includes objects (information elements, commands), object descriptions, constraints (metadata, metarules), the applicable

---

6 The original idea was advanced by Dr. Charles W. Bachman, who is the father of IDS. However, in this text, Bachman's approach has been fully restructured in order to integrate the concept of *meta* and its associated *constraints* which should dominate systems design.

data description language (DDL) statements, process control parameters, and a stream of advanced application programs.

A methodological approach is shown in Figure 4. The X and Y axes, typically used to divide mathematical graphs into four quandrants, are employed to graph information: technology concepts, data, rules, metadata, and metarules.

· The vertical axis places information system concepts to the right and multi-media concepts to the left.
· The horizontal axis locates descriptions, rules, and metarules above the dividing line and the objects and functions they describe below the line.

In the graph shown in Figure 4 we find the business functions and constraints, hence, the planning and individual control part, in the first quadrant. This is the location of the real world.

Manufacturing companies, merchandising concerns, financial institutions, government organizations, and individual people all address this first quadrant. The aim of solutions to be provided is to assure an answer to the questions: *what, why, when,* and *how.* The answers to such questions are part of this first quadrant.

Programs and procedures, files and databases, the detailed programmatic interfaces necessary to run jobs, as well as their online, real time execution are found in the second quadrant. This is the store of resources developed over the years.

Progress should be done sequentially. Its required supports will be, by and large, stored in a repository, preferably in a fully modular fashion with reusable software. Whether or not he likes it, the database administrator cannot perform his functions in an able manner — which means he cannot work in the second quadrant — unless and until he has first elaborated all the details associated with the first quadrant.

· Much of the mismanagement that exists today with information technology is due to the fact that the first quadrant has not been properly studied.
· This means that organizational aspects have not been considered at all, or were evaluated only slightly and in a disconnected manner.
· No vendor can help a user organization in this analysis — when it comes to business organization the user company has to help itself.

In essence, what the different software vendors provide is addressed to the needs of the second quadrant. But software does not solve the problems of the first quadrant; brainware is the answer.

The third quadrant has the multimedia information elements as we know them and use them: data, text, graphics, image, and voice. In short, these are the objects supporting the real world. It is here that computer files, paper files, drawings, plans, messages, and mail are found.

In this sense, the third quadrant typically functions as database server, certainly a role that expands. By combining the third and the first quadrant, we open up a

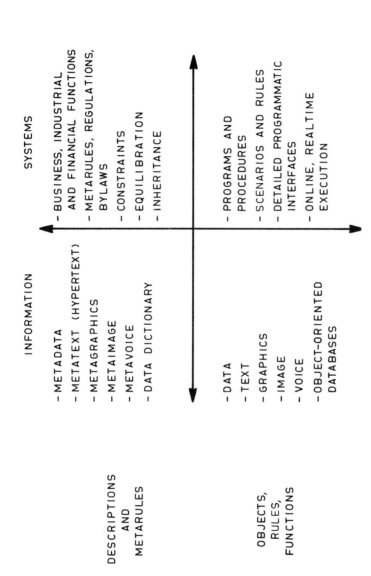

Figure 4   The four quadrant space for data and metadata; rules and metarules.

wider range of applications which require online performance as well as increasingly larger storage capabilities.

The fourth quadrant (top level, left side of the graph in Figure 4) is the *meta* level of the third. It includes data dictionaries that have been designed as repositories for data descriptions, constraints, and controls. But it also holds a completely new set of references collectively known as the *meta* level: metadata, metagraphics, metatext, and so on. These constitute the conceptual schema from the enduser's and the database administrator's viewpoint.

New applications, spanning engineering and science all the way to manufacturing, merchandising, and financial transaction processing, demand database systems with improved complex query performance and high transaction volume. Up to a point, this is guaranteed by the combination of the second and third quadrant pairing processing requirements and database facilities.

Beyond that point, solutions must rest on the predicates provided by the fourth quadrant, that is the metalevel. This metalevel fits well, at the upper half of the graph, with the business system description. In fact, its parallel role is to interpret any valid approach to information technology the business sense of the function has to perform.

We will talk again of the four quadrant system in Chapter 10, after having introduced the concept of intentional and extentional databases. It is quite rational to have these two concepts work in synergy; this helps magnify the impact of every one of them.

Services Provided by a Rigorous Functional Analysis

To appreciate the services a rigorous functional analysis can assure, we need to return to the fundamentals, briefly recapitulating the message given since the beginning of this chapter. Today all major organizations, whether manufacturing companies or banks, face the problem of managing large and sprawling databases. Typically:

- The databases are distributed on different machines and locations.
- They run under different OS and DBMS.
- They tend to have different data structures.

Therefore, like it or not, these databases are incompatible. They have difficulty in interoperating unless something is done to solve the heterogeneity bottleneck.

The bottleneck created by old technology became worse because the new wave of applications, particularly those of analytical queries by managers and professionals as well as the growing range of long transactions, require cross-database access. We also said that such access has to be fully transparent, as the manager cannot be bothered with database heterogeneity.

Since, in the larger number of cases, this problem was not present 10 or even 5 years ago, tools with a lifecycle of 10, 20, or 30 years[7] cannot be of any assistance. Time spent with them is time lost. Period.

Not only are new concepts and new tools necessary, and we spoke of them throughout this book, but also a more efficient methodology. This is the scope of the enhanced four quadrant system: offer a means for systematic analysis of requirements in a complex environment.

Accuracy and efficiency in the process of analysis and mapping business functions is the reason why the *meta* quadrant has been introduced. We must integrate at the meta (higher-up) layer of reference, which provides a logical view of

· Constraints
· Predicates

Ten years ago, some people might have said that database integration might be done through a unique, universal schema. However, as we have already seen, this approach has been tried and not given commendable results. It is useless to spin the wheels in a vacuum.

A better possibility is a very high level language with object orientation and a knowledge engineering solution. It should be well chosen to be applicable all the way from analysis to design and coding, as well as the definition of multimedia information elements. This is what has been suggested since the beginning of the previous section.

Taken together, the four quadrants of the system target the integrated applications which are at the heart of major industrial and financial activity today. Such a functional approach to the organization of information technology implementation is important for efficiency reasons:

· The number of cooperating functions is large, and that of the databases increases.
· The database and applied programming structures are becoming awfully complex, and something has to be done to simplify them.
· Multimedia information elements have taxing requirements, which were not there with simple data.
· The processing logic reflects business policies, which are very dynamic and often change.

---

7   Introduced in 1958, Cobol has had, so far, a 35-year lifecycle. Fortran is a year older, and PL/1 and APL are each a quarter century old.

If no other reason existed than the last one being stated, it would still have been necessary to alter our concepts and tools. In investment banking, for instance, there are financial products that live just one day — others live up to a month. It is simply illogical to take 3 years to develop software able to serve them.

Hence, more powerful mechanisms are necessary to design and implement the information systems we require for our business. Just the same, it is important to be able to describe interactively, in real time, what we have to do.

The knowledge enriched four quadrant modules in Figure 4 can help address all, or major segments of, the database operations we currently run or project. But any serious work should start with a business model that has three descriptive categories:

· The information required to operate
· The functions that create and use this information
· The rules by which the subject functions run

Such descriptions must be sufficiently complete to permit prototyping of new information system perspectives, as well as test how they respond to simulated input.

Both qualitative and quantitative approaches are necessary. The former defines the nature and magnitude of the database structure we address. The latter involves configuration descriptions, covering available computer hardware, software, communications, and storage resources.

If we wish to institute a database architecture, this enhanced four quadrant study is the first thing to do. This is written in appreciation of the fact that, like the database administrator, the database architect is not put into place just to create a bottleneck. His goal must be to really help the organization and its endusers through solutions that are both agile and comprehensive.

10

Requirements for Virtual Database Integration

Introduction

Whether we revamp or redesign our database system, we need to enumerate our requirements in a factual and documented manner. The key to successful requirements analysis is *discovering* and *identifying* a set of applications oriented concepts to be served through a virtual database integration.

This is precisely the purpose of the quadrant system suggested in Chapter 9. Its observance forces a methodological approach that should definitely characterize the solution to many problems with which we are confronted in information technology work.

The best identification of the functions for which support should be provided would come from the domain experts, which means the *endusers*. For their part, the database specialists and systems programmers should provide the integrative capabilities. This is written in recognition of the fact that

- *Data* and *process* components that were handled in the past have often been put together in a monolithic manner
- *Managerial* and *professional* requirements have been ill-defined, or even simply guestimated.

Today, these approaches are no longer viable alternatives. Gone is the time when management visibility of computer operations was remote or nill. Interactive systems have put managers and professionals at the frontline of information technology and its implications.

Since endusers have growing and diversified needs, a basic goal in database development and administration should be the achievement of conceptual integrity leading system solutions that are relatively simple and straightforward, yet modular and useful over time. As leading manufacturing companies have discovered, traditional methods and tools for

173

- User requirements analysis
- Distributed database design

typically lack formal foundations. They do not provide for quick changes and cannot be easily extended or evolved. Hence, they present a poor basis for systems development. At the same time, since the lifecycle of our databases is long, and tends to be even longer, extreme care should be paid to quality since the early design stage.

This is also true in terms of providing solutions to cross-database requirements, which cannot wait unsupported for long. The preferable alternative is virtual integration along the federated lines we discussed in chapters 6 and 7. Hence, prior to proceeding to Part III with real life case studies, let's elaborate a little more on how this can be done.

What Is Meant by a Virtually Homogeneous Database?

The databases shown in Figure 1 may be thousands of miles apart. However, this topological reference is of no particular importance to the way they cooperate and integrate with one another. Some of the applications may be common, others are specific to one of the databases, and still others concern just a small group of them. All these references should be fully transparent to the endusers.

The proper technology in confronting this effort is the one that provides for continuity in integrative perspectives while observing architectural requirements. The latter include both computers and communications, since the two are today indivisible.

What is more, the applications addressing the structure Figure 1 has presented can be expected to evolve as a function of time. The same is true of the information elements. The *metalevel* of

- Applications
- Information elements
- Systems constraints

should be mapped into a data dictionary with Pareto's Law used to decide which object definitions, access authorizations, applications linkages, and system constraints should be distributed and which should be handled centrally.

In principle, frequently accessed entities in the data dictionary should be distributed. Shown in Figure 2, Pareto's Law suggests that between two related entities a small part of one variable, for instance data definitions, corresponds to a big part of the other, e.g., accesses to the data dictionary by user entities.

One of the crucial issues to be addressed in the process of virtual database integration is that of synonyms and homonyms. It is a major challenge encountered during integrative work and has to do with sorting out contradictions and

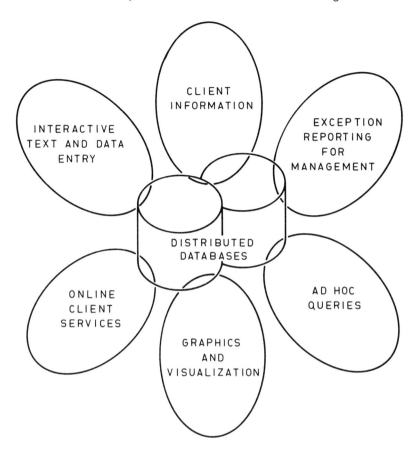

Figure 1   Kernel functionality in a distributed database environment.

incompatibilities. Using knowledgebank principles, some organizations have been able to catch about 90% of synonyms automatically.

The difficulty in sorting out synonyms and homonyms has to do with the fact that there is a complex relation between processes and information elements. A solution to the synonym problem is a microscopic issue. At Ciba-Geigy,[1] for instance, the analysts applied the following queries to each data type using an object-oriented shell:

· Tell me all the relations that are relevant to this information element.
· Tell me all data types related to this one and its versions.

Both *relations* and *related data types* have been handled as *objects* in a fully interactive manner. Visualization was assisted by the fact that the chosen shell

---

1   Switzerland's largest chemical company.

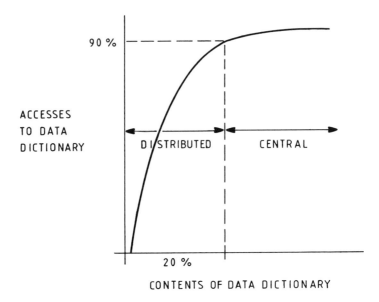

CONTENTS OF DATA DICTIONARY

Figure 2   Pareto's Law can be instrumental in deciding which part of a data dictionary to distribute and which to keep central.

uses different colors per class of queries, in a departmental sense: blue for marketing, green for design, and red for finance.

·   Distinct colors greatly help in visualizing overlaps and substitutions.
·   Much of the tool's power also came from the principle of inheritance.
·   Synonyms were used advantageously: the *classification* and descriptor jobs were enormously assisted through identification.[2]

Also instrumental was the fact that the tool permitted a soft delete operation, keeping databases and sections thereof in a dotted form of representation on the interactive diagram. This visualization acted as a reminder in all subsequent work.

Problems with synonyms and homonyms also exist with centralized database implementations. In most cases, they are at the origin of difficulties that exist in regard to the integration of the discrete islands running on mainframes. What is said in these pages is applicable to all environments, more or less independent of their architecture.

To recapitulate, several problems connected to information elements have to be addressed to obtain a cross-database solution with virtual database integration:

---

2   On classification and identification see D. N. Chorafas, *Handbook of Relational Databases and DBMS,* McGraw-Hill/TAB Books, New York, 1989.

· Synonyms — different identifiers are used in different databases for the same entity.
· Homonyms — the same identifier is employed for different information elements in the same or different data repositories.
· Domain mismatch — incompatible perceptions of what the real world entities are exist.
· View mismatch — inability to generalize description of various information resources.

The effects of each one of these four classes are detrimental in terms of reusing data resources and adequate specifications. Sorting out these differences and correcting them is instrumental in obtaining a homogenized representation, therefore in supporting database interoperability.

Industry's Changing Patterns and the Need for Flexibility in Database Design

The previous section underlined the need to create a virtually homogeneous database. Since the problems being outlined get aggravated with time, every effort should be made *now* to protect our company's competitive position in the late 1990s — and this takes lots of foresight.

Flexibility in database design is absolutely necessary to respond to the changing pattern of industry. Flexibility can be assured through a distributed, modular approach, but the modules must be compatible with one another or at least virtually so.

No company is immune to the waves of change, and their impact on its databases. A study by Siemens[3] demonstrated that:

· In 1975, three quarters of its income was derived from electrical engineering, and the balance from electronics.
· In 1985, the income was practically divided 50-50 between electrical engineering and electronics.
· The forecast is that in 1995, three quarters of the income would come from electronics, radically changing the business and profits profile of the firm.

This change impacts products, process, and business sources — also partnership relationships. Hence, it affects the company's databases, their structure, usage, and contents.

Daimler Benz made the forecast that by the year 2000 some 10% of the value of a motor car would lie in its electronics instead of a mere 0.5% today.

---

3 Germany's largest electrical and electronics company.

- We can expect a similar transformation to happen in practically all products and services, and should get ready for it.
- The virtual integration of heterogeneous databases is key to the design and offering of new products, and this is increasingly true the higher the technology we use.
- But virtual integration needs a great deal of research, including activities directed towards a better use of the knowledge and information we have available.

We simply cannot pass up business opportunities that blend product design and market appeal — they clearly affect the bottomline. New products and services are an avenue for future growth, and they also feature a higher profitability than older products.

Changing products and processes magnify the fact that the implementation of information technology has reached a point where the field of database applications has grown very wide. However, in many cases the tools at our disposal have not changed accordingly.

- This situation is further complicated by the fact that the leading computer manufacturers have provided neither the necessary architectural solutions nor new tools.
- With low technology, it is quite difficult to handle the growing range of heterogeneous databases, even if a user organization stays with the same vendor.

Still another major challenge lies in the fact that the basic notions in DBMS design, therefore the accepted methodology for structuring a database, are changing every decade or so. This, user organizations say, destabilizes much of the work already done.

As we have seen in the preceding chapters, until recently the relational model was commonly accepted as the leading trend, leaving behind the traditional hierarchical and networking approaches to database management. Now there is less consensus about how far the relational model can serve in the 1990s. This is true even if the relational model is still a source of much research, and vendors continue announcing new and improved relational database products.

- There is no denying that new database paradigms are emerging, and research circles now classify the relational model as "traditional".
- Even vendors who, till the end of 1991, bet on relational solutions as their strategy for this decade are now moving into object approaches — IBM and DEC are examples.

User organizations should appreciate that new departures are not made for fancy reasons. They are due to the evolution of real life situations. The already existing database methodology is no longer responding to certain problems in an able manner:

· The complexity of long transactions
· Ad hoc analytical queries
· Advanced applications requirements
· Further out database management perspective

That is why it has been repeated on several occasions that the object-oriented approach is destined to play a leading role in solving reference problems, particularly as fully distributed environments gain strength.

Most likely, however, object-oriented database solutions will not completely take the place of relational approaches. The database community is about to enter a period where various models and paradigms coexist. This further underlines

· The need for a solid architectural solution that addresses *our* company's oncoming requirements
· The fact that an organization should be immediately preoccupied with the coexistence of heterogeneous databases.

As Chapter 9 has underlined, this job must start without delay. Every passing day makes the task more difficult. The preceding chapters have also brought into perspective the fact that the best approach is complemented with ideas from the object-oriented model:

· The knowledge-enriched layer constitutes the *intentional* database and lays over the *extentional* database;
· The *extentional* database can be served through relational management models.

Figure 3 exemplifies this reference, explaining where intentional and extentional databases reside. Both are highly distributed, and this concept fits well with a client–server architecture.

Developed by the New Generation Computer Project (ICOT) in Japan, the concept of an intentional solution resides in each client and each server in the system. By contrast, extentional databases are at the server side. This duality fits object orientation. It constitutes an area where knowledge-based artifacts and object orientation meet.

Database Applications, Rules, and Metarules

When we study the database structure, we have to blend the existing resources with those we project. We should also proceed in a logical, organized manner

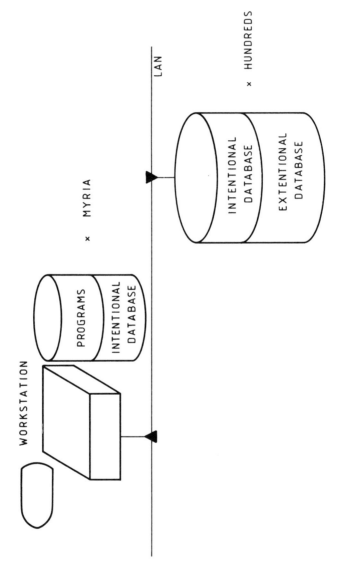

Figure 3   Intentional and extentional databases are a simple concept, yet a powerful one.

from the description of the current system, its inputs, processes and outputs, to projected new perspectives.

During this process, a clear distinction should be made between functions to be performed by the elements included in the distributed database and the way these elements interact:

- Day-to-day interactivity identifies the most frequent access to information elements — by location.
- Multimedia warehousing capability regards a not so frequent access but volumnous information.
- Backup and recovery requirements provide the security infrastructure that must be handled online rather than by batch

Since the database is a living body, fed by its input and sustained by the transactions and queries it receives, error sources must be identified and corrected. Always remember that an error is *not* something strange or necessarily unwanted. It is the basis for system regulation and control. But we must

- Identify these errors and their sources
- Establish acceptable ranges for their variation
- Project measurement metrics and associated procedures
- Establish the control action that should be taken

This must be done throughout the range of supported databases, the interaction taking place from workstation(s) to distributed resources and back. This reference focuses to the total system accessible by the user: person, program, terminal, or host.

The access mechanism to the database has to be studied in detail. The approach we choose for structuring it will greatly impact overall system performance.

- Hierarchical structures, for example, are simple *if* relations are one-to-one or one-to-many.
- They can become very complex if the relations between the information elements and the processes are many-to-many.

The organization of a distributed database as a whole, and of *each* of its component elements, should be thoughtfully projected, integrated, and implemented. This must be done in a way that makes it simple to institute the process of successive database generations.

Frequent restructuring of the interrelations characterizing the information elements becomes necessary when dynamic solutions dominate. For this reason, relational models are more advisable and they are today increasingly used. Yet, relational models too have their limitations, hence the concept of object-oriented solutions.

Information needed to support current applications and to build new ones should contain reusable classes for the application domain, as well as guidelines to help the developer during the specification of requirements. They should support a uniform representation of all information elements, such an approach being composed of two categories:

· A lower level defining the reusable information elements, as well as managing them
· A metalevel providing the guidelines for reusing the class, which makes the intentional database we spoke of earlier

Each level is defined as a set of roles. Lower level roles specify the information elements themselves, the extentional approach. Higher level roles map the characteristics the information elements can have in the application domain.

Metalevel roles convey knowledge, assisting the application developer in deciding how information elements can be tailored to the needs of a specific application. Such roles address themselves to database design aspects that need to be considered, as well as other requirements like functionality and security.

Associated to each metalevel role, hence at the intentional level, is descriptive information concerning relationships and the knowledge to drive the database design process. Such definitions include

· The characteristics of the application domain for which an information element or a group of them is intended
· Design information useful for the implementation, typically dynamically created and kept up during the specification process
· Messages in metalevel roles defining the design operations the developer can perform on information elements, as well as rules associated to metalevel roles
· Textual description and other definitions, stating purpose, functionality, and interrelationships
· Possible dependencies, as well as required interfaces: class, relationships, component parts, and so on.

Application domain characteristics and their metalevels have to do with information elements and commands, but they may also be addressing the functions performed by interfaces in connection to network controllers, bus repeaters, graphic systems, analog-digital converters, and so on. All these may be part and parcel of a concurrent file system which permits the building of a distributed but massive storage facility transparent to the user.

Goals Followed with a Metalevel Solution

To be successful in our effort to develop and implement a virtually integrated database, we must state, in black and white, the goals to be reached in our information technology environment. Unless we have decided on the objectives we wish to accomplish, we will not be able to direct our resources toward commendable results.

For instance, a goal may be to optimize the access structure in spite of incompatible database systems, or to pay particular attention to specific applications requirements that work interactively with databases. Subgoals to this last reference are

- Improving the efficiency of management control functions
- Making feasible a global risk management capability
- Providing a valid basis for experimentation prior to commitments
- Sustaining the profitability of day-to-day operations
- Enhancing productivity, particularly that of managers and professionals

Today the productivity of managers and professionals is a focal point worldwide and is badly served through old data processing. This is not surprising since management productivity can only be effectively supported through heuristics and agile databases — and old data processing is awfully weak on these two counts.

Statistics confirm this. For instance, in meetings during the research that I did in New York in 1992, several participants stated that *less than 5%* of applications on mainframes have a senior management orientation in them, and the majority of these applications are not satisfactory.

Clear-eyed companies are not looking for solutions that are monolithic, but instead involve a modular approach. In practical terms, this translates into an aggregation of self-controlled subsystems providing the ability to replace any one of the more or less centralized procedures currently available with a modern, distributed structure. This system should evolve by

- The accelerating process of innovation, which touches every walk of life
- A sense that the database is a corporate resource and should be managed accordingly
- The needed restructuring operations to meet organizational prerequisites
- The short software lifecycle that results from rapid evolution in today's environment.

In recent years, the frequency and amplitude of changes has increased, and this has had a significant impact on the way systems projects should be managed, particularly database oriented applications.

The increasingly competitive marketplace obliges us to develop solutions that permit faster managerial decisions and their online connection to operations. In turn, this demands wide access to text and data, as well as a rapid software development process.

As I have underlined in practically every chapter, no solution can be efficient without accounting for the wave of change. The time for minor, relatively slow alterations is past. In any projected solution, proper attention should be paid to the fact that systems tend to become more unstable, particularly if the feedback loop is too weak to respond.

Whether we talk of databases or any other project, the managerial and supervisory processes must not only keep control of events but also make feedbacks available to themselves for corrective purposes. The challenge is one of implementing such solutions

- In a manner that can be properly studied prior to commitment
- Without any disruption of current operation
- Within a reasonable timeframe in terms of putting it into practice

Here again, knowledge engineering could provide a significant degree of assistance by elaborating a conceptual model and working with it. Figure 4 shows such an approach which, as it should be expected, integrates a feedback mechanism.

What has been stated regarding business operations is just as valid with database technology. Any new plans for greater database coherence and integration must always take into account the fact that the diversity in DBMS and data structures a company presently has available will continue to be around; it cannot be disinvested.

This is precisely where some of the intentional database capabilities of which we spoke earlier come into the picture. The same is true about parallelism in database access, to which has been devoted part of Chapter 9.

A knowledge enriched parallel file system will see to it that users can create virtual logical storage facilities that are accessed via a global file directory. We have already spoken of the importance of data dictionaries.

How to proceed in terms of defining the characteristics of database applications in this environment is an issue that has already been addressed in Chapter 9, when we talked of the enhanced four quadrant system. Now that we have discussed intentional and extentional databases, the concept of metadata can be better appreciated:

- Intentional, hence metadata concepts, reside in quadrant 4.
- Extentional, therefore information elements, are in the quadrant 3.

Besides stating dependencies between classes, within the metalevel role of quadrant 4 rules define the evolution of a given class or object. This way, a dynamic design process is suggested to the development and maintenance phases driving the selection of classes and roles at the application level. For instance, metalevel roles can help the developer define document handling, security procedures, or presentation aspects within a specific application. Other metalevel roles may address basic specifications, assuring that they are complete, noncontradictory, and consistent.

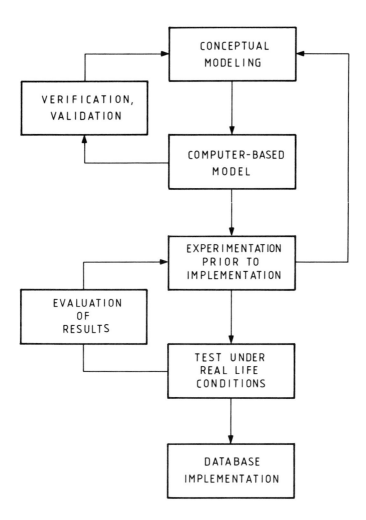

Figure 4   From conceptual modeling to database implementation.

Putting Intentional and Extentional Databases into Practical Use

Not only is the probability of having diverse and incompatible computer-supported databases high, but chances are that there are still manual files that hold vital information and whose online integration is quite important. Therefore, an approach to the creation of an integrative database structure must start with the systems architecture.

Like any other architecture, the grand design of a system cannot come forward with piecemeal suggestions that do not form a pattern everyone would understand.

The grand design must not only cover all applications, be effectively used by them. The solution to be developed should be able to

· Integrate the database elements today, found piecemeal under different incompatible applications domains
· Create a coherent, homogeneous, and comprehensive system

The present status has to be modeled, and this requires considerable research. In any organization, it is difficult to say, off hand, how many different data structures and incompatible OS-DBMS environments are involved. Only a careful study can provide a valid answer and assessment the problem. Such a study should be user oriented and very focused.

Once this is done, the basic work for the implementation of an intentional approach to distributed database management is already in place. From that point on the aim must be to create what is also known as a distributed *deductive* database structure.

The mapping and firing of the rules necessary for database management, in a deductive sense, will be done through knowledge engineering. We have discussed repetitively how important that is:

· At planning and development time, business knowledge, metarules, and metadata will guide the designer's hand in developing the system.
· At execution time, the predicates embedded in intentional rules will see to it that we have a virtual database integration.

Such a solution does not require any intermediate layers of data storage, as those promoted through information centers and other warehouses. Everything can be stored in an *episodic* memory form, the episodes constituting the extentional database.

One of the *worst* ideas that have come out in the search for a way out from current incompatibilities is that of creating an intermediate database — sort of decision support structures as presented in Figure 5. In a number of instances, this intermediate level server is supposed to act as an aggregation level of sorts.

· All pertinent transactions running in central or department machines under different DBMS will leave a trace on the InfoCenter.
· For their requirements, company executives and professionals will be expected to access the InfoCenter, not the transactional databases.

Such an approach is not uncommon, but it also fits the proverbial saying that a camel is a horse designed by a committee. Besides this, it looks backwards towards the 1970s. The information center concepts are now past because they largely rely on batch processes, which should definitely be weeded out of the system.

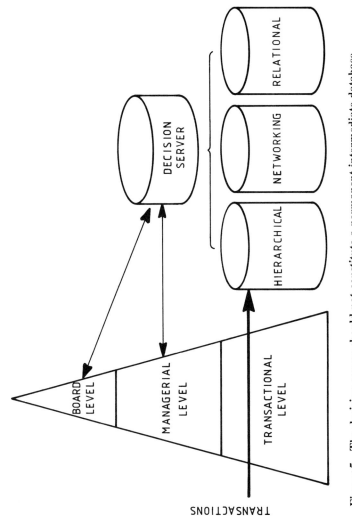

Figure 5   The decision server should not constitute a permanent intermediate database layer.

·   *If* the intermediate level includes a complete mapping of information elements with any-to-any connectivity
·   *Then* this approach will practically double the organization's current database in terms of size

It is evidently out of the question to double the database. Hence, choices will have to be made — and any filtering done today, even the best, will be obsolete by the time the InfoCenter database goes into operation.

The great diversity of data structures currently prevailing in a large majority of companies simply does not permit inputting the same database information elements pertinent to

·   Different transaction domains
·   Different procedures
·   Different data structures

There are three possible ways in case we want to remedy this situation: (1) sit down and change the programs, which is practically unthinkable with an inventory of Cobol statements running in the millions; (2) try to create a universal schema into which all other schemata will be converted (this, we said, has been tried and failed); (3) create a deductive database solution worked out along intentional and extentional lines — this option requires imagination, ingenuity, and technology, contrasted to the other two options which rest on brute force.

Concurrency Control in a Distributed Environment

There is one more subject we should discuss prior to starting with case studies, and it has to do with concurrency control. Its implementation requires a solid concept, basic algorithms and heuristics, as well as trusted approaches for avoiding performance failures.

Concurrency control involves locking, timestamp ordering, and validation methods assuring network-wide consistency. A concurrency control project must account for the fact that the networks of distributed databases have to support hundreds or thousands of simultaneous communications while

·   Avoiding the bottlenecks inherent in systems with significant contention
·   Assuring that consistency is being upheld at all times

Conflicting updates in a distributed database environment can be avoided by granting what is wrongly called "ownership" of information elements to specific sites, restricting updates only to the owning sites. However, flexibility must also be assured, and this cannot be done through centralized approaches.

Information elements may get out of date in applications that have much harsher time needs than the typical commercial systems. This is the case with real time applications featuring critical response time requirements that may not be able to be acted upon within a pre-established time delay.

As the transaction load increases, organizations are searching for low-delay consistency protocols. The exclusive writer protocol, developed by the University of California at Los Angeles,[4] is representative of the protocols a distributed real time system needs:

·   It designates a single task, called an exclusive writer, for each shared resource.
·   All update requests must be sent to this task, which alone has the right to update its assigned information elements.

Since the exclusive writer protocol uses neither locks nor timestamps to guarantee correct processing order, it avoids delays and overhead due to locking protocol synchronization, deadlocks, or timestamp rollback. These can be prohibitive in a real time system, where files consist of data in main memory and which use no high level data model.

Unlike real time systems, real-enough-time (deferred update but online execution) applications do not need up-to-date data immediately and do not have to pay the associated overhead. Hence, the solution to be selected should permit the organization to choose the variables associated to overhead, performance, and concurrency of data, depending on prevailing requirements.

Solutions to the concurrency problem are more important as a failed site may contain information that is replicated elsewhere and updates may occur to the replicated copy while its twin site is down. Distributed databases need a technique of synchronizing the replicated files after recovery.

One approach[5] employs two techniques for the synchronization chores, with the choice depending on how long the site has been out of operation:

1. The DBMS assumes that if a site is down for a long time, many changes in information elements have occurred.

Therefore, the DBMS ships a block of data containing the replicated and updated information elements to the recovering site. Upon reception and verification, that site replaces its copy with the new one.

---

4   In collaboration with the Ballistic Missile Defense Advanced Technology Center (BMDATC) of Huntsville, AL.
5   By Computer Corporation of America, Cambridge, MA.

2. The alternative approach is used when the site has not been down for very long and the number of replicated information elements updated elsewhere is small.

Under this hypothesis, the DBMS uses a spooler to hold the update messages sent to the site during its failed time. It then reprocesses them as part of its recovery scheme. In other terms, instead of viewing the site as having failed, database management reacts *as if* it has merely taken a long time to receive its update messages.

These are examples, not universally accepted approaches. The solution to be adopted by a given manufacturing firm should definitely avoid deadlock problems. These apply to two machines or tasks that each have a resource the other one wants. But neither one will give up its resource until it also gets something from the other.

While deadlock problems also occur in a centralized environment, they are slower to detect in a distributed database setting because nodes must send messages across communications links. In cases, not only does the deadlock span multiple sites but there are not enough controls at one site to detect a deadlock.

Intentional database solutions can help remedy this situation. In fact, some DBMS amended for distributed database applications have, in every node, a process whose function is to

· Monitor waiting transactions
· Determine what resource they are waiting for

The process sends a message over the network to find out who else is waiting for that resource. Subsequently, the monitoring process detects potential deadlocks.

Not only should detectors flash out deadlocks, they should avoid detecting erroneous ones. This dual safeguard is necessary even if erroneous deadlocks do not happen very often, because the amount of distributed node activity is usually low compared to the activity concentrated at a local site. If a deadlock is detected

· The monitor scans the transaction log to determine how much work each transaction has done.
· It then rolls back the one that has done the least amount of work, thus relieving the deadlock and allowing the other one to complete.

Data dictionaries and their directories are pivotal to such activity within a distributed database environment. But, as information elements change location, directories and dictionaries have to be updated.

Access paths have to be automatically regenerated to trace the new location(s) so that users (persons, programs, computers) can still access the information elements in a transparent manner. This too is one of the requirements for achieving virtual database integration.

III

Case Studies with Real Life Applications

11

Successful Projects with Integrated Databases

Introduction

The five chapters in Part II have demonstrated that a number of principles must be observed in designing, implementing, and maintaining distributed database systems. These range all the way from site independence to nonstop operations for long transactions and query processing and the interconnection of heterogeneous database structures.

- In terms of independence from site, the principle is that local information elements should be managed locally.
- The local data should not be affected from other site conditions, but when necessary made available in a global sense.

Nowhere is this principle better demonstrated than in the first case study we will see in this chapter regarding the Database Integration Architecture developed by TRW in answer to cross-database military requirements at large, and most particularly those connected to Operation Desert Shield and Operation Desert Storm in Iraq from 1990 to 1991.

This principle of local database independence, while at the same time assuring global connectivity, is no exclusive policy, valid only for military operations. It is applicable to all applications domains that require a degree of independence from the center site.

- Sound design principles suggest that all sites of the distributed database system should be treated as equal to each other (peers).
- They should not depend on a central point for storage retrieval, dictionary services, or recovery control.
- All data should be handled *as if* available at the local site.

As we will see in this chapter through practical examples (and most particularly CRONUS by BBN, the second case study) records partitioned and objects stored in multiple sites should be handled logically as a single reference.

- Sometimes the information elements are partitioned and distributed in order to give the distributed database system a higher performance.
- In other cases partitioning has happened by chance, or as a result of *database mergers.*
- The background reason should make no difference to the solution we adopt.

Even if copies of information elements are reproduced, users should not need to know at which site this happens or which data is the copy. If the objects are modified, their copies should be automatically modified as well.

The reader will appreciate that both case studies in this chapter observe the principle of independence from OS and DBMS of which we have spoken all along in Parts I and II. The distributed systems are constructed to integrate a multiple number of network architectures and communication media, both local and wide area.

Finally, the networked databases should work nonstop — this is precisely what both the TRW and BBN solutions are doing. That's why this chapter covers some of the best examples in the domain of effective cross-database solutions, particularly those made for military and civilian paramilitary operations.

TRW and the Data Integration Engine

In 1984, TRW decided to leverage its software technology, leading itself toward business operations and out of sole dependency on military contracts. At that time, a study demonstrated that in the late 1980s and throughout the 1990s

- Database know-how will be in significant demand as new markets develop with no well-established players in database connectivity.
- Interest in the integration of heterogeneous databases represented a business opportunity due to last 15 to 20 years.

Based on these forecasts, TRW decided to focus on the integration of heterogeneous database environments. So far, its projects involve IMS, DB2, Sybase, Ingres, and RDB. They also include knowledge engineering approaches, which the company considers fundamental in any successful solution to heterogeneous database challenges.

The chosen approach, as was said during a meeting held in Los Angeles with a TRW executive, has been dictated by experience. TRW's main effort along the integrative databases line has been the TRW Data Integration Engine (TDIE) project. It uses a knowledge engineering-enriched integration advisor (IA) and works source to target, where

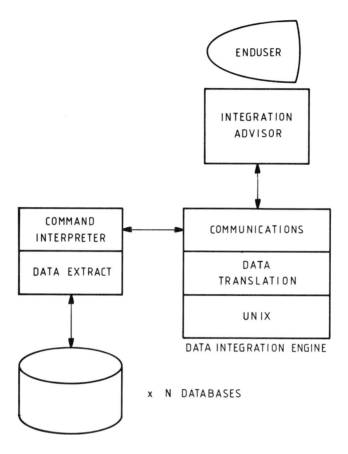

Figure 1   Using IA in a heterogeneous database environment.

- The source is the *owner*
- The target the *user*.

The way the IA interfaces with the system is shown in Figure 1, which identifies, at workstation level, the main modules of the TDIE. Resources distributed in "n" databases include the command interpreter and data extra routines.

   This architecture is not well known to the public, yet the results obtained through it were consistently in the news during the first 2 months of 1991. TRW was the contractor that integrated the heterogeneous databases of the American military for Operation Desert Shield — then Desert Storm — and the TDIE project underpinned this effort.[1]

---

1   The mechanics of the TRW Data Integration Engine are examined in the next section.

TRW outlined the benefits the TDIE architecture has provided, as well as the services obtained through the knowledge engineering artifact. To the judgment of the company's specialists, approaches to database integration based on expert systems prove to be increasingly valuable. They provide an important contribution in modern information systems environments where

- Each DBMS is different from the others
- There is a steady need for configuration control
- Work must be consistently done on data mapping
- There is an overriding requirement for systematic transfer of know-how
- User friendliness implies that add-ons eventually done by endusers are very simple

At TRW, object-oriented applications have also been undertaken to understand diverse database mappings, leading to input and output listings which help clarify the information background. "There are three ways to handle integration," the specialist suggested, based on his experience from this project:

- When queries are made
- When one makes changes
- At preset automatic update times

In each instance, the TDIE engine polls the different databases and massages their relevant contents in order to satisfy query requirements. This is the solution that was applied in connection to Operation Desert Shield.

In this and several other real life implementations, the workstations attached to the system use Sybase and X-Windows. All information is timestamped. Critical and frequent requests are kept on the local database (under Sybase). If the next query is satisfied by the locally kept information elements, there is no reason for initiating a global access routine; otherwise, a global networking application is launched.

Let's make sure that nobody thinks TDIE is a solution only for the military. TRW's own manufacturing division has implemented this approach, interfacing the different databases used in the factories. On a consulting basis, TRW has also provided a similar solution for British Gas.

At the conceptual design level, TDIE can be valid for many companies. The principles underpinning it rest on the implementation of a frontend that handles ad hoc schemata. The solution is dynamic. "Nobody can define the enterprise global schema *a priori*," said the TRW executive.

In a nutshell, the procedure is as follows: After sign-on, the user defines the schema of his choice. The system employs its data dictionary to display the different information elements from the databases being accessed. The engine's frontend (Unix OS on Sun, HP, or IBM 6000) will

- Match the information elements
- Convert the data strings
- Compile them for presentation

All code is in C. As a shell, Nexpert Object has been used and found to be helpful with the object-oriented relations. However, only some DBMS are supported, and interfacing to nonsupported DBMS must be custom-made, though the range of supported DBMS can be expected to increase over time.

Database Integration with Operation Desert Storm

At the heart of the Global Transportation Network/In-Transit Visibility (GTN/ITV) System of the Department of Defense is the TRW Data Integration Engine which we saw in the previous section. As a software system, it:

- Integrates data without impacting host databases
- Helps in saving investments in technology and training, while providing the needed integration

The diverse computer systems in the network are able to share accurate, current data to any extent needed. The DOD uses this operational solution to rapidly track personnel airlifts, cargo shipments, and weapons and ammunition supplies, to name but a few logistics that need realtime control.

At the time the meeting took place, TDIE allowed about 30 worldwide users at the commander-in-chief level to simultaneously access six external databases. Eventually the system is expected to connect hundreds of worldwide users to dozens of varying, geographically dispersed databases. The application perspective is shown in the form of a block diagram in Figure 2.

There are two major components of TDIE: the integration advisor is the development tool kit; the integration engine (IE) is the runtime tool kit. IA assists in the integration process per se, while the IE is a collection of executables and object files that work together with application-specific code generation and configuration.

- At runtime the IE does the required actual data movement and translation.
- IA assists the process of generating application-specific codes and handles any subsequent changes.

In this sense, the IA can be seen as a computer aided software engineering (CASE) tool which serves as an aid in the analysis and description of information to be integrated in distributed computers. It is also used to specify the mechanisms by which distributed systems communicate. IA produces two primary artifacts:

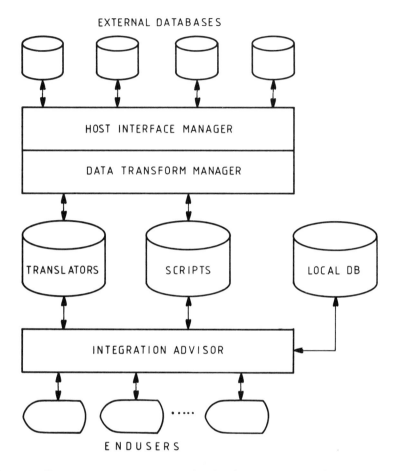

Figure 2   Heterogeneous database solution for Operation Desert Shield.

· Data translators
· Communications scripts

A primary design goal has been that IA is organized as a collection of loosely coupled cooperating tools, each working in its own specific domain of integration: script generation, script simulation, schema analysis, and translation generation.

All of the tools post status about their activities to a central message posting center, which acts as blackboard. Various options are supported and consequent actions depend on the state and content of the current set of posted messages.

Maintenance is a particularly critical issue, since it is common everywhere. As user interfaces do change, the IA scripting tool addresses the change problem by providing automatic script generation through

· Session capture
· Graphic script visualization and manipulation

Translators map data from one semantically equivalent format to another (source to target), and may optionally perform integrity constraint checking. TDIE supports two translator implementations: standalone and intelligent translators. The latter uses the knowledgebank to augment the translation process.

Through schema integration two or more independent forms of information are analyzed to determine their semantic equivalence. IA accomplishes this through understanding the inner relationships of the attributes and entities in a network graph, which is similar to entity relationship data modeling.

An essential contribution of TDIE is the provision of assistance in creating the communication script and translator components of the IE:

· Scripts are needed to direct communications between the TDIE and the databases being integrated.
· TDIE provides a scripting language, called SLANG, for script implementation.

Since one of the goals of this project has been to minimize the impact on existing information systems, the chosen general method for intersystem communications is emulation of user terminal to host sessions. SLANG scripts are representations of finite state machines mapped as finite state diagrams.

Part of the TDIE design philosophy is to deliver information as closely as possible to the time it is needed. This is done by real time job scheduling mechanisms which can be time based or on demand. The solution also supports the incremental delivery of information for specific database management systems, featuring a backend integration approach.

One of the basic products of the IA is a translator (written in C) that embodies the user's requests, mapping between input and output information. When compiled and linked with a runtime library, it provides the user's translation specification, employing a tool known as the transform grid.

As a solution, TDIE integrates existing dissimilar computers with the software applications running on them remaining unchanged. Integration can be done incrementally, providing the ability to add new applications to existing systems. Shared information is automatically available to users by means of expert systems, which help to control the integration. The integrity of the data is maintained during operation, and with Operation Desert Storm this has given very satisfactory results.

Project CRONUS by Bolt Beranek Newman

BBN has been for many years one of the best-known companies in high technology. Therefore, it is not surprising that today it has considerable experience in database integration work. One of the best projects it has undertaken is CRONUS.

CRONUS has been designed to work within a distributed computing environment, across a range of hardware and software platforms, and it has three key facets:

· Object orientation
· Location independence
· Data transparency assurance

This project started in 1981, funded by the U.S. Air Force (Rome Air Force Base Laboratories) to support command and control (C2) applications. It is now installed at 20 sites, of which 6 have 50 or more database machines. In large measure, these are Sun and VAX running under Unix and Ultrix.

As Figure 3 indicates, the server-to-server communication is assured CRONUS kernel-to-CRONUS kernel, interfacing the client processes, i.e., the applications. Software supports generally provide anything the user wishes to handle:

· Configuration
· Authentication
· Type definition
· Directory services

As with all other cross-database solutions, the goal of this implementation is to amortize existing machine investment. However, there is no mainframe implementation of the project. "No one has funded us to bring CRONUS on mainframes," suggested an executive during the research meeting I held with BBN in 1991.[2]

As stated during the BBN meeting, one of the reasons a mainframe environment is far from ideal lies in the fact that IBM mainframes do not do a good job of supporting TCP/IT, on which rests the transport facility of CRONUS. The same, incidentally, is true of all other mainframes.

CRONUS interprocess communication supports operation invocations from clients to services, whether the invocations are synchronous or asynchronous. Such support can have one or many targets and is implemented as a series of layers. The system relies on standard communication protocols embedded in the native operating mode at and below the transport layers. The protocols are

· Transmission control protocol (TCP)
· User datagram protocol (UDP)
· Internet protocol (IP)

---

2 Which is not surprising since clear-eyed companies interested in CRONUS-type solutions are very cool on mainframes.

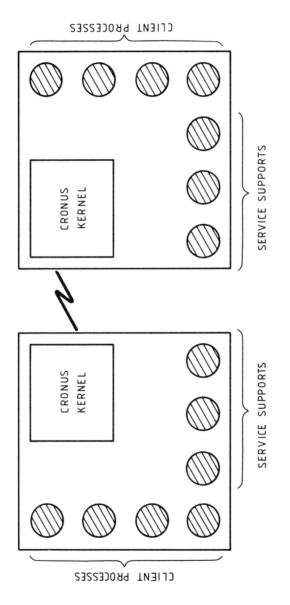

Figure 3   The CRONUS database to database solution.

Supported DBMSs are Sybase, Oracle, and Informix. Anyone of them can be reached online both for predefined and ad hoc queries.

Release 2.0 includes additions, enhancements, and improvements over previous releases, and it contains the following major components: kernel, commands type definition manager, manager development tools (in C and Common Lisp), bug report manager, development libraries, authentication manager, configuration manager, database managers, directory manager, and monitoring and control system manager.

A basic assumption underlying CRONUS programming support is that large-scale applications will be developed in accordance with the object model, just as the system itself is. Key to this policy is the definition of new object types to represent application-specific resources and the development of new services embodying the newly defined object types.

Currently supported languages are C, Lisp, Fortran, and Ada. CRONUS is written in Lisp. The code to be generated is specified by the user. If the code is in C, then it is portable between supported platforms. Cobol is not in the language list, but an implementor can do cross-language calls if necessary.

Through the tools featured by the system, the implementor can also provide additional interfacing with databases. This is done through

·   SQL type queries, handling a string that is completely ASCII-compliant.
·   Application-specific queries, for instance, string manipulation in a tailored interface.

One of the interesting implementations is a video database server. It is using CRONUS to access the information elements, catalogue them, and produce replicated instances. Other applications include command and control in a system designed for distributed telemetry data collection and analysis, as well as radar tracking information in space and time.

There is also a LAN-oriented implementation that integrates formerly distinct implementation islands. Still another application integrates database accesses running across a number Sun, VAX, and personal computers in connection

·   Parts management
·   Inventory control

The Chemical Substance Information Network (CSIN) is, as well, another example of heterogeneous databases successfully handled through CRONUS. It was originally developed for the U.S. Geological Survey.

CSIN connects 20 incompatible databases. It runs on Sun and keeps track of all details necessary to dial and manipulate the networked databases:

·   Calling up each one of them

- Bringing records back and forth
- Presenting the obtained information elements in a standard form.[3]

CSIN is extendable and can be adapted to other types of databases, for instance, cartographic and bibliographic. At user's end, the access mode is menu driven.

With a great deal of experience in integrating heterogeneous databases, BBN has been a good source to question the chances a global schema approach may have. Learning from the source of knowledge is always a sound policy.

"There are customers of ours who tried the global schema approach," said the same BBN executive during the research meeting at Cambridge, MA. "None completed it yet. All of them have found many more problems than they thought they would encounter."

An Object-Oriented Solution to Database Challenges

CRONUS adopts an object-oriented paradigm in providing network-transparent, host-independent interprocess communication (IPC) in a heterogeneous distributed environment. Tightly integrated with this IPC model is an object storage facility embedded within applications; in many cases it replaces local file references.

The system is designed to execute distributed applications across a diverse set of operating systems and hosts. Incorporating structured data storage facilities within these applications makes it feasible to customize

- Data concurrency control
- Access control

It also permits better supervision over the availability and consistency of replicated information elements, which is of primary importance in all interactive database applications.

CRONUS provides support for customizing storage mechanisms on a type by type basis. Object addressing and retrieval is based on referencing individual objects and their associative database access.

The basis for customization has been assured by combining the general purpose query language offered by conventional relational databases with application embedded, object-oriented storage facilities. This approach

- Made it possible to represent structured data from system-wide event collections

---

3 Up to a point its architecture seems to be similar to that of Lotus' DataLens and IBM's EDA/SQL — it predates both of them.

- Permitted query processing over the distributed information elements in a standard fashion.

The supported query language for associative data access is an extension of the "Select...From...Where" statement of SQL. A client process located on the query site invokes a query operation of a given type:

- The system automatically forwards the query to a manager module for this type.
- The manager module receiving the invocation becomes the coordinator responsible for overseeing the distributed query execution.

Among the tasks involved in a coordination are those of contacting the other object managers, gathering their responses, and forwarding the answer to the client at the request site.

Using the object-oriented programming paradigm, each application is structured as a group of types. A type defines a set of objects as well as the operations used to manipulate them.

CRONUS provides the system types, such as hosts, processes, files, directories, users, and groups of users. Object types created during application building correspond to the basic resources maintained by that application.

The adopted solution treats system types in precisely the same manner as it treats applications. Objects and the components that use them are implemented in a variety of ways, but their implementations can be described using a basic set of concepts and tools:

- The component interactively accessing an object is a client
- When a client invokes an operation on an object, the system delivers the invocation request to the object's manager.
- Clients may be short-lived or long-lived processes, such as user interfaces.

Once the type interface is defined, codes in several languages can be generated automatically to implement the low-level, routine functions found in virtually all object managers. This permits developers to concentrate on application-specific functions.

The focal point of the design is to support coherent integration of heterogeneous computers, providing an effective, general purpose, distributed database environment. Such an environment is composed of hosts with different hardware and operating systems.

Implementations realized so far with this approach have given commendable results. BBN also expects that the chosen approach will promote a comprehensive basis for the development of large scale distributed applications.

The systems philosophy underpinning the CRONUS approach is to provide a set of services and communication layers on top of native operating systems through the object model:

Table 1   Operating Systems Supported by CRONUS of BBN

Hardware Family	Operating System
Alliant FX/80	Concentrix 5.0
BBN Butterfly GP1000	Mach 1000
DEC RISC	Ultrix 3.x, 4.x
DEC VAX	VMS, Ultrix 3.x, 4.x
Encore Multimax	UMAX 4.2
Masscomp 54xx, 55xx	RTU 4.x
Sun 2, 3, 4, 386i	SunOS 3.4, 3.5, 4.x
Sun 3	Mach 2.5
Symbolics	Genera 8.0.1

· Each system resource is an object
· Each system resource is accessed through operations defined by the object's type.

This assures the necessary extensible architecture, permitting software developers to cast application-specific resources in terms of new object types. Type definitions are organized in a type hierarchy, allowing new types to be defined as subtypes of existing types.

Heterogeneity is handled by a bypassable layer of abstraction between application programs and native operating systems outlined in Table 1. Through this approach, application programs gain access to a coherent, object-oriented system interface, regardless of the specific computer base. At the same time, they retain conventional access to native operating system resources and services.

Objects are accessed by clients through operation invocations, assuring information hiding and data abstraction. Processes are the active entities in CRONUS. Composed of one or more processes, an object manager is responsible for manipulating all of the objects of one or more types on a host, using the operations defined by the types.

The object manager is generally implemented as a long-living process. On receiving an invocation request, it manipulates the representation of the referenced object and returns the results to the client. However,

· A manager may manage more than one object type, and several managers may manage the same type.
· When the managers of a type cooperate in implementing that type, the group of managers is called a service.

New types can be created and new object managers of existing types can be started. They can interact with existing ones, cooperating to provide a service. This demonstrates how flexible CRONUS has been in its conception as well as in its implementation.

Hidden Data Replication and Parallel Computation

Data replication is hidden from clients accessing a replicated object. When a client program invokes an operation on any object, it simply names the object. CRONUS automatically locates any copy of the object using a combination of multicast and location caches. It then routes the invocation request to its manager.

Data replication is also transparent to the developer of a type implementing replicated objects. The object manager maintains a complete copy of each object it supervises, as well as

· The object's access control list and version vector
· The list of sites where the object is replicated

A CRONUS manager always knows where all of its peers are located, i.e., other managers of the same type. It is also informed on the status of their availability.

The adopted system design embeds the databases within the application instead of centralizing the data outside the application. This has been done on the premise that, by moving the information elements into the application, the developer has better control over data representation and manipulation as well as the potential for improved efficiency through colocation.

In CRONUS jargon, *computational structure* refers to the structure of interactions established between object managers during query execution. There are two aspects of a computational structure:

· Parallelism[4]
· Coordination

There are three types of computational structures: serial computation, parallel computation with centralized coordination, and parallel computation with distributed coordination.

As the title suggests, with serial computation execution proceeds serially from one site to the next. This approach could lead to parallelism when pipelining is possible, which occurs only when processing multiple operations in a query.

In parallel computation, several sites simultaneously handle parts of an operation. A centrally coordinated parallel structure may, however, have several execution sites but only one coordinator that controls the execution. The latter is referred to as a centralized coordination. Much more flexible is the distributed coordination.

In CRONUS, object level resource management is applied according to the principle of policy mechanism separation. The system provides a set of mechanisms enabling the cooperative enforcement of type-specific policies. The mechanisms include the following facilities for object managers:

---

4 See also the discussion in Part II on the need for parallelism.

- When implementing a service they can execute on different hosts for each type of object.
- They can question the status of their peers, and if necessary redirect requests to peers.
- Clients can indicate preferred hosts where operation invocations are routed.

Some of the interesting features are *migration* and *replication* of objects. Facilities for replication offer the developer a number of tools that help to customize the actual replication mechanisms: version vectors, voting options, incremental or whole object updates, and automatic replication.

Every replicated object has a version vector containing a list of host location and version number pairs. Options are provided to specify the number of votes necessary for read and update operations.

Sometimes it is necessary to update remote copies of an object by performing an operation locally and then sending a copy of the new object to the remote site(s). With CRONUS, developers have the option of specifying whether updating copies of objects should be performed by replacement or by operation.

Automatic replication of objects can be *implied* as part of type definition, which also specifies the number and type of different hosts for which the object should be created. The actual locations are determined at creation time, permitting load balancing across multiple managers.

CRONUS uses a nonprocedural program development specification language. It permits the developer to provide nonprocedural specifications of a new object type. Subsequently, a code is supplied or automatically generated for skeletal object managers, including

- Remote procedure call stubs for clients
- Multitasking for concurrent operation processing
- Data conversion between canonical and system-specific data representations
- Message parsing and validation
- Access control checks
- Operation dispatching
- Stable storage management

Extensive subroutine libraries, including interprocess communication routines, data conversion routines, and interfaces to CRONUS objects are part of the programming endowment. The same is true of user and operator commands, operations inherited by different objects, source management software, a bug tracking facility, and monitoring services.

A significant real time resource is the CRONUS authentication system. All activities are capable of being access controlled. When a user executes the login command, his identity is verified by the Authentication Manager using a principal (user) name and password combination. When the user executes application commands object managers

- Automatically check his identity
- Verify that he has permission to perform the requested operation

The newer release redesigned and reimplemented the Authentication Manager facility, using concepts developed for the Kerberos network authentication system.[5] The latter was developed by MIT's Project Athena for distributed computing environments where neither hosts nor users can be trusted. Timestamps are added to prevent playback. Other Kerberos characteristics are that no cleartext passwords should be sent over the network, no cleartext client passwords should be stored on network servers, client and server keys should only be minimally exposed, compromises should only affect the current session, authentication lifetime should be limited, the system should function transparently during normal use, and minimal modification should be required of existing network applications.

Benefits from a Knowledge-Oriented Methodology

Two issues the BBN and TRW cross-database projects have in common is the focus on object-oriented solutions and on knowledge engineering as the way to solve the challenges posed by heterogeneity. Indeed, research has provided plenty of documentation that by far the best approach to interoperability rests on the implementation of artificial intelligence.

A convergence of knowledge engineering and object-oriented tools can provide an answer to wider applications requirements. A framework within which this concept can effectively operate is shown in Figure 4. Notice that the knowledgebank management system (KBMS) supports the intentional database solution introduced in Chapter 9. Both TRW and BBN made use of this concept, though not necessarily under the same name or with exactly the same tools.

Figure 4 advances a layered approach which rests on one physical and seven logical levels. Four of these layers identify part of the functions of the KBMS; the difference between the contents of a knowledgebank and those of a database is that

- In the knowledgebank is knowledge contained in rules and programs.
- In the database are information elements, events, and values.

---

5   Kerberos is also used in connection to the ENCINA transaction processing monitor.

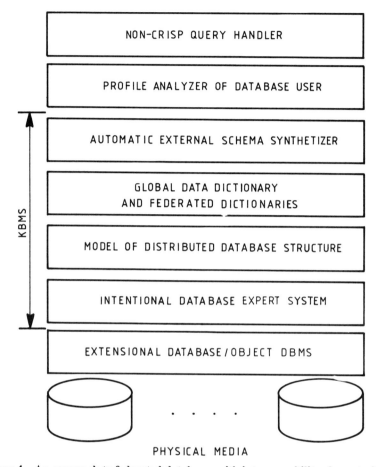

Figure 4 An approach to federated databases with interoperability characteristics.

Both are interactively accessible in computer storage. The rules in the knowledgebank help in interpreting schemata and in combining certainty factors or are oriented to the handling of meaning, hence, the semantics of external schemata — those prevailing in the distributed database environment.

The information elements in the global distributed database may, for example, include facts and figures about a particular inventory problem being analyzed. The knowledgebank will have the rules to be observed in the analysis and associated assertions:

· History of replenishment solutions
· Results and conclusions dependent upon them
· Problem status and plausible alternative concepts for a solution

As the TRW and BBN case studies demonstrated, when we work on an interoperability project we should plan to effectively distribute not only information elements, but also the application logic across different vendors' machines. At the same time, we should pay close attention to data structures and communications protocols.

Let's notice that, when properly implemented, the modular solution we saw in Figure 4 permits more functionality to the system, e.g., a security layer. This layer could assure that all text and data contained in the distributed database is cryptographically protected against unauthorized use. Within such a reference platform

·   Each user can be endowed with a private key that not only authenicates him but also describes the information elements that he is allowed to retrieve.
·   Each data block transmitted over the network can be encrypted with the specific master key of its source.

In one application similar to those we have seen in this chapter, the bulk encryption algorithm employs a linear feedback shift register with a nonlinear output function. An authentication and authorization protocol is also integrated.

Enriched with security algorithms, a federated databases solution, like the one we will examine in Chapter 13 by GTE, can face the information protection challenge. The demonstration made on this application[6] used the example of

·   Five databases that must be accessed, each having its own security level

Under classical DBMS approaches, just the coordination of the different security mechanisms is a major task. By contrast, GTE's KBMS incorporates modules that take care of security refinements. IA constructs see to it that the system is able to protect itself universally, throughout the spectrum of database usage.

What is the investment in time and cost that might be required in order to develop and implement a similar solution? The answer to this question can best be given by analogy.

The development of a cross-database implementation by the GTE Laboratories required a team of five knowledge engineers and database experts working for 4 years. Hence, it represents 20 man-years, or about $2.4 million. A number of qualifiers should, however, be attached to this metric:

1. As a time expenditure, this statistic represents the development, testing, and implementation of two events: a shell (IDA) and an application (CALIDA).[7]
2. This was one of the first projects ever undertaken in this direction, hence, it includes quite a bit of basic research.

---

6   During the visit at GTE Laboratories, Weltham, MA.
7   The details are given in Chapter 13.

3. It was done by a team of very learned and dedicated knowledge engineers, with a proven record of practical accomplishments.

Items 2 and 3 do not necessarily counterbalance each other. A less knowledgeable, or less dedicated, team can take ages and never provide any results. What can happen is precisely what happened to a number of expert systems that were done half-heartedly in "this" or "that" organization — and the same is true of cross-database projects that failed.

The success of a mission, any mission, is tightly linked to the ability to use the human capital, driving toward a well-established goal. Apart from trivial cases, such a goal will not be otherwise attainable without leadership and dedication.

Hence, I will strongly advise that after the work to be done has been properly defined, firm timetables are set and the best qualified personnel are set to work under firm leadership. This is another lesson that can be learned from TRW, BBN, and GTE.

12

From California to Japan: The Search for Interoperability Solutions

Introduction

Two separate conferences took place with the Hughes Aircraft company in the Los Angeles area: one at the Fullerton plant with the department that addresses itself to the integration of hetergeneous databases for Air Traffic control, the other at Hughes Research.

Hughes Research is currently in the middle of a major project under contract with NASA for the integration of the databases of five different laboratories in the U.S. All of them exploit

· Spacecraft
· Satellite data

but so far have not been kept on a homogeneous basis. As practically everybody else in America, Europe, and Japan, they are using, among themselves, incompatible database technologies.

Like all defense contractors, Hughes Aircraft aims to direct a significant amount of its current efforts into a conversion process from defense to civilian applications. In a manner similar to TRW, it has chosen system expertise in database technology as a main line in this conversion.

The contracts currently undertaken by Hughes along database homogeneity lines not only represent vital American interests in the exploitation of Space and Air Traffic activities, they also blend well with much of the work Hughes has done in the past for the military. Therefore, it comes as no surprise that the work executed by Hughes in this domain is

- · Characterized by fundamental thinking on database integration
- · Involves a great deal of basic theory on how to approach problems posed by heterogeneity
- · Employs knowledge engineering as the way to reach effective solutions

Less sophisticated but also very interesting are the approaches taken by two Japanese software houses: Toyo Information Systems (TIS) and Japan Research Institute (JRI). They have been purposely added to this chapter to show that there is more than one way to approach the problems of database heterogeneity.

There are two other reasons for the TIS and JRI case studies. First, contrary to the TRW, BBN, and up to a point, Hughes examples, they address the challenges posed by mainframes. Second, they are implemented in a financial environment which represents an aspect of manufacturing we have not considered so far: that of treasury and accounting operations.

The careful reader will see that there are also negative overtones in the case study of the JRI approach for a major Securities house. They suggest many things which should not happen but do. Quite often, we learn much more from negative examples than from positive ones.

The Air Traffic Control Implementation

The integrative air traffic control study by Hughes concerns a real time distributed databases system aiming at data consistency. An open architecture has been adopted, appropriately configured by the number and type of locations.

A goal of the Hughes solution is to support the characteristics of a *deductive database*[1] able to modify its own contents and automatically inform all interested databases in the distributed environment as well as the endusers.

- · In air traffic control, it is critical that the system is able to do flight precontention calculations.
- · This requirement is valid in many fields, e.g., those of sophisticated financial, medical, and robotics systems.

The deductive database solution elaborated by Hughes for Air Traffic control is integrated with the North American Airspace Monitor and Control system, which is used for both air defense and air traffic. The adopted solution features a dynamic data ownership protocol, which is not difficult to migrate to other application domains such as the manufacturing floor, medical science, or financial.

Not only is a cross-database deductive capability crucial, but attention must be paid to the fact that there is no single point of failure. For deductive reasons, a

---

1 Hence, as we saw, enriched with knowledge engineering.

neural network implementation is under examination to help reduce noise inter-ferences. But in air control, the job to be done seems to be too massive for current neural network (connectionist) technology.

Fuzzy engineering, Hughes suggested, seems to be another promising field for an advanced implementation. Fuzzy engineering has not yet been applied in detail, but Hughes analysts undergo training for its real time applications.

Fuzzy set applications can have a great future in specific domains such as locating, positioning, giving type, and estimating probability. Possibilistic con-cepts[2] can find fruitful implementation by extending into landscapes with a certain scarcity of precise, crisp input signals.

Only 65% of Canada, for example, is under radar coverage. In the rest, traffic goes, so to speak, blind. Heuristic solutions can make up for part of the fuzziness in the estimates, and the same is true of rapid seamless access to distributed databases.

The database to which the air traffic control system addresses itself is distrib-uted and replicated in different locations in a nearly homogeneous manner. Each location has a local database which holds subsets of records, with the result that the same record resides in multiple local databases.

The distribution of primary and backup copies, as well as group coordination and group membership, is shown in Figure 1. A local data manager is responsible for transaction execution and sets up the distribution lists and notification lists.

A distribution list contains record assignment, as the bulk of the information elements is not sitting in any specific location but is partitioned and replicated.

· There is a *primary location* for consistency and integrity reasons.
· *Any-to-any transactions* update the primary database.
· Only the primary database can update the *secondary copies* of a given information element.

In other terms, the location responsible for the primary or "official" copy of an information element is responsible for updating the distributed secondary loca-tions, where a read-only copy of data resides.

For backup reasons a special secondary location has been designated which contains the same information elements as the primary and takes over primary responsibility if the primary location fails. Each primary database can have zero to "n" backups.

Local data management is based on the concept of dynamic data ownership assisted by a data dictionary. The owner is the software application task that resides at the primary location of a record. The owner updates the primary copy

2 For a definition see D. N. Chorafas, *New Information Technology. A Practitioner's Guide,* Van Nostrand Reinhold, New York, 1993.

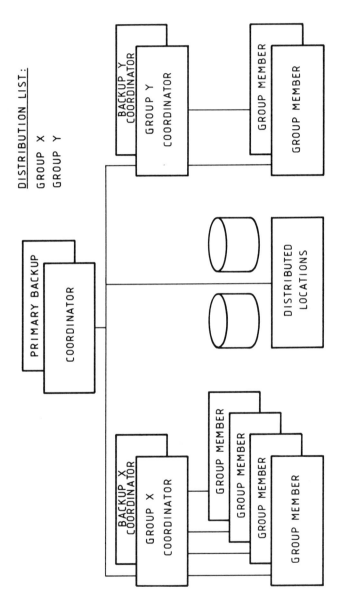

Figure 1   Primary, backup, coordination, and membership functions.

of the record and initiates secondary updates. In case of a crash or another emergency, the owner may transfer ownership to another location.

· A distribution list tells the owner where to send secondary updates. Group membership is the key to reduced communications requirements.
· This leads to the concept of a group coordinator, operating along applications lines to reduce communicating requirements through concurrent update.

A location within a group is responsible for accepting updates addressed to the group. It distributes the updates to group members, accepts acknowledgements from group members, and forwards one acknowledgement for the group to the primary location.

The basic concept is that when there is a three-digit number of computer systems in the network running thousands of terminals, it is necessary to partition them into more or less homogeneous groups. This discipline led to the message and transaction sequence management and can be applicable with smaller configurations.

Research on Heterogeneous Databases by Hughes Aircraft

Five different laboratories in the U.S. have, up to now, addressed themselves to the storage and exploration of space data, from the West Coast to the East Coast: JPL, EDC, NSIDC, GSFG, and LaRC (Figure 2). These five compounds of the Earth Observation Satellite Distributed Information System (EOSDIS) were originally designed quite independently, each being different from the other. Now they are brought together.

The Heterogeneous Databases Project has been initiated by the Artificial Intelligence Center, Hughes Research Laboratory. This center is actively working on the interoperability of heterogeneous databases with the goal of supporting seamless access to information elements stored and managed by different DBMS.

The project uses Itasca (Ex-Orion), an object-oriented DBMS by the MicroElectronics and Computer Development Corporation (MCC), as well as query language. Considerable attention is also placed on the task of building an intelligent data dictionary.

Like the real life examples we have seen in Chapter 11, this project is tuned to seamless integration. In approaching this challenging issue, Hughes has projected a three-level strategy for short, medium, and longer term.

· The *short-term* solution, which provides a workstation with distributed database connectivity through a passthrough facility
· The *medium-term* approach, which rests on federated databases (every leading American company in this research is working on this at present)

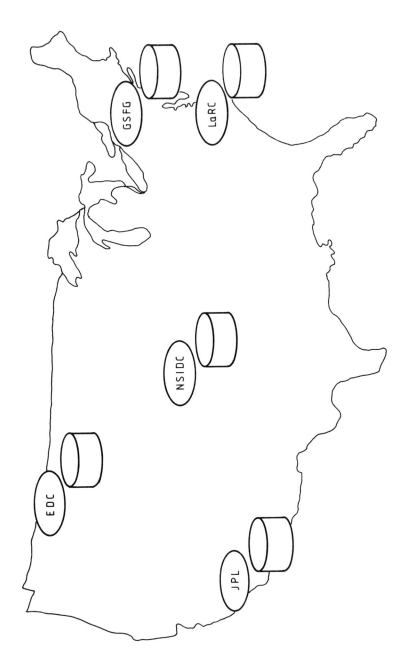

Figure 2 Distributed databases and smart data dictionary for EOSDIS (satellite data).

· The *longer term*, where there might also be a more tightly coupled solution addressed to a low one-digit number of heterogeneous databases that have some communality.[3]

In a manner quite similar to the discussions that took place with other systems integrators, the evidence at Hughes has been that the global schema would be a tough nut to crack. Theoretically, the global schema provides the tightest control over the underlying heterogeneous databases. Practically, this approach has seen consistant failures with organizations that tried it.

At Hughes as elsewhere, federated solutions are regarded as a better alternative at the current state of the art, but evidently they have prerequisites. One of them is that tasks have to be notified whenever records are updated. This can be performed on a file basis within a location.

Also, regarding the system-wide distribution list, the researchers suggest that updates have to be sent to locations on a record basis across the distributed database. Other researchers, however, consider the object basis to be a better alternative.

Hughes aptly pointed out that another important characteristic of a valid federated solution is fault tolerance. Fault tolerance must be assured along with recovery from dropped messages:

· Multiple simultaneous updates may have to be made to a single location.
· The system should apply updates in correct order when messages are received out of order

In the implementation example in the next section, there is protocol continuation upon primary location failure, backup location failure, or group member failure. Procedures for recovery from failure are also one of the prerequisites.

Recovery is a major part of the Hughes distributed database design. The challenge is how to reconstruct the database after half the network has died. The solution we will see supports a real time distributed database operation and is characterized by an open architecture. The overall result is rapid access to the expanding database landscape.

Another point worth bringing to the reader's attention is that networked databases should work nonstop, with the system unaffected by addition or deletion of sites and modification of the database configuration.[4] Under the worst conditions, the least number of sites should be affected from any given modification.

---

3 For instance, all of them being relational or produced by the same vendor. Yet, the failure of IBM to link IMS to DB2 for transaction purposes makes this second criterion questionable.
4 A reference also made in the introduction to Chapter 11.

As Hughes and other systems integrators have underlined, this principle is necessary to support 24-hr per day, 7-day per week distributed transaction management. Information elements in multiple sites should be steadily renewed by the transaction stream, with

·   Simulation or deferred update
·   Data consistency among sites
·   Recovery from system failure

All three functions should be steadily assured, and deadlock should be predetected and avoided. We spoke of this need at the end of Chapter 10.

The same principle is valid regarding distributed query processing, including analytical queries. It has been underlined on several occasions that the distributed database system should be seen and treated as a virtually homogeneous construct by all users. This is what companies with experience in the cross-database domain strongly suggest.

Artificial Intelligence and the Heterogeneous Databases Project

To assist in reaching the goals of the project we saw in the previous section, Hughes developed a smart data dictionary (SDD) prototype to support seamless database access. Its practical implementation is connected to the EOS DIS which is composed of geographically dispersed information systems:

·   Pilot Land
·   Pilot Climate
·   NASA Ocean

The users of information stored on incompatible databases in this distributed landscape are not computer scientists; they come from many different disciplines. Hence, the decision that the cross-database solution must be simple, seamless, and user friendly.

Today, data is stored in relational databases, file management constructs, and spatial systems. The interconnection being provided node-to-node has been characterized like a nude wire. Hughes researchers, therefore, decided to proceed with the SDD towards schema integration and the development of a global architecture.

The premise on which the Hughes Research Laboratories worked is that a very large data dictionary that can do all the mapping for all databases in the network is not a feasible alternative. A better way is to cluster into a set of relatively homogeneous operations with correspondingly simpler solutions. Hughes' SDD is defined by a two-layer architecture:

- A knowledge structure layer for modeling semantic relationships
- An object structure layer for modeling physical object relation information

The object structure layer is composed of object hierarchies that capture the structural relationships of the data model, such as hierarchical, relational,[5] and object-oriented. A set of constructors is provided for the creation, update, and manipulation of the objects. Data distribution properties are also captured through this composite hierarchy.

During dynamic schema integration, a high level of abstraction has been found to be useful for representing the interrelationships among local schemata and modeling distributed applications views. A knowledge layer is imposed on semantic relationships.

An object-oriented and knowledge engineering-supported query browser and editor (QuBE) facility has been established. It constitutes a cross-database high level query interface permitting

- The handling of predicates
- Efficient cross-database access
- Provision of an integrated knowledge and object-oriented data model

Apart from assuring data/knowledge integration, QuBE also represents both knowledge and data. The facility includes similarity and string matching. It works along case-based reasoning lines for schema integration — as well as for classification and structure mapping.

The system's knowledgebank incorporates reasoning capabilities during the formulation of queries, as well as query interpretation and schema integration. A layered architecture supports a multilanguage approach by giving application programmers the ability to directly traverse and manipulate objects in the object structural layer.

As file, edit, browse, and query options are executed, query results can be displayed as in Figure 3. SDD provides an intelligent user interface with automatic query formulation and interpretation. It also supports knowledge intensive applications requiring access to heterogeneous databases.

- SDD has the knowledge of the inner workings of each component part in connection to data, metadata, and relationships.
- As such, it allows some degree of access optimization, features reasoning capabilities, and provides control over the knowledge and data interaction.

---

5 In this particular implementation, the goal is to provide for valid interconnection of mainly relational DBMS: Sybase, Oracle, Ingres.

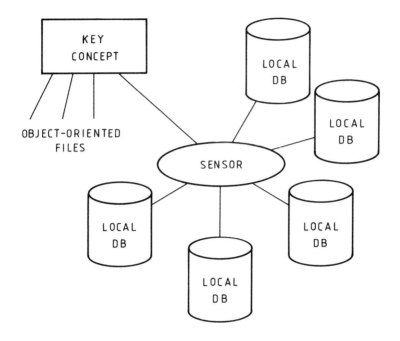

DISPLAY OF QUERY RESULTS

	DB 1	DB 2	DB 3	DB 4	DB 5
QUERY 1	GRAPHICS	TABLE			TABLE
QUERY 2		TEXT	GRAPHICS	TEXT	TABLE
QUERY 3			IMAGE	IMAGE	
QUERY 4	TEXT		IMAGE	TABLE	

Figure 3   Seamless access and display of results.

QuBE supports a visual interface for knowledge and data retrieval through a view mechanism, thus assisting concept formulation. Users query, browse, and edit federated views, relationships, and local views using a directed metaphor.

The smart data dictionary accepts a concept retrieval request from QuBE. Depending upon the definition, it may call upon the distributed query processing method to decompose the global queries into local queries using a replicated, fragmented optimization algorithm. It also coordinates the local query processing and integrates local results into final results.

- The graphics processing method executes two dimensional graphic algorithms.
- Image handling is supported by appropriate algorithms for the image storage format display requirements.

Retrieval of SDD information such as structure mappings, graphic presentations, and relationships, essential during queries, is performed by traversing the SDD abstract model using system or user-defined approaches. Schema integration is composed of two major phases:

- Data discovery
- Schema reclassification

During data discovery, real meanings of attributes are captured from queries, data, schemata, and the database administrator's interaction (if necessary). By contrast, in schema reclassification concept hierarchies produced by the first phase may be handled again when integrating new schema objects to form a unified view.

Schema integration process involves taking the concept hierarchies acquired from the data discovery phase and encoding them as an input specification. Reclassification depends upon these results, for identifying the similarities and differences of schema objects.

Transformation criteria for schema reclassification, such as generalization and aggregation, are encoded as rules that are AI-enriched. The concept behind the whole approach is dominated by federated semantic views.

Cross-Database Solutions by Toyo Information Systems

As it will be appreciated, problems connected to the exploitation of distributed databases exist in every industrial and business domain. The financial industry is not alien to them. If anything, it needs as much seamless cross-database solutions as manufacturing does.

Increasingly, companies turn to assistance in developing the needed concept and supporting software for systems integrators. Typically they choose third parties with a certain renown, not the hardware vendors that brought them the problems in the first place.

In Chapter 11 and in this Chapter we have seen how TRW, BBN, and Hughes Aircraft have been helping their clients to solve their cross-database problems. It is now time to take a look at a different environment as well as different methods that have been used in attacking database heterogeneity problems.

Toyo Information Systems (TIS) is one of the foremost Japanese software companies. It is also a firm with good experience in knowledge engineering, having developed BRAINS, one of the best shells based on KEE.[6] However, it

· Extends over many different platforms, from PCs to minis, maxis, and mainframes
· Works not only with frames but also with rules and scripts

TIS has developed and implemented the project *Rainbow* for the integration of frontdesk and backoffice operations of a leading Japanese bank. It places emphasis on cross-database interconnection of seven incompatible OS/DBMS environments shown in Figure 4.

Rainbow assures real time data transfer between these dissimilar hosts, including transaction handling and file exchange. Searches of databases residing, for instance, on Hitachi and Fujitsu computers, can be carried out from terminals connected directly to the IBM host. Through data classification priority orders can be created for the transfer route.

· Displays of operating conditions and changes to system configuration can be performed with operator commands, while the system runs nonstop.
· Log information can be extracted and interhost statistical information acquired.
· The progress of an internal task operation can be easily traced.
· When obstacles occur in the transmission path an automatic switch to a reserve channel is performed.

These features have been found to efficiently handle real time connections between dissimilar host machines. Not only is it possible to assure one-to-one connectivity of incompatible hosts, but also to configure any-to-any linkages involving multipled hosts.

Most importantly, this solution can be used without making additional modifications to existing applications. For instance, in the case of VTAM, the interface to the online system simulates a secondary station. From the application program viewpoint, the connection appears as a virtual terminal performing terminal emulation.

Any-to-any access is supported in this manner in the IBM world, including IMS, DB2, and Adabas. However, the protocol is IBM's Logical Unit 0 (LU0) hence batch level. The reason for the LU0 choice, TIS stated in our meeting, is that it creates a common denominator for the attached platform, though LU6.2 would have been easier to implement.

---

6 Knowledge Engineering Environment.

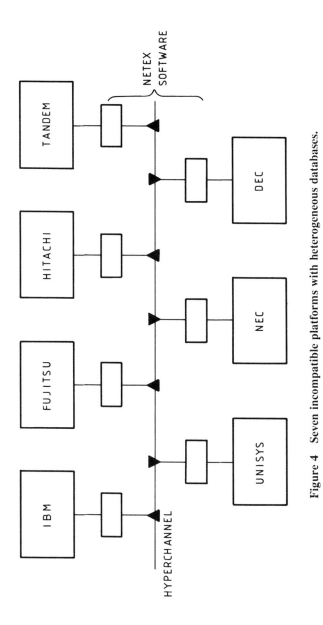

Figure 4 Seven incompatible platforms with heterogeneous databases.

The integration of a Cray computer is under study. Because of high rate requirements, Ultranet rather than Hyperchannel will be used in connection with the Cray implementation.

A similar concept dominates interdatabase connectivity at the frontdesk level, but the equipment is different: Sun, News (by Sony), Hewlett-Packard 9000, and PC 9800. The LAN is Ethernet and the protocol TCP/IP.

The introduction of this system into financial institution operations has come by stages. Phase I of the implementation integrated transactions, commitments, client information, and a general ledger, as well as quotations and confirmations. Phase II interconnected traders and salesmen of financial services. It emphasized file servers and incorporated expert systems. Many new AI-based applications have been developed from scratch. Phase III, which is currently in process, will substitute mainframe-run databases by a database computer (DBC). This is expected to provide significant improvement in response time and systems reliability. A similar finding has been underlined by American financial institutions and manufacturing organizations.

An Approach by the Japan Research Institute for a Major Securities House

This and the following sections present another cross-database example for heterogeneous databases in the financial industry. The Japan Research Institute has been involved in different applications concerning a leading broker, and came up with interesting findings it is wise to keep under perspective.

As in all other cases, the goal has been to simplify the overall information systems and procedures by assuring seamless cross-database access. ABC Securities[7] currently has two methods of data handling with two workstations per trader desk because of two big but incompatible database structures that have been developed over the years.

- · *Portfolio management* is on IBM 3090 with PS/55 workstations interconnected through token ring.
- · *Market data feed*[8] and backoffice operations are on Fujitsu Facom. Some 500 traders use nonintelligent terminals connected to this database.

As many other security houses know by experience, organization-wise these two jobs are highly interrelated. Each trader is also a salesman who handles his own customers. The IBM-based network emphasizes the sales support. The Fujitsu machine focuses on the trading chores.

---

7   A fictitious name.
8   From the Tokyo Stock Exchange (TSE).

Updating and calculating, including unrealized profit and loss (P+L), is done in real time. The database handles 6000 different positions dynamically. However, a consolidated view cannot be supported because the customer information files (CIF) are on another heterogeneous database.

Consequently, management has made the decision to evaluate two approaches:

· *Virtual integration* of the two heterogeneous database structures through software
· *Real integration* by changing one of the two sources of information the systems supply

Keeping in mind that, of the two major applications, the one on IBM was the newer, the broker's own specialists and a consulting company were commissioned to evaluate at depth the results to be obtained with OS/2 and the future of IBM's SAA architecture. The answer is that

· OS/2 does *not* have enough functionality to integrate a market data feed of 25 to 30 prices per second.
· SAA was evaluated as an architecture still in process, hence it was decided not to adopt it because of performance reasons.

Among other technical characteristics that weighed in a decision to move the integration away from the IBM environment is that, at the time of the original installation, the mainframe salesman was able to sell supports that were not available, let alone operational. Hence, the nonintegrated conditions that prevail today.

Also, the software was missing pieces, which saw to it that the system could not be fully controlled in crashes taking place in remote environments. This handicapped the work of the traders/salesmen, beyond the fact that the crucial statistical information is split over the dual Fujitsu and IBM environments.

All this has been instrumental in making management realize that integration is a critical issue — but the fact that there were *political* pressures was somehow forgotten. In fact, as a cognizant person suggested, system integration is

· 80% politics
· 20% technology

As if the sales/trading split among incompatible databases was not enough, there are other issues connected to the need of integrating the company's decision support system (DSS):

· The DSS application was developed on the IBM machines as part of the trading support system (TSS).

· There has also been as a totally separate development of a DSS application which uses an AS 400 database within the IBM world.

The securities house management contracted IBM for the needed job of this particular all-blue integration. Subsequently, IBM subcontracted it to two other companies that were expected to do the legwork. This legwork is yet to be done. In the meantime, the results continue to be substandard, further magnified by the fact that management asked for both TSS and DSS upgrading.

Interestingly enough, IBM gave the same list of requirements to the two different subcontractors. Each one of them worked on it up to a point, so the list is now twice half-done and the results are

· Incompatible
· Suboptimal
· Suffering from ballooning costs

Unhappy with the developing situation, the management of the brokerage started talking to the second of the two IBM subcontractors directly to short-circuit the mainframer. If you think that this problem is still a long way from a solution, you are correct.

Evidently, there are lessons to be learned from this experience, and they should not escape anyone's attention. "If you wish a job to be done," advises an old proverb, "You do it yourself. If not, you delegate it." And proverbs pack a lot of experience into a short sentence.

The Management of Workstations in a Networked Setting

A couple of the case studies we considered in this chpater made reference to replicated information elements among distributed databases. They also presented the approaches taken by systems integrators in solving the database consistency problem, but they missed the necessary emphasis on integrated workstations.

Consistency in the process of updating distributed information elements is so much more important as, in many cases, replication is a key factor in sustaining greater availability and lesser communications flows regarding the distributed database system. But replication also makes mandatory synchronizations to assure

· Correctness of database contents
· High availability of all resources

The distributed database network can be seen as a layer enveloping the communications network, each with attached file servers working peer to peer. This solution has no shared central memory — only a communications medium for message passing.

Shared-nothing approaches help provide an increased degree of concurrency, and at the same time, assure coordinated access with little or no contention. Network-wide, logical execution should guarantee the same dependability *as if* the database system was centralized through

· Conflict resolution
· Consistent image

As Hughes Aircraft suggested, the best approach is that of an open architecture. But this is not simply a networking problem. Computers can be ISO/OSI[9] compatible but still have different bit structures, and within one of those, say, the 32-bit:

· Machines can structure their bits in many different ways.
· Even otherwise homogeneous computers may handle different database managers, interpreters, word layouts, and data structures.

Incompatibilities interfere with the transfer mechanisms needed for distributed databases. And there are other problems in implementing open solutions — not very different, in fact, than those closed solutions present.

To distribute text and data, as well as to maintain directories in a dynamic manner, it is necessary to always know the location of the information elements. The problem is that quite often companies do not know where their data is. Typically in large institutions, names appear in a database four or five times, or even more. They can be found at the same or different locations; we spoke of synonyms and homonyms in Part II.

Only a few of the complex technical problems connected to networked databases could be resolved with the cooperation of the different vendors. The reason is that:

· Datacomm experts know little about databases and their contents.
· Most database people do not even know what a seven-layer OSI model stands for.
· Only a few computer specialists understand the synchronization problems involved in networked databases.

Synchronization is a prerequisite for implementing concurrency in a distributed database, and as we saw in many examples, the success of modern systems depends on the ability of multiple users to simultaneously access the same information elements, possibly at different locations. The architecture to be adopted must therefore support the consistent manipulation of objects, including

---

9 International Standards Organization/Open System Interconnection.

· Documents (messages, memos)
· Tables (relations)
· Menus (for user interaction)

Specific implementations should also reflect the characteristics of a given applications environment, not abstract ideas. Transaction-oriented solutions need tight database integration, but old status information does not need to be retained in any other place but the journal. By contrast, office-type applications have different prerequisites.

Several experiences encountered in America and Japan indicate that, with most office automation systems, the user needs to interact with the database while a change takes place, such as a message being received. Also, past information persists after the new transaction, and there is a constant need for annotations.

Since office automation environments are communications-intense, the workstation typically acts as a communications engine that may at times work standalone and at other times online:

· It is definitely single user.
· It employs a simple language.
· It is endowed with a small database.

It used to be that the workstation and its database posed no particular concern for security; its DBMS could feature rather limited facilities, compared to other DBMS for bigger machines. However, this is no longer the case. Both security and sophisticated DBMS features are important today. A workstation database can be part of a fully distributed structure:

· It accesses distributed database servers with shared files.
· It must be provided with fourth and fifth generation languages, as well as embedded programming products.
· It has concurrency capabilities, hence, it must be security oriented (lock, commit, rollback).
· It needs password identification and authorization controls (grant, revoke).

Besides this, it is simply illogical and inefficient to have two or three workstations per desk, as the case study in the previous section showed — and some vendors seem to advise.

In other terms, a workstation solution must be streamlined and rich in tools for applications development, but it must be endowed with multidatabase facilities able to handle heterogeneous DBMS on the same network. Emphasis is on the sharing of resources through a unique interface.

13

The Intelligent Database
Assistant (IDA)

Introduction

A number of practical examples have demonstrated that different companies follow diverse approaches in solving cross-database access problems for themselves and for their clients. In Chapters 11 and 12 saw several of the solutions that were chosen. In this chapter we will follow an application in detail, examining the conceptual infrastructure behind the project.

We simply cannot discontinue ongoing operations in any significant scale. The solutions to be found regarding heterogeneous databases have to take full account of the need for continuity; otherwise, they will remain theoretical.

As the preceding chapters documented, there are no effective means for sharing heterogeneous databases in a classical programming sense. At the same time, lack of cross-database capability brings inefficiency in operations. Worse yet,

- The development of the same applications under incompatible DBMS and through different languages results in major costs.
- Duplicating information elements at different locations leads to data inconsistency, particularly if there is no effective means for cross-database access.

During the last couple of years, however, experience gained from the application of knowledge engineering in diagnostics and real time control has suggested the use of reasoning methods and data management techniques in the handling of databases. We have seen some real life examples in this direction.

Along a similar line of thinking, GTE developed a knowledge engineering construct that provided for the coexistence of many different DBMS by looking at them as diverse but cooperating components in a heterogeneous database structure. The challenge has been one of providing effective means for sharing information elements. This is what GTE does with the *Intelligent Database Assistant* (IDA).

Scope and Functions of the Intelligent Database Assistant

IDA has been designed as a generator for building knowledge enriched database access mechanisms and application systems. Its architecture is conceptually similar to that of expert system development shells, but it is focused on the exploitation of heterogeneous databases. IDA contains four major functional components:

· An enduser interface
· Database expert modules
· A network communication module
· The system knowledgebank

This GTE artifact operates through the four generic components and a set of online knowledgebank editors. Each new application includes IDA modules, but it also has its own knowledgebank, built using the editors.

Many issues are connected to the development and utilization of expert systems for accessing and manipulating information elements stored in multiple heterogeneous databases. Some are technical, others strategic, for instance,

· The increasing number of public and private databases with different data structures and database management systems
· The fact that private databases get increasingly distributed over multiple sites

Taken together these two factors suggested to the GTE laboratories the wisdom of embedding the expertise of experienced database administrators and systems programmers into a knowledgebank, making this expertise automatically accessible to users.

After all, which are our alternatives? Organizations that tried to standardize on a single DBMS and one only data structure found this unworkable. There is no single DBMS that satisfies all applications requirements and runs on all machines, or for that matter under all available OS.

Even if this was not the case, and there was a unique best solution, transition from one DBMS to another is so expensive, error prone, and time consuming as to be impractical. Nobody has been able to justify the required high conversion cost. Furthermore, technology is rapidly changing.

· Say that a new standard DBMS is chosen to replace an old one — how long are we going to take advantage of new technology?

Besides its many weaknesses in terms of future developments and the fact that this "unique DBMS" approach does not answer the need for public databases, it is unthinkable to substitute current DBMS through interruption of ongoing services, even if their performance is substandard.

Therefore, the rigorous strategy adopted by GTE can be a model for other developments. For example, a primary goal of the intelligent database shell is to overcome data access problems posed by

- The diversity of hardware in which the distributed heterogeneous databases reside
- The existence of operating systems with incompatible primitives and commands
- Database management systems ranging from hierarchical to network and relational approaches
- Diversity in query languages, starting from native instruction sets, to low level Cobol statements
- Naming and scaling conventions, which exhibit a lack of a unified view of corporate resources
- Approaches used for the interpretation of the different data structures, as well as a variety of database exploitation philosophies

The GTE researchers decided to confront these issues in an instrumental manner, identifying not only cross-database problems but also the fact that these do not come solely from the existence and utilization of diverse database management systems.

In fact, the six points do not even represent all of the list. GTE suggested adding, to the stated issues, the challenges posed by the new high density mass storage devices (both magnetic and optical disks), which:

- Require program intelligence that can arrange, store, and dynamically link vast archival and control blocks of information
- Call for solutions to overcome the handicaps posed by such multifunctional diversity while assuring easy to comprehend man/machine interfaces.

To meet the latter goal, IDA includes a high-level query specification language which permits flexible and friendly communications with the user. Another supported function is that of making transparent network connections to remote databases.

Enriched with knowledge engineering, IDA primitives allow the user to create, edit, and browse data dictionaries. The system protects data from unauthorized use and permits the automatic creation of multiple database integration programs.

The learned reader will appreciate that this is an important conceptual evolution in database management. We can look at it from the standpoint of milestones, which have characterized our handling of databases as shown in Figure 1:

- In the 1950s and early 1960s, the first data processing approaches concerned simple files and were function driven.
- As information volumes multiplied, data driven solutions became necessary. The hierarchical, network and inverted file DBMS appeared in the mid-1960s.

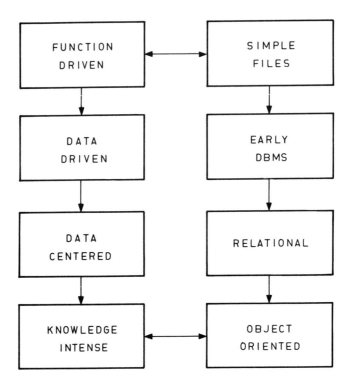

Figure 1   Evolution in the handling of files and databases.

- The inflexibility of hierarchical and other aging DBMS in the data centered environment that started in the 1970s led to relational approaches.
- With knowledge intense solutions becoming the peak of technology, and the proliferation of distributed databases, object-oriented solutions seem to be the answer for the 1990s.

Research results increasingly demonstrate that information management is one of the areas most amenable to intelligent information processing. As databases continue to grow and the nature of stored information continues to change, unique requirements are emerging — some of which are connected to heterogeneity in databases.

Understanding this background helps in appreciating the approach GTE has chosen. IDA capitalizes on the best possibilities technology can offer. That's why it is important to look at its development step by step.

Exploiting the Impact of Knowledge Engineering

IDA stores and utilizes expert knowledge regarding different databases to execute multiple integration procedures that generate lower level queries from higher level specifications. The shell estimates the size of the responses requested by the user as well as the needed database access, and assures an efficient, user-friendly operating environment.

Part of the mission of the knowledgebank is to incorporate rules that map the company's database environment and allow

- Specification
- Access
- Editing

This is achieved while making transparent network connections to remote databases. It also allows the user to create, edit, and browse data dictionaries while protecting the information elements contained in the database from unauthorized use.

As we will see in the following section, the first major implementation of IDA was access to and integration of GTE's corporate marketing databases. Since 1989, the Southern California-based application, CALIDA,[1] has run in a production environment.

The main components of the IDA artifact are shown in Figure 2. Like a coin, this construct has been designed to have two faces: one facing the system programmer and the other the user. The main components are

- Human window
- Query language specification
- Data dictionaries
- Loader/editor
- Estimator
- Communications protocols
- Gateway

These components are common to all applications, with the exception of the data dictionaries. There is one data dictionary for every heterogeneous database addressed by IDA.

In terms of real life implementation, the use of IDA has dramatically reduced the elapsed query processing time, in many cases from hours to minutes. This is well documented through field results and proves the feasibility of simultaneous online access to heterogeneous databases belonging to the GTE operating company in California. For instance, in a sample of 30 cross-database queries, which have been timed in terms of response time,

- Classical data processing required from about 1 to 1100 min (over 18 hr) to provide a response.

---

1   For California Intelligent Database Assistant.

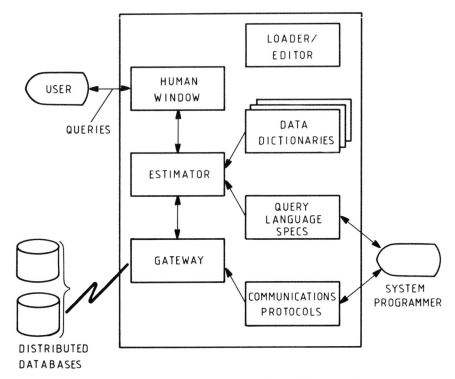

Figure 2   The main system components supporting IDA functionality.

·   IDA presented a reponse to a query in a timeframe that ranged from a couple
    of seconds to 70 min.

In terms of the *minimum* response time required, the difference between CALIDA
and classical data processing was a full order of magnitude in favor of the AI-
based solution. This difference was even greater (more than 1.5 orders of magnitude) in regard to the *maximum* response time.

Most importantly, CALIDA's results have been *high quality* while DP results
were *low quality*. High quality results are always those whose statistical distribution is characterized by a small standard deviation. Low quality distributions have
a wide spread, for instance, response time can range from seconds to hours.

Most significantly, IDA performed best where the old data processing system
was the poorest. Notice, however, that in 2 cases out of 30 the old data processing
approach was slightly faster — due to the higher overhead of knowledge engineering.

Though on comparative terms to old data processing IDA's performance
within a heterogeneous database environment was exceptional, I was somewhat
bothered by some of IDA's response times, which required several minutes.
Therefore, the question was posed to Dr. Gabriel Jakobson, who helped design

IDA: "What holds the system back? Why is the response time minutes rather than seconds?"

Dr. Jakobson's reply is quite significant, as it identifies some of the issues every company will most likely encounter in a solution to the problem of heterogeneous databases:

· The multiminute delay is *not* CALIDA's; the expert system works in subsecond speed.
· The delay is caused by getting the query through DP and accessing the different databases, which are organized in a less than optimal manner.

Even if access is done online, linkages consume a lot of minutes because the current databases are not organized for *ad hoc* searches. Dr. Jakobson further underlined that without IDA some of the searches necessary to respond to ad hoc queries would have been impossible. As some of the 30 test cases indicated, the searches necessary to respond to ad hoc queries took nearly 2 days when done through classical approaches.

Performance optimization has come at a price, and the price is changing the company's culture so that it is able to use high technology. To many readers this may seem evident enough, therefore, no particular explanation or attention is required: however,

· Only leading-edge companies, like GTE, appreciate the impact of knowledge engineering and use it to their advantage.
· A large number of companies still live in the paleolithic age of technology and resist getting out.
· Still another group of companies see it difficult, or even impossible, to integrate knowledge engineering and classical DP.

Seen under the perspective of a competitive solution for the requirements of the 1990s, this case study speaks volumes about the wisdom of hybrid solutions, that is, the merger of DP and AI into one well-knit operating environment.

The lack of a concept capable of bringing together old data processing with knowledge engineering, and making symbiosis a feasible proposition, is not only irrational but also most regretable in strict profitability terms. We can neither throw away past investments all of a sudden nor lose the benefits of new technology. We must know how to take advantage of both.

The technical problems in the background of this reference are embedded in the integrative capabilities of the different DBMS used in the daily operations environment, as well as the overcoming of prevailing incompatibilities. This is a challenge faced today by all major organizations; that's why the GTE example is so valuable.

Facing the Challenges with Large Databases

Today, it is not unusual to store trillions of bytes (terabytes) of information online. As we saw in Part I, the Lawrence Livermore National Laboratory, for instance, has more than 10 trillion bytes stored online. Several money center banks have more than a terabyte, a few of them reaching 4 terabytes.

Today it is also not unusual to store very different kinds of multimedia information elements, which must be interactively accessible by endusers. These information elements may range from

·   Conventional computer data to pictorial and voice information

What many computing centers fail to appreciate, or even resist in doing so, is that within this radically changed landscape knowledge engineering solutions offer great promise in the management of large diverse databases.

Some of the latter approaches implemented with large databases include natural language processing and expert systems, which interact with heterogeneous databases in specific problem domains.

·   Though this is not the case with IDA, it is proper to keep this possibility in mind.
·   The object of this presentation is to identify what is *possible* rather than just describe one single system.

Like others of the foremost solutions approaches in this steadily enlarging domain, IDA technology can be customized according to the specification of a given application. This is true from the generation of low-level database queries[2] (based on high level query descriptions) to the estimation of the size of the requested report before the actual database access.

In several respects, the challenge is one of dynamic customization facing the situation as it develops, even if it involves a moving target. Typically, customization covers some or all of the following functions:

1. Domain specifications, including the concepts and terminology of a specific domain

In the GTE example that we consider, this can be done by the database specialist using the IDA user language macros.

2. Database specifications with goal adaptation to and from the file structures of accessed databases

---

2   As we will see in the next section.

In a practical sense, this has been accomplished by loading database dictionaries into IDA and using them for identification, search, and editing reasons.

3. Query language specifications, to help generate queries in a way that conforms to the accessed databases

Such a mission of adaptation to prevailing heterogeneity can be performed by a system programmer using the solution's universal, high-level nonprocedural language. The latter has been designed to work with multiple heterogeneous databases.

This approach allows the user to specify queries against relational and hierarchical databases. In Chapter 14 we will see a different approach developed by the General Motors Research Laboratories, known as as DATAPLEX.

DATAPLEX is an application environment rather than a shell. In the GTE world, the application environment is CALIDA. Its structure is shown in Figure 3:

- The modules composing CALIDA reflect IDA's functionality, the latter underpinning the way CALIDA works.
- The generic setting of CALIDA extends its implementation to cover a network of large, incompatible databases.

A prerequisite to this action is the existence of appropriate data dictionaries (one per supported heterogeneous database) and knowledgebank editors. Taken together, Figures 2 and 3 show that these prerequisites are being fulfilled. Some of the problems encountered in this enlarged view of database management include

- Data fusion, as well as image understanding and analysis
- Distributed approaches aimed at solving problems within and beyond command and control

Short of knowledge enriched solutions, the ability to collect, assemble, and process ever increasing amounts of diverse information can vastly complicate the conceptual issues.

Surprisingly, not every company appreciates the truth behind this statement, and few really do something about it. Those who fail to take action find significant difficulties in their work with databases, all the way to management information systems (MIS) problems.

A different way of looking into the same fundamental issue is to bring into perspective the managerial impact of solutions behind IDA, CALIDA, DATAPLEX, and their kin. Such impact can best be appreciated when we realize that we are confronted today with databases reflecting polyvalent business and industrial requirements.

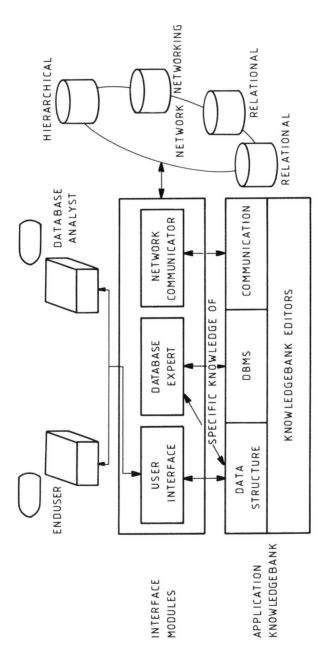

Figure 3   Structure of the California Intelligent Database Assistant (CALIDA).

· There are thousands of descriptors and millions of objects necessary to define a given business situation — and literally billions of individual bits of raw data.

· Without knowledge-based approaches we are waging a losing battle in our struggle to absorb, assimilate, and quickly analyze the flood of relevant and essential information required for intelligent response and action.

During the 1990s, the GTE Laboratories suggested, solutions of the nature we are discussing, they will be increasingly employed to assist in meeting the massive databasing, information processing, and analysis challenges. Knowledge engineering will be used with greater objectivity than man to evaluate distributed database organizations and forecast appropriate evolution based on the results of that evaluation.

This does not mean that human ingenuity will be superfluous. Skilled people will be always valuable, but they will not be in a position to do the job required without the appropriate technological assistance.

Handling Ad Hoc Queries in an Able Manner

CALIDA's query editing facilities provide a flexible and effective environment. The editor uses the same communications controller employed for query specification, assuring that semantic and syntactic correctness is preserved.

Editing features include the ability to erase values in a query section, replace values in a section, and/or add values. The editing of queries follow the same type of interaction as the course of specification. Users can

· Identify any portion of a query section they wish to highlight
· Add items before or after the selected portion
· Replace or modify that portion in the way that suits them best.

Given that menu options during editing are guided by the same procedures as during specification, the postedited query is assured to be syntactically correct. This is quite important from a global operations viewpoint, since an integrative approach includes not only queries but messages and (up to a point) transactions as shown in Figure 4.

Enriched through AI, CALIDA's user interface module provides an interactive, menu-driven environment. The query is specified by mouse selection, but the user can customize the interface be defining macros. Two major components help in doing so:

· The communication controller
· The frame transformer

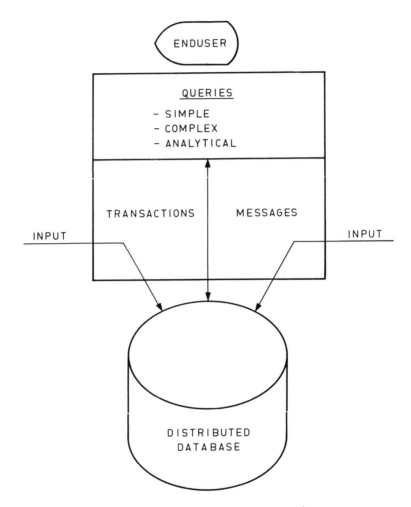

Figure 4   Inputs, outputs, transactions, messages, and queries.

Macros allow users to customize their environment and improve their productivity by reducing the number of menu selections during query formulation. A macro is a sequence of

·   User specified values
·   User language keywords
·   Field names

User defined macros introduce key concepts connected to high-level applications. During query specification, the enduser can define a macro by selecting its beginning and end. An embedded mechanism guarantees that defined macros are syntactically correct and can be reemployed.

Two methods have been chosen by the developers of IDA to assure flexibility in the menu interface. Both can find applicability in other projects as well:

1. Many of the command options are available to the user during any part of query processing.

In other terms, the user does not have to wait until a query is completed to redo a section or quit. This approach increases flexibility.

2. The query language is nonprocedural, so the user can create or edit the query in any order.

A query expressed in CALIDA's nonprocedural language may contain seven sections: output, selection condition, sort, totals, record limit, report title, and month.

There is also a range of command options for editing and session generation: **New Query** starts a new query specification and **Redo Section** erases the query section currently being specified and allows the users to start the section over.

Other commands are **Undo,** erasing the last item selected or typed; **Quit Session,** aborting the CALIDA session; **Define,** allowing the user to define and save macros; and **Run.** The last processes the query and returns an estimate of the query result size. The user then has an option to send the request or abort. The command menu is organized into four parts:

· Top-level commands such as New Query, Undo, and Run are employed to control the user/CALIDA dialog.
· Logical, arithmetic, and comparison operators help specify the output and the selection condition of the query.
· The selection of keywords starts the specification of the corresponding section, such as **Show** for output.
· Database options and miscellaneous submenu items are also available for housekeeping reasons.

Selecting a database option creates a pop-up menu of all the files in the database. Similarly, selecting a file creates a pop-up menu of all the fields in the file.

Through the interface, the user formulates, edits, and runs queries. This module contains the full range of constructs needed to describe: output, selection conditions, sorting, totalling, and logical and arithmetic expressions. The interface is interactive and easy to use. Valid menu options are determined by the grammar of the user language. Menu options can be guided by semantic integrity constraints of the application domain.

The user language does not require specifying file joins, as CALIDA determines the joins automatically from the query. User-defined macros reduce the number of menu selections during queries, thus easing the man/machine communication problems.

Another benefit from user-defined macros is that they make the implementation of high-level application-specific concepts feasible. In turn, these save time and prevent errors.

The user can define a macro by selecting its beginning and end, while the system sees to it that only valid beginning and end positions are selectable. This is a facility that has not been fully exploited with other query management approaches. Yet, it is very user-friendly as well as helpful in systems terms.

Designing and Implementing the Dialog Window

The IDA developers have paid particular attention to the design of the interface screen. Overall, this is divided into dialog window, query and menu options, report title, "sort by" key (including month and record), totals, output, and selection conditions.

The *dialog window* displays information about menu choices. It is employed by the endusers to type those portions of the query, such as field values, that cannot be selected from the menu. Hence, it is both a display and an input medium.

Enriched through knowledge engineering and projected to respond to a changing implementation environment, the *query planner* produces the execution plan:

·   If the query refers to only one database, the plan is simple and amounts to translating the query into the target language.
·   When the query addresses multiple databases, the planner performs global optimization to choose the appropriate sequence of single database requests and data transfers.

As it has already been stated, knowledge about the CALIDA database structures resides in the IDA data dictionary. In addition to the usual information, such as field names, types, and sizes contained in data dictionaries, this facility also has information about implicit joins, DBMS languages, and bit sequences: ASCII or EBCDIC.

Designed for this application, a Universal DELPHI language is a multidatabase, jointless version of the DELPHI query language. In a way it is similar to other user-oriented languages; but it also differs from other languages, mainly in its LISP-style syntax.

These facilities make IDA's user interface an interactive menu-driven system. All syntactic constructs needed for query formulation, such as logical and arithmetic operations, comparisons, conditions, sorting specifications, and output, are entered by menu item selection. Menus are also used for specifying databases, files, and fields.

Structurally, an IDA query has nine sections. They are all optional, except that either a condition, output, or summary section needs to be specified. These nine query sections are:

- *Report title* — as the name implies, it specifies the title of the report asked for by the query.
- *Report limit* — it tells IDA to stop after finding the specified number of acceptable accounts.[2]
- *Compute* — it helps define new variables that can later be used in other query sections.
- *Join* — it specifies the join field for a user-defined file.
- *Condition* — it assists in establishing the condition for accepting or rejecting the data record or account.
- *Sort* — it specifies the sorting and grouping order of the output.
- *Output* — it focuses on the tabular input fields and column headings.
- *Summary* — it helps make references to the aggregate computations for each group (as defined by the user) and for report summary reasons.
- *Destination* — it assists in specifying the destination of the query output, i.e., terminal, file, and so on.

A query structure editor permits the user to edit various query sections. It is based on the same mechanisms employed during query specification. Knowledge engineering sees to it that edited queries are always syntactically correct.

Another major component, which we have been discussing all along, is the group of database expert systems performing three major tasks:

- *Planning and optimizing* query execution by way of integrating database accesses in the distributed environment
- *Transforming* the query execution plan into target database queries, within the distributed database landscape
- *Estimating* the number of records to be returned before actually accessing the distributed databases.

To perform these tasks, the expert system module of IDA uses the application section of the knowledgebank containing the data dictionary of each database, and associated software generators. The latter are necessary for generating the target database program.

---

2 The limit is tested only on those records that satisfy certain conditions.

An estimator module applies itself to problems such as estimating the number of returned records. IDA uses precalculated database file and join statistics for this purpose. Such a feature is useful in preventing expensive and lengthy queries, as it helps provide low, middle, and high estimates before the query is actually processed.

Finally, the editor/browser permits IDA users to easily modify the data dictionary itself. Employing a menu-based interface, system programmers, database administrators, and authorized users can add, delete, and modify file, record, and field specifications.

Network Communications and Security Perspectives

IDA's network communication processor links the attached workstations to the remote databases. The gateway in Figure 2, is adjustable to different network protocols and logon procedures. It helps in making the communication links transparent to the user, and

·   Monitors logons
·   Responds to the network operating system
·   Addresses DBMS prompts

A special IDA security package sees to it that only authorized users access the system. It has a database of all the authorized IDA users and their passwords, which can be modified only by the database administrator or a designated system manager.

As it will be appreciated, this functionality goes well beyond what is classically available in DBMS facilities. It provides means of organizing files into data dictionaries, controlling access to them:

·   The attributes of files needed for this utility are stored by the operating system in locations associated with the file, in addition to the contents of the file itself.
·   The attributes are the file name, creation date, block size, and creator name, whether it is contiguous or noncontiguous or created, used, and updated online.

The addition of facilities knowledge engineering goes beyond that level of reference, attacking the very essential problem of prevailing heterogeneity in the database setting.

IDA's designers have taken care of the fact that with the proliferation of high performance workstations, a company today has many users who are extremely proficient in their area of expertise — at the same time, they are not computer experts. They should not be required to know operating systems, network protocols, file transfer utilities, and data access routines.

Hence, the aim has been to insulate the user from the skills needed to effect actions associated with daily work. Knowledge engineering is instrumental in reaching these aims. It is also instrumental in

· Projecting truly user-friendly man/machine interfaces
· Assisting with communications protocols
· Providing the means for assuring the needed level of security

The message given by the preceding paragraphs is that the assistance of artificial intelligence artifacts is indispensable when we handle very large databases, whether these are centralized or distributed. In either case,

· A myriad of terminals are accessing the databases online.
· The requirements such terminals pose are quite different from one another.
· The data structures they access are diverse, and so are the DBMS.

In conclusion, IDA and CALIDA are typical of a well-focused research and implementation oriented to the design of intelligent computer systems, with such capabilities as virtual homogeneity within a heterogeneous environment. The suggested solution includes machine representation and acquisition of world knowledge, understanding of meaning and relationships across distributed database resources, and the handling of objects and events. Classical approaches are simply not made to address these problems.

At the core of the chosen solution by GTE is the provision of automated techniques for performing such intelligent functions as database access, data abstraction, and data filtering. What IDA is doing essentially is exploring the potential of machines to

· Perform spatial and temporal integration
· Recognize the nature of man-made queries
· Respond to complex queries by exploiting global resources

Other goals have been to detect and correct possible errors and anomalies that exist in heterogeneous environments, accommodating and adapting to change, as well as eventually providing a corporate memory of past decisions.

For many of the topmost organizations today, the support of a corporate memory facility is a goal increasingly coming into perspective. IDA does not have all of the tools to meet the further objectives of corporate memory facility. Presently, its aim is limited to the provision of a global approach to a distributed heterogeneous database environment, but the system can develop.

14

The DATAPLEX Solution for Heterogeneous Distributed Databases

Introduction

DATAPLEX has been developed by General Motors Research Laboratories,[1] as a heterogeneous distributed database management system. Its concept rests on the use of the relational model as a base reference and of SQL as a query language.

The DATAPLEX prototype interfaces the IMS database management hierarchical system under MVS, and the Ingres relational DBMS under VMS. Its current implementation allows users and applications to retrieve data from IMS and Ingres with a single SQL query, with database location transparent to endusers.

Embedded in a C language program, distributed SQL statements address themselves to the IMS and Ingres worlds. Supported formats are characters, variable length text, fields with maximum 2000 bytes, integers, floating point numbers, and packed decimal numbers.

DATAPLEX features an open architecture which provides a defined interface that can be extended to different DBMS. The available construct has been shown to

- · Effectively interface relational and nonrelational DBMS
- · Correctly process different test transactions
- · Exhibit a reasonably acceptable performance in its operation

The first to be executed during development has been a rapid prototype which includes four processes: user interface, IMS interface, Ingres interface, and a distributed query manager.

---

1 In collaboration with Relational Technology, Inc.

The distributed query manager has been designed to perform the following functions: distributed data dictionary management, query parsing, query decomposition, and generation of an execution plan of distributed queries, as well as execution of transaction procedures through communication with local DBMS.

As we will see in the second half of this chapter, a major difference between DATAPLEX and IDA (as well as other cross-database solutions like IBM's EDA/SQL, DataLens by Lotus, and DAL by Apple) is that

· DATAPLEX can handle both queries and transactions.
· IDA, EDA/SQL, etc. are mainly query oriented.

The efficiency of the DATAPLEX prototype has been measured in terms of query processing and response time (clock time). The average query response time was found to be about 37 sec when the prototype system runs on an IBM 4381 or a DEC VAX 11/785. With an IBM 3090, the average response time is 12 sec.

A distributed execution strategy can be passed to an execution monitor responsible for coordinating the execution of command sets, returning the results to the user. A federated schema helps modify global queries, which are handled by software processors that generate sequences according to a plan laid out by a query optimizer facility.

The developers have observed that the bottleneck for processing queries is the IMS interface. This has been the element with the largest overhead, but as database size grows, the fraction of the overhead to the total processing time decreases.

A Different Look at Accessing Distributed Databases

Like any other effort aimed at braking the barrier of database heterogeneity, DATAPLEX aims at providing a flexible approach to the access of diverse databases. The aim is one of simplifying the retrieval and update of distributed information elements under different DBMS, but the concept and tools being used are not necessarily the same as those of IDA,[2] or for that matter of other cross-database solutions.

The DATAPLEX architecture is relational. The basic design concept rests on the fact that different data models used by incompatible databases

· Structure data in different ways
· Present incompatibilities in terms of local schemata

---

2   We will compare the two methodologies in the second half of this chapter.

DATAPLEX sees to it that data definitions of all shared databases are transformed to an equivalent relational type definition, a *conceptual schema* that includes

· Shared data objects
· Local database views

Attention is being paid to each user's view of data in the heterogeneous distributed environment. Each one of these views is an external schema event, consisting of conceptual, often semantic, entities reflecting the user's requirements.

The choice of the relational model has been made on the basis that is is easy to understand, supports query languages, and sees to it that relational transactions can be translated to lower level nonrelational data manipulation language. Also the derivation of global views poses no great difficulties — and the same is true in terms of schema translation.

In other terms, the hypothesis underlying this specific implementation has been that the advantages from a relational approach seem to outweight the disadvantages such a solution might present. As a result, the adopted strategy translates transactions

· At each computer in which information elements are stored and referenced by the transaction
· As opposed to translation at the location of the computer from which the transaction originates

This approach of translation at a data storage level necessitates replication of only the crucial information, such as the conceptual schema and the directory in the DATAPLEX dictionaries, at every location. By contrast, the queries involving access at multiple locations are handled at the user location.

A given query is decomposed into subqueries, each of which addresses itself to a single database location. The overall solution features 14 component modules:

· User interface
· Security manager
· Application interface
· Query parser (for SQL)
· Distributed query decomposer
· Distributed query optimizer
· Enriched data dictionary
· Distributed database protocol
· Distributed transaction coordinator

- Local DBMS interface
- Translator
- Relational operations processor
- Error handler
- Controller

The functions performed by these 14 basic modules are explained in the following section. Such a description is based on the present design and performance of the DATAPLEX system.

This well thought-out list of functions helps document the well recognized DATAPLEX problems involved with information retrieval software. The development of the appropriate modules has reflected the difficulties of structuring a heterogeneous distributed database environment so that

- It looks homogeneous to the user.
- It is suited to the dynamic interrogation needs of a particular situation.

With the DATAPLEX example, the necessary functionality is addressed by the design of adaptive data retrieval concepts. Bringing this solution one step further, we can see situations where database organization is automatically reconfigured to permit optimal response to changing user query requirements. Three levels of reference and the component parts of such extended solutions are shown in Figure 1.[3]

A well-designed inference engine will have to address several problems. For instance, user organizations know of few issues of more concern to the enduser than the high error content of databases. Here, DATAPLEX has begun to make a contribution, with automated methodologies designed to detect and correct a variety of errors such as accidental data recording and erroneous relationships.

Designed with concurrent engineering in mind, the DATAPLEX approach has been oriented towards providing needed answers to the handling of complex queries and long transactions. But the relational approach is not necessarily the best answer in this domain, as other organizations comment. They point out that

- Long transactions can be best assisted through object-oriented approaches, hence, the attention a number of cross-database projects are now paying to object solutions.

According to the definition by Hughes Aircraft, which is based on extensive research, IMS, Adabas, DMS, RDMS, RDB, DB2, Oracle, Ingres, Sybase, and the different file management systems that preceded them are all oriented to short transactions. Assuring the handling of short transactions is necessary but not

---

3   We will return to these levels of reference in the section on "Extending the Domain of Interdatabase Connectivity".

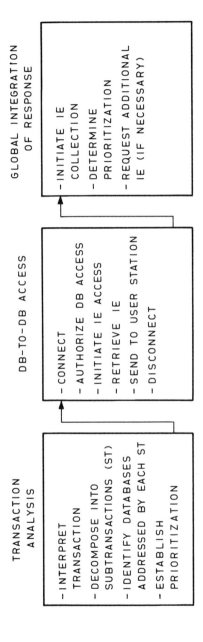

Figure 1   Deployment environment of an intelligent database solution.

enough; much more is needed in terms of functionality in order to answer the cross-database requirements of long transactions.

Functions Supported by DATAPLEX Modules

At the core of DATAPLEX are four modules: controller, error handler, relational operations processor, and translator. Each addresses itself to a specific mission. There is also an enriched data dictionary. Value added modules include a distributed query optimizer, query decomposer, and SQL parser.

The function of the DATAPLEX Controller is to invoke and sequence necessary modules to process a transaction. The exact procedures depend on the transaction type.

The error handler corrects recoverable errors. The relational operations processor addresses itself to relational database activities, manipulating queries, and obtained results at the local level. Transactions are handled in a distributed way and the update mechanism provides for

- Concurrency control
- Deadlock handling
- Data recovery

On a local basis, all three issues are assured by the local DBMS. The real challenge with distributed concurrency control is that of going beyond queries in a transaction oriented implementation.

DATAPLEX addresses the subject of concurrency control by globally performing a two-phase locking. There is also a two-phase commit to enforce the update procedures for recovery reasons.

- This consists of a prepare-to-commit, followed by an actual commit.

The job of the translator is to convert SQL transactions to another relational transaction or to a nonrelational data definition. This module also translates between global and local names using data dictionary facilities.

Translation of data definition and data manipulation language statements is necessary to overcome the differences prevailing in a heterogeneous database environment. DATAPLEX aims to provide a relational model as a common denominator and uniform user interface.

- The major difference between the relational and the nonrelational approach is in the way of modeling relationships among entities.
- As its name implies, the relational model represents the relationship between two entities.

· The hierarchical and network models represent such a relationship by using a pointer, which is an approach widely used with file management.

The DATAPLEX solution for translating a nonrelational data definition to an equivalent relation is through a key in the owner record. It is used as a foreign key in its member records. This method normalizes a simple set of relations.

The local DBMS interface passes the translated transaction to the supported local DBMS and gets back the results. The distributed transaction coordinator requests both lock and unlock operations on local data. The system also enforces update chores within the perspective of a distributed update.

The distributed database protocol interfaces the underlying communication protocols, exchanging commands, and information elements. It is doing so by using the file and message transfer facilities. It also detects and reports any problem associated with accessing remote information elements.

The role of the enriched data dictionary, which assists the DATAPLEX mechanism, is quite important. Supported facilities include the ability to question or update information by identifying the location of referenced data.

The distributed query optimizer collects statistical information on data volumes as well as on local DBMS results, helping to define and schedule the best data reduction approach. The job of the distributed query decomposer is to break up a distributed retrieval query into local queries and user location queries which merge local results.

The SQL parser scans and parses query statements to check syntactic errors, for instance, whether a query references correct names of relations and attributes and so on. It also transforms a query that references global views of information elements coordinating with local views. The application interface establishes the link between an application and DATAPLEX. It also identifies SQL statements in the application and records an SQL transaction in the transaction log.

The job of the security manager is to enforce content-independent access control using the global data object names and user identification. The database administrator creates a section in the DATAPLEX dictionary and grants access privileges to users.

The assignment and management of user access privileges is done with the assistance of knowledge engineering, particularly by means of predicates, e.g.,

· IF the global object requested by the user corresponds to a local data object managed by a given DBMS
  THEN the user becomes authorized to reach the local object, accessing it where it is stored
· IF the global object is a view covering one or more local objects
  THEN DATAPLEX becomes the authorized user of the local objects at their location

The assurance of a distributed data security mechanism with DATAPLEX is done in content-dependent access, whose rules include a predicate focusing on the content of information elements. By contrast, in a content-independent access mode rules are defined only on the types of data. The security arrangement is enforced in two steps: at DATAPLEX level and by local DBMS, whose access control mechanism preserves its autonomy of action.

In this sense, when a user issues a query to the DATAPLEX module at his location, the system performs a content-independent security check employing

· The user ID
· The global data objects referenced

A query will be handled only if the check gives a positive outcome. In case global objects included in the query are stored in other locations, the query and the user ID are sent to the locations in reference. There, the local DBMS checks for security.

Users formulate queries through the relational view of the distributed database. The location and type of the actual database where the information elements they need are stored is transparent to them. The interface prompts the enduser to issue SQL queries and messages as well as results returned to his workstation.

Comparing the Solutions Adopted by CALIDA and DATAPLEX

We have seen, to some detail, two approaches intended to provide a degree of homogeneity with heterogeneous distributed databases: CALIDA by GTE and DATAPLEX by GM. Both have gone through a rapid prototype level of implementation which permitted their designs to improve the artifact on the basis of experience.

In both cases, the applications made it feasible to recognize the importance of such factors as accuracy and dependability and appreciate the anomalies and inconsistencies that may be present. The prototype implementation provided the possibility to modify the behavior of these systems by reconfiguring their primitives and component modules.

Learning from actual experience is the best way to adjust to the complexities inherent in distributed databases and their associated control procedures. It is also important for the negotiation that should take place in steps, e.g.,

· Analyzing a complex ad hoc query into subqueries
· Automatically routing these subqueries to the information element sources at the various databases
· Automatically reconstructing the answer to the query as a function of responses to subqueries, after the appropriate format changes have been done

Table 1   Common Elements in the CALIDA and DATAPLEX Solutions

1. Designed for a production environment
2. Address two heterogeneous databases: a hierarchical and a relational
3. Use knowledge engineering tools and concepts
4. Emphasize friendly enduser orientation
5. Interaction is only at higher level
6. Support SQL interface of sorts
7. Design is not object-oriented

If we compare the adopted solutions with CALIDA and DATAPLEX, we will see that the approaches being taken are not the same, though the goals are fairly similar. The careful evaluator will discover that there is commonality among the two approaches, and Table 1 focuses on this common ground.

Both CALIDA and DATAPLEX have been designed and implemented to operate in a production environment. To this end, their designers have selected two heterogeneous production databases: a hierarchical and a relational. Also, their field test has been based on processing data requests, both with the old mode of operation and with the facilities offered by the new constructs.

CALIDA has been projected to offer database pass-through capabilities connected to marketing operations. DATAPLEX addresses engineering problems and the approach has to be more polyvalent, as Figure 2 documents.

The databases for computer aided design (CAD), computer aided manufacturing (CAM), bill of materials, purchasing, general accounting, personnel, and operations planning can be quite diverse from one another. Because they grew like wild cacti, such environments typically involve lots of technical incompatibilities.

Both in the cases of CALIDA and DATAPLEX, artificial intelligence has been a rewarding experience. In both cases, the use of knowledge engineering concepts and tools was instrumental in producing results. Both constructs

· Emphasize a user-friendly orientation and can demonstrate that it has been well implemented
· Present to the enduser a comprehensive homogeneous response, in spite of the underlying nonhomogeneity of the databases

In terms of man/machine communications, both DATAPLEX and CALIDA support a variation of SQL, though the latter goes beyond that by providing a more powerful linguistic interface: the CALIDA-88 artifact.

In both cases, the interaction is only at a higher level. Both solutions automatically generate the low level target language queries from higher level queries specified by the user. Just the same, they both see to it that user queries are checked for consistency and correctness.

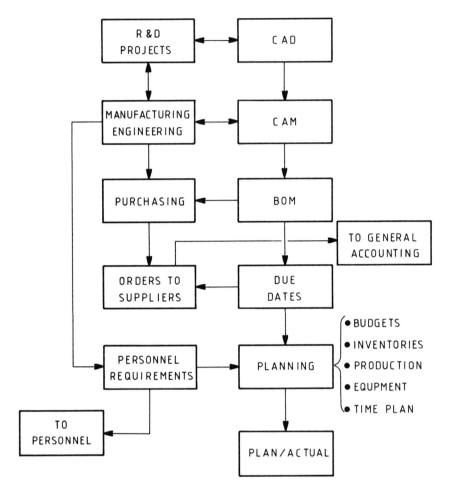

Figure 2   Cross-database problems in a heterogeneous engineering/manufacturing environment require flexible solutions.

Finally, neither DATAPLEX nor CALIDA are object-oriented solutions. While at some later day the incorporation of object-based versions is not impossible,[4] this approach does not characterize the current state of the art of the two artifacts.

The common ground ends at about this point, and from here on start the differences. The differences have been classified in three basic issues and are shown in Table 2.

---

4   Particularly for applications in computer aided design, computer aided manufacturing, office automation, complex financial transactions, and computer assisted software engineering (CASE).

Table 2   **Differences in Conception and Implementation of CALIDA and DATAPLEX**

Issue	CALIDA	DATAPLEX
1. Target Applications	Management information system, marketing, and office automation	Technical issues, design automation, and computer integrated manufacturing
2. Base Language	Lisp	C
3. Shell Usage	IDA	—

- The target population of CALIDA is of the management information system type, including office automation and customer oriented queries.
- The focal point of DATAPLEX is technical and engineering applications, facilitating computer aided design as well as computer integrated manufacturing (CIM).

Ironically, while neither CALIDA nor DATAPLEX emphasize object orientation, the domains to which both constructs appeal are those most difficult to address through classical approaches — also where an object orientation has given the best results. Hewlett-Packard's Open ODB, Versant's Versant Star, and DEC's RDB Star are examples documenting this reference.

Linguistic Issues and Cross-Database Solutions

As Table 2 has shown, DATAPLEX chose C as its programming language while CALIDA bet its future on Lisp. There is, as well, another difference in linguistics; CALIDA is built through a shell, the Intelligent Database Assistant (IDA). By contrast, DATAPLEX features no shell.

Whether their finer programmatic interfaces are in C or in Lisp, both constructs aim to support a high quality of query handling as well as expandability and functional completeness:

- *Functional completeness* addresses the issues of query specification, query estimation, database integration, and network communication functions.
- *Expandability* aims to keep the options open in determining the population of databases that can be accessed and in estimating the amount of effort involved in extending the construct to other database types.
- *Quality of query* is a function of the ability of the solution to access a range of databases from user specification(s), in a manner transparent to the enduser.

All three issues have a great deal to do with the linguistic solutions being chosen, as well as with the amount of knowledge engineering embedded into the system. Have these goals been achieved?

GTE identified several advantages it obtained by using CALIDA over the old method of request processing, for instance, no syntactic errors, no misspelling errors, no data type errors, and quite importantly, fewer database semantic errors.

As an example of the last reference, CALIDA's macro facility permits an experienced analyst to define all the domain concepts that he needs. This feature not only eliminates some types of semantic domain errors but also improves the user's productivity. DATAPLEX offers a similar facility.

- Both solutions are able to handle the requests that fall within their design specifications.
- By implementing additional features both can extend their coverage to include complex queries.

This frame of reference addresses the issues of integration of multiple heterogeneous databases, accessing corporate data from both relational and hierarchical databases as well as variable record type files.

Cognizant information technologists, however, comment that further developments are necessary in order to meet the efficiency requirements of a growing range of implementations, particularly for multimedia applications. The same is true in regard to environments that include photonics storage media (optical disks). Different platforms must be included in a range of implementations, suggested in Figure 3.

It is also proper to add that neither GTE's CALIDA nor GM's DATAPLEX are unique architectural solutions. The Lawrence Livermore National Laboratory (LLNL) has developed LINCS.[5] This is a distributed architecture designed to integrate diverse operating systems and heterogeneous DBMS.

In contrast to IDA and DATAPLEX, LINCS is a communications based integrative solution that exists side by side with the approaches implemented in previous generations of effort (like old Octopus), which are being phased out. According to LLNL, this transition is facilitated by

- Software gateways that effectively translate between differing formats and protocols
- Gateways for terminal interaction, allowing terminal drivers conforming to one generation to interact with applications conforming to the other

In a manner quite similar to that of GTE and GM, the Lawrence Livermore National Laboratory is using some of its rich experience in artificial intelligence to achieve this goal.

There is, as well, a global database management project American Airlines has undertaken with knowledge engineering assistance. As in the case of DATAPLEX and CALIDA, this project addresses itself to the challenge of conceptually inte-

---

5   LINCS standard for Livermore Interactive Network Communications System.

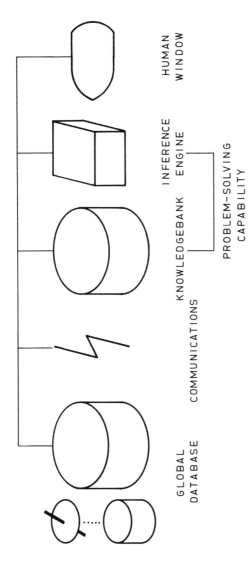

Figure 3 Areas to be simultaneously addressed through a logic programming language.

grating the existing multiplicity of heterogeneous databases currently in operation at the company.

American Airlines is also trying to gather all data in its distributed environment into a homogeneous format for all future database usage. This led to the DATATABLE concept. By all indications, the first application of DATATABLE will be with the Teradata Database Computer, using a single format and employing semantic approaches.

As these examples help demonstrate, there are alternative goals, approaches, and tools used to solve the problems of cross-database access in a heterogeneous environment. Such alternatives have common points, the strongest among them being that they all come from user organizations.

Apart from the cases we have just seen, there are vendor offerings to which a rapid reference has been made in preceding chapters. As a memory refresher, these are DataLens by Lotus Development, DAL by Apple Computers, and EDA/ SQL by IBM/Information Builders.

Extending the Domain of Interdatabase Connectivity

The present section presents some technical hindsights into what needs to be done in order to maintain the flexibility of a cross-database solution, focusing on the specifications that are necessary. One of the aims is planning for and automatically generating database access programs for the enduser:

- Starting with high level queries
- Considering schema and primitives
- Providing programmatic interfaces for low level database queries

The first requirement of a user-friendly approach is that of making all network connections transparent, permitting the user to create, edit, and browse information elements in storage. As we have already seen, this requires the assistance of data dictionaries.

Since we talk of databases, hence corporate resources, a parallel requirement is controlling unauthorized access and the associated utilization of the elements they contain. Hence, authorization and authentication are two issues at top of the list.

Generalizing from the IDA and DATAPLEX experiences, and taking transaction processing as an example, we can express this mission in the concept outlined in Figure 1 of this chapter. Three levels of reference were brought under perspective:

- The analysis of a transaction into subtransactions
- Provision of database-to-database access
- Global integration of the response

The best way to handle this approach is to see to it that a supervisory expert system manages the deployment environment of the intelligent database, supervising the solution we are after. Each main function should be assisted through a knowledge engineering construct, starting with analysis of a transaction into subtransactions.

A similar approach will be taken with queries, analyzing each user query into subqueries. As an example, suppose there is only one user request but the subqueries address three heterogeneous databases. There are also joint fields involved in the query in reference.

Contrary to SQL, which has to say explicitly: "Select... From... Where", hence providing no transparency, CALIDA defines a query without saying which are the joint fields. The expert systems will do this job.

For instance, the user's query may be: "Find me a client company whose last 3 month average in billing was less than last month's." In the GTE environment, this requires online interaction between the

- · User workstation
- · IDA shell
- · Heterogeneous databases attached to the network

The joint fields algorithm is implemented in the database expert module. IDA takes care of the differences in DBMS primitives; the user does not need to know about them.

Since the accessed databases are heterogeneous, there are incompatibilities in schemata and primitives. The mosaic of options is controlled by the expert system through frames. A frame holds information about an object, for instance a record:

- · The structure has slots, which resemble fields in a record and may be filled or unfilled.
- · Slots can hold single values or multiple values, and may also have a procedure attached.
- · This procedure is invoked automatically when the value of that slot is required.

Rules are expressed as frames that have an antecedent slot and a consequent slot. Artificial intelligence modules see to it that the interface is protected against

- · Domain errors
- · Syntactic errors
- · Semantic errors

IDA builds up a knowledge representation of the database structure using the frames and their slots as parameters and constraints. A message passing algorithm helps provide the connectivity between artifacts.

Constraints may be simple or complex. For instance, they may include built-in comparisons. This is a good example of the system's practicality, as well as the federated database solution's procedure.

A financial example can help focus this discussion. Say that we have five nonintegrated databases and each gets served through its own parochial programming products as well as local DBMS:

- · Forex
- · Commodities
- · Securities
- · Futures and options
- · Treasury

Then, let's assume that for risk control reasons we need to access simultaneously all five databases. We have to do so online, without spending precious time in changing schemata and searching through the rules or protocols which access each one of the databases in reference separately and manually.

The IDA solution provides the needed support to automate this type of service. It makes the difference in data structures, DBMS, and internal schemata, which exist among the databases and assures an integrated response to the user's query, transparent to the user.

Through the IA-supported services of IDA, the risk control request will be examined and analyzed in subtransactions. These will be directed to the appropriate databases in a parallel fashion and processed locally. Each of the five responses will be returned to the workstation to be integrated in a manner comprehensive to the enduser — even if incompatible information elements have been employed.

Benchmarking the System Response and Its Cost-Effectiveness

The preceding sections have demonstrated the type of functionality provided through knowledge engineering solutions elaborated along the lines of IDA. The more accurate way of expressing these services is through the reference "nearly integrated databases", and this is written in a functional sense, suggesting the type of applications that can be served in a valid way.

Other organizations have chosen different approaches. As an example we have seen General Motors' DATAPLEX. Like IDA it uses an interfacing processor that significantly benefits from knowledge engineering — but unlike IDA it provides for tighter coupling among databases, hence the ability to process transactions.

The fact that in both cases knowledge engineering proves to be the key to a solution is not surprising. IA research is polyvalent and addresses many fields:

- · Providing the means for the development of smart systems

· Building intelligent interfaces
· Minimizing error occurrences through software that has failsafe features.

The thrust of this research is in interfacing, and it has a great deal to do with error prevention, at the same time reducing and controlling the opportunities for a mistake. Another aftermath is cutting down programming work associated with cross-database access — and therefore associated programming costs.

These results are being achieved by automating the total process of developing or writing complex machine code and data translation routines. By being two of the original efforts made in this direction, IDA and DATAPLEX are now seen as classic examples of distributed problem solving and distributed information processing mechanisms.

As it cannot be repeated too often, the pressure by the leading user organizations in regard to solutions supporting geographically and functionally distributed database assets has been dictated by

· The complexities of operating decisions
· The volume of information flows

At the same time, incompatibilities in data structures, DBMS, and other issues saw to it that valid integrative approaches must be provided to enhance database usage.

But what is the efficiency of the approach that sprang up as the result of ongoing research in this field? Can we measure performance in a way that gives confidence that operational requirements will be fulfilled in a valid manner?

The answer is "yes". We can do it through benchmarking, provided that the necessary preparatory work has been done. For instance, object code optimization may not only be in software but also in hardware terms, assisting in the determination of which hardware and/or implementation gives the most performance.

The benchmarks should be exactly the same on all software/hardware machines, tested and portable enough to run on all of them. They should exercise specific, known functions of the operating system and compiler implementation:

· Containing tests of overall performance by simulating typical user activities
· Executing background processes that may characterize complex transactions
· Focusing on foreground processes to see how the system responds under a multitasking load

Benchmark timings should be made using a method that is both consistent and accurate. Some operating systems can help in this connection. For instance, Unix has a standard timing mechanism that reports elapsed and processor times used by a process. The processor time is further divided into user and system times.

Further to the point, benchmarks tuned to federated database solutions should be able to differentiate between the responses of the different databases, as well as their processors, OS, and DBMS. Real time (elapsed time) should be measured for each database response, with a log kept over a number of subtransactions to obtain a distribution of values, as background processes may account for much of

15

Project Carnot by MCC

Introduction

A case study must be a representative project retaining the attention of committed learners. It should be fairly well documented in its presentation, able to be worked out in a nearly complete manner and with a solution that leaves a clear message to the reader.

These are the principles that have been followed with the case studies we have seen in Chapters 11 through 14, and this is also the basis on which Project Carnot will be presented. Undertaken by the Microelectronics and Computer Development Corporation (MCC),[1] Phase 0 of Project Carnot started in 1990. Its goal has been the definition of an architecture:

· The standard to be used for cross-database integration, in connection with the adoption of the remote data access (RDA) protocol.[2]

Phase 0 was followed in 1991 by Phase 1, which aims to practically apply RDA, the Information Repository Dictionary System (IRDS),[3] and transaction processing monitors currently under development. Norms established by X.400 and office document architecture (ODA)[4] are being observed.

In 1992, Phase 2 of Project Carnot continued extending the original prototype and started incorporating enhancements specifically connected to some applications under way. One of the standards in that phase is the Common Management Information System (CMIS), by ISO.

---

1 This project is conducted in direct conjunction with the SQL Access Group and is building everything in compliance with standards by ANSI and ISO.
2 Normalized by ANSI and produced by the SQL Access Group.
3 By ANSI and the National Institute of Standards and Technology (NIST), formerly NBS.
4 By the International Standards Organization (ISO).

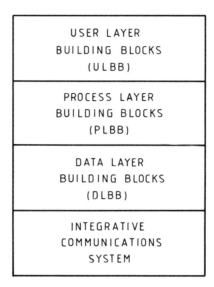

Figure 1   Layers of the communications software fabric project by Bellcore.

Carnot is intended to grow through application development projects culminating in final deliveries in late 1994 — well beyond Phase 2. Participating vendor firms will produce and support the different tools in observance of decisions reached by various standards bodies, assuring compliance with them as well as implementation results.

A number of MCC departments and projects contribute to Carnot. One of them is Itasca, the successor to Orion object-oriented DBMS — which is in Lisp. Other inputs come from knowledge engineering. Two of the MCC shareholders promote the project, having officially stated that they do so because they need

· Interoperable databases
· Network-wide knowledgebanks

Among frontline level expectations is that of generic solutions, which can be transferred into the day-to-day activities of corporations. Bellcore, one of the sponsors, is working on a Communications Software Fabric (CSF/OSCA). The concept rests on the layered structure shown in Figure 1.

Physical Connectivity and Logical Connectivity

Like every other project in the cross-database domain, Carnot is working on the realistic assumption that organizations have 30 to 40 years of investments in information technology that cannot be thrown overboard. Hence, the solution is to build a bridge between the

- Closed centralized systems of yesterday
- Open distributed systems of today and tomorrow

A basic grand design objective is that of integrating the four layers we saw in Figure 1 into one system and showing that this aggregate is usable. Among the specific goals is a network-wide protocol definition. The project's aim is to alleviate the current need, where most companies still have to build different protocols and interfaces ad hoc.

The basic hypothesis underlining this drive is that when a network-wide database protocol is defined, commodity products will start coming up, helping to provide standard parts under a communications software fabric. This hypothesis has been pursued for some years by Bellcore in connection to its OSCA project.

OSCA has been a strategic initiative aimed at an integrative architecture able to provide software interoperability between heterogeneous machines. The basic concepts reflect the fact that

- Databases are a corporate information system, and are growing in number as well as diversity.
- Files exist not only in central and departmental computers but also at the user layer and its components (ULBB in Figure 1).
- The process layer and its building blocks also carry their own databases, which are largely incompatible (PLBB).
- The data layer building blocks essentially act as repositories for the whole system (DLBB).

Within this context the research done by Carnot aims to develop tools that permit open applications, which can be integrated with information stored on existing closed systems.

According to Bellcore, and by extension the Project Carnot, telecommunications facilities and databases are not two distinct or disconnected levels of reference:

- They must be seen as one integrative implementation field, with the digital network being the link.

Therefore, the goal is to specify and prototype a platform that will provide physical and logical connectivity, both of them implemented in a seamless manner.

Physical connectivity regards transactions, messages, and queries, including long transaction processing — not just the standard short transactions. Conventional two-phase commit-based distributed transaction processing is available as a transaction service from participating computer vendors.

The aim of *logical connectivity* is semantic integration and integrity, with support for appropriate human interfaces. Top to bottom, the corresponding layers are

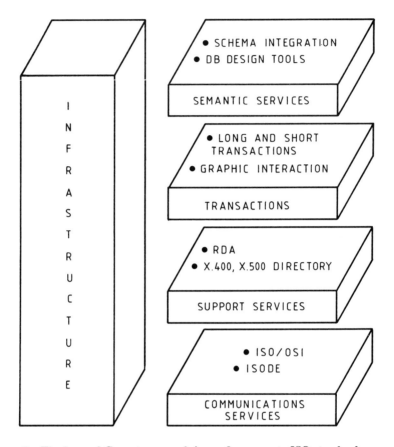

Figure 2   The layered Carnot approach in conformance to ISO standards.

·   Semantics
·   Transactions
·   Supporting services
·   Communications

Figure 2 presents the four-layered solution advanced by Project Carnot.[5] The ISO Data Exchange Standard (ISODE) is the core function of the communications layer, within an open system interconnection (OSI) architecture. The latter features Internet and other services, TCP/IP being an option.

Remote data access (RDA), X.400, and X.500 directory services constitute the core of the supporting services layer. Other vital components are interfaces to CASE tools and electronic document interchange (EDI).

---

5   The integrative infrastructure has two main components which will be discussed in the next section.

Transaction Scripting and the System Knowledgebank

Transaction services, the third layer bottom up, addresses the transaction processing protocols. While current emphasis is on short transactions, further plans include long transactions. Other vital components are the graphics interaction environment (GIE) and its lower level transaction scripting.

Data access protocols are utilized for transaction scripting. MIT's *Rosette* has been chosen as an environment for doing transaction operations, with SQL and OSQL[6] used as query language, as well as Itasca, a Lisp-based, object-oriented DBMS by MCC.

OSQL is an object SQL (originally developed by Texas Instruments) with distributed database functions. The dual object orientation of the Carnot project, at query and DBMS levels, rests on the choices made during developmental work.

The way Carnot works is distributed transaction/query generators build Rosette scripts. The generators develop the scripts through interactions with

- Directory services
- Repository managers
- Deductive knowledge in Carnot's knowledgebank

Known as the declarative resource constraint base, this knowledgebank consists of a collection of predicates that express business rules, inter-resource dependencies, consistency requirements, and clauses.

Developed by MIT, Rosette is an open system information handler based on the *Actor* model with lightweight threads. The software reflects more than 2 years of work on formal theory and experimentation, providing

- A shell-like environment
- The possibility for rapid prototyping
- Debugging and examination calls
- Supports for remote evaluation and interactions
- Fan-In/Fan-Out data flows

Rosette permits process synchronization through reliable broadcasting, dynamically incorporating functions through foreign function call. The shell makes building an extensible environment feasible, as well as bringing a number of services online and integrating them.

Semantic services are handled at the top layer identified in Figure 2, which is database oriented. Expressed in a layered fashion, top to bottom, it includes

- Common sense knowledge
- Schema integration

---

6 Object SQL, which is *not* a standard.

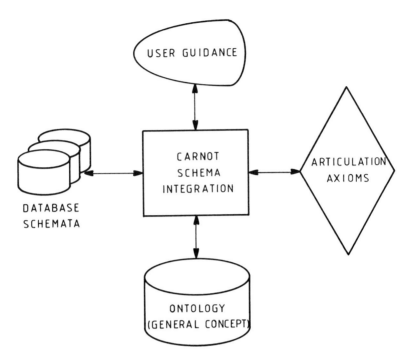

Figure 3   Component parts and their integration into MIT's CYC.

·   Database design tools
·   Communications agents

Carnot utilizes MCC's CYC knowledgebank as a part of the framework. CYC ontology and reasoning mechanisms are being used as a backdrop for representing sets of concepts that may be found in various databases.

CYC encodes semantics and provides the representation and inference mechanisms needed for expressing relationships among information resources. The resulting service assists in facing semantic integrity, at least as an initial approach to solving the associated integrative challenges.

Figure 3 shows the synergy behind concepts and functional parts, which creates the CYC approach. These components provide for interactive user guidance, the manipulation of database schemata, and a knowledgebank of articulation axioms. Ontology assures the general context.

A Framework for Developing Applications

Project Carnot takes advantage of standards being developed, as well as of projects like Rosette and CYC which are already advanced. As another critical building block, Carnot uses MCC's Reasoning Architecture software to provide mechanisms for independent communicating agents.

· Such agents encapsulate chunks of expertise as separate active entities within Carnot.
· The framework includes schema integration and database design tools for reconceptualizing, updating, and generating schemata.

An interesting capability that may arise with the addition of reasoning agents into the semantic services layer is an inversion of the notion regarding the way standards work. This approach aims at providing the conditions under which Carnot can adapt to evolving user needs.

The notion about inverted standards rests on the use of a declarative knowledgebank, capable of dealing with contingency requirements by selecting standards as needed rather than having pre-established norms. MCC has done a risk analysis connected to this proposition and proven that it leads to high payoff with relatively low risk.

In an architectural sense, the networked and file server components of Carnot are shown in Figure 4. They fit within an infrastructure, which is divided into two major components: *applications framework* and *basics*.[7]

· The applications framework intends to integrate different applications modules, consisting of both commodity software and inhouse developments.
· Another goal of the applications infrastructure is to present a friendly, adaptable environment.
· Basics aims to effectively support graphical interactivity, as well as cooperative data manipulation functions.

Part of the reason for the distinction being made is that a Carnot objective is to provide a flexible structuring of services by level of reference. Among the major questions remaining to be answered, however, are the efficient use of resources (particularly MIPS) and semantic integrity in a network-wide sense.

At the infrastructural level, Carnot has correctly paid attention to human window requirements. The man/machine interface includes tools providing for graphical interaction:

· Graphic objects can be selected and then dropped onto active regions of the screen, causing various actions to take place.
· The tools come with application libraries that may be modified and extended to build interfaces for new domains.

---

7 This infrastructure has already been shown in Figure 2.

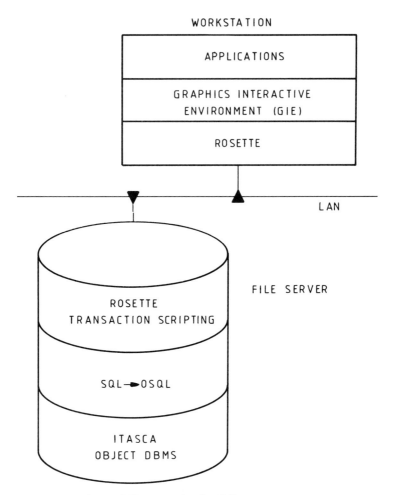

Figure 4   Workstation and file server levels of Carnot.

Navigation and graphical metaphors of the information space are focal points of the design.

Support is also provided for structuring dialogues involving data entry, where incomplete or erroneous information may be discovered. Further extension will include human interfaces for multiple cooperating users accessing and updating common databases.

Declarative languages are being developed for associating the semantics of application data to grammars. This helps both in parsing and in interactively generating visualizations.

As it will be recalled from the second section, the choice of Carnot's basic components aimed at offering a common semantic framework. It reflects a global enterprise-wide view of all the resources integrated within the system, where the same language can be used for intercommunicating. The chosen approach is aimed at achieving resource integration by resolving semantic incompatibilities among disparate information resources, helped by the global ontology provided by CYC.

Project management understands that the chosen linguistic approach must support semantic integration of autonomous information resources, focusing on a composite approach for accessing a multidatabase environment. The language must provide a unified view for application tasks, expressed as an integrative schema of the individual resources.

A user should not be aware of differences among components of the environment and should issue queries and transactions against the unified view. The options are

·   To craft a new multidatabase schema each time a collection of information resources is to be integrated, or each time a previously integrated resource is altered
·   Use a knowledgebank as a pre-existing integrative schema, capitalizing on artificial intelligence

Correctly, Carnot chose the second solution and employed CYC in bringing it alive. The schemata of individual resources are related to CYC independently, which makes an integrative schema easier to construct and maintain than in previous attempts at implementing a composite approach.

The researchers at the Carnot project suggested that most of these previous attempts to schema integration can be characterized as some combination of four alternative strategies. We will examine them in the next section.

Alternative Strategies for Schema Integration

The previous section made reference to alternative strategies as representative of previous attempts to schema integration in a multidatabase environment. These are preintegrating, conforming, comparing, merging, and restructuring.

The scope of *preintegrating* is that of choosing the schemata to be integrated as well as the order of integration, as well as a possible assignment of preferences to schemata or portions thereof. This can be achieved through a set of integration policy rules, as well as assertions among views that will merge into the integrative schema.

The goal of the *conforming* mode is to detect and resolve conflicts. Since automatic conflict resolution is not feasible in a generalized sense, different scenarios must be developed based on interaction with users so that some compromises can be achieved and mapped into solutions.

The third approach is *comparing*. It analyzes and compares schemata to determine the correspondences among concepts and detect possible conflicts. Finally, *merging and restructuring* superimposes and reconciles schemata into an integrative schema that must be understandable, complete, and correct.

To a significant extent, the methodology chosen by Carnot differs from those just described in several aspects. In this project, *resource integration* means more than schema in the accepted sense of structural description of the local schemata resolving semantic differences. The aim of Carnot is not only to reconcile structural primitives of data models supported by the distributed database resources, but also to

- Reconcile integrity constraints as well as metadata and metarules
- Take stock of specifications regarding data usage, as well as doing something about them
- Represent information about the resources themselves, including those of an organizational and managerial nature

This can be called a fifth strategy for database resource integration, and it is more generic than either of the four described at the beginning of this section. However, to be implemented effectively, it requires knowledge about the individual information resources and the way in which they work.

An example of knowledge that must be available is schema information regarding the structure of data, integrity constraints, and allowable operations. Another example is resource information concerning the description of supported services, such as

- Data model and languages
- Data dictionary
- Lexical definitions of the names for data objects
- Interactive guidance from the schema integrator
- Comments from the database designer and administrator

Other approaches, too, feature these or similar requirements, but not necessarily the organizational information which is a "must" with Carnot. By organizational information is meant the rules defined by the organization to which the resource belongs.

Organizational rules specify the contribution of the different database resources in the heterogeneous environment and some characteristics of the user organization itself. Specs oriented toward information technology organization are

· The natural language used to communicate
· The methodology implemented.

With the strategy Project Carnot has adopted, the different heterogeneous schemata prevailing among the incompatible databases are compared, conformed, and merged with the CYC ontology, but not with each other. By contrast, during semantic transaction processing,

· CYC will compare these schemata to determine the most appropriate local resources to process queries and updates.

This is a good example of what was meant in the proceeding section, when it was said that the knowledge already in CYC offers a platform for managing heterogeneous database properties. With Carnot, the knowledgebank contains the equivalent of 50,000 entities and relationships expressed as frames and slots.

· CYC encodes the semantics for a significant portion of consensus reality to which a particular database resource can be related
· It provides the knowledge representation and inference mechanisms needed for expressing the relationships among information elements.

The artifact can represent dynamic properties of information elements through predicates attached to the slots of the frames. It also assures a set of mechanisms necessary to construct, represent, and maintain an integrative schema.

By enforcing rather elaborate integrity constraints, CYC can prevent violations of semantics. However, these phases of the schema integration methodology are strongly influenced by the data model that has been chosen to represent the conceptual local schema. We will see what this means in the next section.

Choosing an Approach for Schema Integration

Project Carnot uses three database schemata: relational, entity-relationship, and object-oriented to aproach problems arising in schema integration. These three schemata are structurally and semantically different, they also represent diverse perspectives in regard to items common to a number of databases.

Say, as an example, that we will be interested in three databases, each providing information about inventories and belonging to different organizations. These organizations can be seen as vertically integrated in a product sense:

· A vendor of raw materials and intermediate manufacturing parts
· The main manufacturing company, its stocks, in-process inventories, and finished products

· A wholesaler's warehoused, finished products, ready for distribution to
retailers and major customers

These are three vertically integrated levels of information, and online access to the
databases of all three organizations is vital. Each wishes to provide its customers
with the maximum amount of information about available inventories, as well as
what can be made available due to future deliveries.

Going all the way to the original source of products, the wholesaler will have
to integrate the local schemata of the three groups of databases in order to get the
total status picture. Through this integrative approach client queries can be handled
in a very competitive manner, however,

· Each organization needs to cooperate with the other organizations responding to client (enduser) requests.
· Structural and semantic diversities of the prevailing schemata should not be
permitted to cause conflicts and incompatibilities.
· Locally, each organization is responsible for the data, programs, and applications accessible by different users.

To solve the problem Carnot proposes a preintegration phase which represents
the schema of a given database resource in the formalism of the CYC knowledge
representation language. This representation consists of a set of frames with slots
residing in a local schema context.

The so-called CYC *microtheory* instances belong to more general units describing the data model used by the schema. If we represent an instance of a
relational schema, the units will be of the types relation and attribute.

Project Carnot attempts to represent the maximum semantics about a schema
in order to automate, as much as possible during integration, the construction of
articulation axioms. Along this line of reference, it has defined a set of CYC units
to represent the characteristics of local resources and their related information
elements.

· A first try is to define CYC units corresponding to the concepts of application, entity, relation, attributes, record, file, system commands, title, and
program.
· Every local schema can be represented as an instance of these units belonging to a local context, with each component resource being a subtype of a
more generic component type.

Along the line of this reference, the component types are *metatypes* under which
can be classified schemata expressed in the same formalism. Schema definitions
may be further specialized if a resource uses a model that cannot be classified
within the above categories or has additional features in comparison to the general
definition of its class.

New specializations of component types may be defined during preintegration, if the model and the language(s) of the resource involved in the preintegration process are not known to CYC. The semantics of attribute domains and integrity constraints must also be represented in CYC. These, however, are not always specified in database schemata.

A unit known as *DatabaseLink* is employed to relate high level concepts to each other, or a high level concept with an attribute. This unit summarizes the common features of a set of link definitions, for instance, definitions of relational attributes, entity relationship attributes, class attributes, or links involved in a relationship. There are two possible cases:

1. The type of resource to be integrated is known to and represented in CYC.

In this case, the system will propose a representation that the administrator of the resource may specialize by deleting slots — or, alternatively, by adding or modifying slot definitions as necessary.

2. The type of resource to be integrated is unknown to CYC.

This means that the database administrator must represent the data model for this resource in the CYC knowledgebank, integrating his new definition into it. The representation of a schema of the resource must be assured whether automatically or otherwise.

In the general case, the preintegration process produces a CYC context containing a model for each database resource. The integration process then builds a mapping between the CYC model and the base context in the system that contains CYC's global ontology and constitutes the integrative schema.

Basically, the mapping consists of articulation axioms that encode correspondence between the semantics of the information resource domain and the CYC ontology, as well as between the local database(s) language(s) and the CYC language.

There can be two CYC representations for the same concept, each allowing different aspects of it to be emphasized. The matching phase of integration is essentially a dual issue:

·   Conceptual modeling for resource design
·   Knowledge representation for expert system design

The problem is that, given a concept from the real world, we have to determine how to represent and model it. For resource integration purposes, the problem becomes: given a representation for a concept, determine the concept.

There are several factors that affect this latter phase: there may be a mismatch between the local and global schemata in the depth of knowledge representing a concept and there may also be mismatches between the structures used to encode the knowledge.

- The local schema may have used one of different structures to represent a concept.
- Alternatively, the schema may have employed one of two different structures to represent a concept.

In the latter case, in terms of relative knowledge, the integrative schema may have more, less, or equivalent knowledge compared to a local schema.

The factor of *relative knowledge* applies to each concept in the local schema, rather than to all of the local schemata as a whole. If the integrative schema knowledge is more than or equivalent to that of the local schema for some concept, then the interactive matching process will find the relevant portion of the global schema knowledge. This knowledge will be in one of CYC's two forms for concept representation.

If the integrative schema has less knowledge than the local schema, then knowledge will be added to the integrative schema until its level of knowledge equals or exceeds that in the local schema. Otherwise, the broader schema would be unable to model the semantics of the different local schemata represented in the database resource.

Parallels Between Complex Financial and Manufacturing Operations

Many origins can be found in incompatibility problems we experience with databases. Though the exact reasons vary from one company to another, and from one case to another within the same manufacturing firm, there are some underlying factors Project Carnot has aimed at addressing.

The cutting edge of technology and the changing landscape with which we have been faced during the last 10 years see to it that organizations lack permanent, formal definitions of methods and systems. Both are continually reevaluated in the course of the work a company is doing, changing in the process the implementation perspectives it follows.

Due to the dynamic nature of the business environment, investments in high technology, including the management of sophisticated database projects, must be seen in the light of the operations into which our organization engages as a whole:

- Management decisions need to adapt fast and accurately to unstable conditions.
- Problems arise that cannot be assigned among the operating departments in a clearly defined manner.
- Research has to be done with specific database implementations in mind, not in the abstract.
- Increasingly, we have to learn how to make design choices when confronted with vagueness and uncertainty.

For instance, just-in-time inventory management requires a complex web of databases and applications, many of which call for extensive access to the company's information technology environment.

Like global risk management application in the financial sector, just-in-time inventory management in industry not only calls for sophisticated mathematics but also involves access to many different and (chances are) largely incompatible databases.

· In the financial world, risk management involves polyvalent treasury operations done at the foreign exchange department, the corporate treasury itself, the general ledger, the loans operations, securities trading, foreign exchange, and so on. All these activities involve joint credit risks.

For a financial institution, and for a multinational industrial corporation, a major issue is overnight exposure — also known as "Follow the Sun Overdraft" — which not only involves interest rate risk and foreign exchange risk, but also the other party's ability to repay.

· In the manufacturing world, the corresponding risk is one of producing for a nonexisting market, either because the market's own whims have shifted or because our own product specifications have simply changed but nobody was informed down the line.

This happens everyday in the manufacturing industry and results in significant costs. To stop the practice we need real time, interactive database access, and this can be achieved either through homemade software products or through commodity projects like Carnot.

As we have seen in preceding chapters, there are many aspects of cross-database interactivity and piecemeal access to information, which in at least some of the cases is an obsolete practice, will not work.

· It will be a nightmare to maintain manual synchronization between the different information elements obtained from databases.
· The search-and-locate time will be too long compared to more elegant, fully automatic solutions,[8] which are today receiving the lion's share of attention.
· The concept of an intermediate database (the InfoCenter approach), contemplated by some organizations, dates back to the late 1970s, and has been abandoned by those who have tasted its results.

Yet in general, the information elements pertinent to each of the areas outlined in the manufacturing and financial examples are in diverse, dispersed, and incom-

---

8 See also the quantitative reference made in Chapters 13 and 14 to IDA vs. classical database access benchmarks.

patible databases. To make matters worse, many companies still have a very heavy batch orientation, which keeps them *uncompetitive*.

There was a time when success and failure depended on mechanistic approaches, when methods were carved in stone, and the duties of everyone were clearly defined on paper. Times, however, have changed. Due to the cutting edge of technology, corporate survival does not permit paleolithic methods.

In years past, the mechanistic approach was the procedure followed by so many firms that the newer technology was confined only to the leaders. But this is not the prescription for success today, where the best procedures are those that are

· Interactive
· Flexible
· Adaptable

Flexibility and adaptability are axioms to follow in order to control not one but a network of projects and processes which are interrelated, interconnected, and must proceed in parallel. This is the way to bet.

Managing Integrative Database Projects

Carnot, IDA, and other efforts demonstrate that the management of a project, whose goal is to revamp and restructure the database, can greatly benefit from what has been learned through theory and practice in other domains. Management theory has been originally developed to increase the productivity and efficiency of business organizations, and there are some outstanding principles from which to quote.

A search for principles that would provide general rules for administration has been undertaken by many organizations and has resulted in such well-known axioms as

· Unity of command
· The need of delegation
· An optimal span of control
· Matched authority and accountability
· The necessity for planning business activities
· The need for action-oriented control

These axioms are sound, but the prescriptions devised for their implementation have not been always satisfactory. To use them effectively we have to adapt them in a specific, well-designed manner to the specific situation we face, rather than the other way around.

Over the years, the study of functioning organizations indicated that no single management system is best for all firms. This is true because of their internal culture but also due to variation in

· Product characteristics
· Market appeal
· Technical methods
· Specific duties
· Working relationships
· The very concept of accountability

Every one of these issues has to be defined by the company, taking into account its goals, past history, and present and projected structure. The implementation of high technology and the specific aims we wish to fulfill cannot be done in a vague way, and specific aims vary from one organization to another.

Hence, while there are basic axioms derived from experience on how a sophisticated database integration project has to be managed, these axioms will best fit a company's needs if they are adapted to its operations and its environment, as well as the specific goals a cross-database project has to address.

There are no blanket-type, good-for-everyone solutions in management, and the management of a database project is no exception to this reference. *Adaptation* is the keyword both with living organisms and in organizational practice.

To a significant degree, adaptation and personalization can be assisted through astute choices of norms and standards. This permits the user organization to

· Feel part of a broader implementation community, while at the same time adapting the chosen cross-database solution to its needs

The forementioned principle did not escape the attention of Project Carnot or that of its sponsors, and the original policy has been that of selecting ANSI/ISO standards, like RDA and X.400, or artifacts likely to become more generally accepted artifacts, such as Rosette and CYC.

However, unfortunately for Project Carnot, Rosette and CYC have not been normalized by international standards bodies, and the choice of Itasca is not helping either. Instead,

· ENCINA has been given the blessing of the Open Software Foundation (OSF) as transaction processing monitor.
· Other object DBMS like Ontos, Gemstone, and Versant have stolen the show[9] — not Itasca.

In terms of adoption, this had evident negative aftermaths on Carnot's standing as a generalized cross-database solution. Carnot will most likely be used by Bellcore and other sponsor companies, but I don't really see it capturing a broad segment of the market. What Carnot accomplished is to present a solid method for

---

9 See also D. N. Chorafas and H. Steinmann, *An Introduction to Object-Oriented Databases,* Prentice-Hall, Englewood Cliffs, NJ, 1993.

integrating separately developed incompatible database resources, enabling them to be accessed and modified coherently.

In conclusion, the best approach is one of achieving integration at the semantic level by using an existing global ontology to resolve inconsistencies. In the overall this concept operates in two phases:

1. Preintegration, in which an information resource is represented declaratively within the global ontology
2. Integration proper with declarative mappings between the resource and the global ontology being constructed

These mappings are used by the transaction tool to translate queries and updates, written against the global ontology. Also to the credit of Carnot is that, in terms of prototyping and implementation, three database models have been used: relational, entity-relationship and object-oriented, i.e., the best possible alternatives. The results are interesting, and the method may become a norm. But one fundamental problem neither Carnot nor other similar projects are addressing in terms of implementation is: *How to change the current company culture?*

Index